ArcGIS Web Development

ArcGIS
Web Development

RENE RUBALCAVA

MANNING
SHELTER ISLAND

For online information and ordering of this and other Manning books, please visit
www.manning.com. The publisher offers discounts on this book when ordered in quantity.
For more information, please contact

> Special Sales Department
> Manning Publications Co.
> 20 Baldwin Road
> PO Box 261
> Shelter Island, NY 11964
> Email: orders@manning.com

Manning Publications Co.
20 Baldwin Road
PO Box 261
Shelter Island, NY 11964

Development editor:	Susan Conant
Technical development editor:	Florian Lengyel
Technical proofreader:	Brian Arnold
Copyeditors:	Lianna Wlasiuk, Katie Petito
Proofreader:	Melody Dolab
Typesetter:	Marija Tudor
Cover designer:	Marija Tudor

ISBN: 9781617291616
Printed in the United States of America
2 3 4 5 6 7 8 9 10 – MAL – 19 18 17 16 15

brief contents

contents

preface

The last decade has seen a boom in people becoming acclimated to location technology. Most users may not fully realize that they're using location technology when they get an alert on their phone that there's traffic on the way home, or when they get a coupon from an app on their phone for a local restaurant. Smart phones are no longer simply devices for making phone calls, texting, and checking email. For many people, they've not only replaced the heavy and clumsy map book that your passenger used to help you navigate, but these "phones" have also replaced the expensive in-dash GPS systems in our vehicles. It's so easy today to say the name of a store or venue into your phone, and in seconds receive turn-by-turn directions. That's not to say that these directions may not try to direct you into a lake, but there's no denying that location technology has become part of our daily lives. We gladly share our current locations with friends and family with as much fervor as when we shared a photo a few years ago. Maps and the information they can convey are great tools that developers should take time to learn to use.

A few years ago, I was tasked with upgrading an enterprise GIS application and bringing it into the modern non-mainframe era. Esri had just started releasing Web APIs for use with their technology. At the time, I built my application with the Flex API, and I delved deep into the world of ActionScript and Flex modular development, but it always felt a bit heavy-handed.

Over time, the Esri JavaScript API became more appealing. It performed better with each release and offered new features that worked with the latest updates to ArcGIS Server. At some point, my focus switched entirely from Flex development to JavaScript, and I immersed myself in every nook and cranny of the API.

I've had the pleasure over the years of building numerous applications with the ArcGIS API for JavaScript, even building a business around creating web-mapping applications. I've tried to follow each learning hump with a blog post or a presentation to share what I have learned. This is my way of paying it forward—paying it forward for all those blog posts I spent late nights digging through, simply to fix some odd bug or solve a problem I was ready to give up on, and for all the presentations I've attended that inspired me to build and learn, to create useful tools and applications, and to strive to learn what I didn't even know I wanted or needed to learn. This book brings together the knowledge I've gained and puts it all in one place. I hope you enjoy reading this book as much as I did writing it.

I also hope you take the foundations laid out here to explore what you can do with web mapping with the ArcGIS API for JavaScript and build some really cool things. Because as developers, isn't that what we all want to do? Just build.

acknowledgments

There are numerous people to thank, without whose help and support this book would not have been possible.

I'd like to thank the people at Esri who provided me with great feedback on the subject matter: Jim Barry, Derek Swingley, Andy Gup, Jeremy Bartley, and everyone on the JavaScript API and Server team who answered one of my numerous questions.

Thanks to the Manning Early Access Program (MEAP) readers who posted comments and corrections in the Author Online forum. Thanks also to all the reviewers who provided invaluable feedback: Adam Krein, Alexander Jones, Andrea Tarocchi, Brandon Titus, Cliff Zhao, David Takahashi, Dennis Sellinger, Jaclynn Wilson, Shaun Langley, Tim Djossou, and Vidyasagar Nallapati.

I'd like to thank the entire Manning editorial staff for helping me every single step of the way in writing this book. My development editor, Susan Conant, helped me brainstorm ideas for this book and was quick to answer all my questions and show me how to teach, not tell. Brian Arnold, technical proofreader, provided incredibly thorough technical guidance in reviewing the code for this book.

I'd also like to thank my parents for always believing in me and supporting me when I needed it the most. A special thank you to my wife Zenayda, who has been my rock since we met, and who pushes me to be better on a daily basis. Thank you to my three daughters Andrea, Zoe, and Abbey Rose, who have taught me the patience that only a father of daughters could understand.

about this book

The ArcGIS API for JavaScript is a library built to work hand in hand with ArcGIS Server technologies. It's designed to provide a wide range of tools that allow a developer to build everything from the simplest web-mapping application to a heavily used and feature-rich tool. What you decide to build is up to you and the needs of your users, but it's been my experience that the ArcGIS API for JavaScript can meet most expectations.

This book, *ArcGIS Web Development*, is an introduction to the ArcGIS API for JavaScript, with a little bit of extra information thrown in to get you up to speed with the Dojo Toolkit that the API is built on.

There are a variety of web-mapping libraries available, and the ArcGIS API for JavaScript is designed to take advantage of the technology provided by ArcGIS Server and ArcGIS Online, both of which will be discussed in this book.

Roadmap

ArcGIS Web Development is divided into two parts: "ArcGIS JavaScript Foundation" and "A Sample Use Case." If you're already familiar with GIS and just want to learn how to use the ArcGIS API for JavaScript, you may be tempted to skip Part 1 entirely. I strongly recommend, though, that you at least familiarize yourself with chapter 3, which covers the ArcGIS REST API.

The first part of the book is an introduction to some core concepts of GIS and terms used throughout the book. By the end of part 1, you'll have a solid understanding of the ArcGIS Server REST API, which is the driving force for ArcGIS web technologies and core concepts of the ArcGIS API for JavaScript.

- In chapter 1, you'll learn how GIS can be used as a tool and the significance of spatial applications.
- In chapter 2, you'll build your first map and learn the basics of spatial data and how to query that data.
- In chapter 3, you'll learn the basics of the ArcGIS Server REST API and be given a sample of how to use it to build a custom legend widget. This is also the first dive into using the Dojo AMD loading system.

The second part of the book walks you through a sample field collection application, which also provides some tips on disconnected editing for mobile applications. In part 2 you'll learn how to structure a scalable application, build a mobile-friendly data-collection application, and even learn some advanced techniques for disconnected editing:

- In chapter 4, you'll set up an ArcGIS Online account and learn how to use Dojo to build your application.
- In chapter 5, you'll learn how to edit features on the map and use authentication to secure your application, as well as how you can use LocalStorage to enable disconnected editing.
- In chapter 6, you'll focus on building an application for use on a desktop browser, freeing you up from some limitations of a mobile environment. You'll also learn how to use OAuth 2.0 with ArcGIS Online and store your credentials to allow users to log in and out. This chapter also covers how to integrate data collected in the field with some non-spatial data.
- In chapter 7, you'll be introduced to more advanced subjects and techniques. You'll learn about the ArcGIS WebMap specification and how to use it to configure your map. You'll also learn how to build your entire application from a single JSON file that will configure your widgets for you. This chapter will also describe an alternative to disconnected editing using a library called PouchDB.

Finally, there are three appendixes that contain supporting information. Appendix A provides some development environment options available for writing and running the code in this book. Appendix B is probably the most valuable appendix in this book, as it covers basics of the Dojo Toolkit that are indispensable for using the ArcGIS API for JavaScript. Appendix C discusses how to use the proxy files provided by Esri in your application and explains why you will probably need them.

Code conventions and downloads

All source code in listings or in text is in a `fixed-width font like this` to separate it from ordinary text. Code annotations accompany many of the listings, highlighting important concepts. In some cases, numbered bullets link to explanations that follow the listing.

Source code for the examples in the book can be downloaded from the publisher's website at www.manning.com/ArcGISWebDevelopment.

Author Online

Purchase of *ArcGIS Web Development* includes free access to a private web forum run by Manning Publications, where you can make comments about the book, ask technical questions, and receive help from the author and from other users. To access the forum and subscribe to it, point your web browser to www.manning.com/ArcGISWeb Development. This page provides information on how to get on the forum once you are registered, what kind of help is available, and the rules of conduct on the forum.

Manning's commitment to our readers is to provide a venue where a meaningful dialogue between individual readers and between readers and the author can take place. It is not a commitment to any specific amount of participation on the part of the author, whose contribution to the book's forum remains voluntary (and unpaid). We suggest you try asking him some challenging questions, lest his interest strays!

The Author Online forum and the archives of previous discussions will be accessible from the publisher's website as long as the book is in print.

About the cover illustration

The figure on the cover of *ArcGIS Web Development* is captioned "La Demoiselle de Compagnie," a young woman who serves as a companion to an older and more well-to-do woman from the aristocracy or bourgeoisie; or as a chaperone for a young, unmarried woman, who could not go out unaccompanied. The illustration is taken from a nineteenth-century edition of Sylvain Maréchal's four-volume compendium of regional dress customs published in France. Each illustration is finely drawn and colored by hand. The rich variety of Maréchal's collection reminds us vividly of how culturally distinct the world's towns and regions were just 200 years ago. Isolated from each other, people spoke different dialects and languages. In the streets or in the countryside, it was easy to identify where they lived and what their trade or station in life was just by their dress.

Dress codes have changed since then and the diversity by region, so rich at the time, has faded away. It is now hard to tell apart the inhabitants of different continents, let alone different towns or regions. Perhaps we have traded cultural diversity for a more varied personal life—certainly for a more varied and fast-paced technological life.

At a time when it is hard to tell one computer book from another, Manning celebrates the inventiveness and initiative of the computer business with book covers based on the rich diversity of regional life of two centuries ago, brought back to life by Maréchal's pictures.

Part 1

ArcGIS JavaScript Foundation

P art one of this book introduces some of the core concepts of GIS and terms used throughout the book. By the end of this part, you'll have a solid understanding of the ArcGIS Server REST API, which is the driving force for ArcGIS web technologies and core concepts of the ArcGIS API for JavaScript, as well as how spatial data is provided to web applications:

- In chapter 1, you'll learn how to use GIS as a tool and the significance of spatial applications.
- In chapter 2, you'll build your first map and learn the basics of spatial data and how to query that data. You'll also learn the details of how a Feature-Layer works and how it's optimized for performance.
- In chapter 3, you'll learn the basics of the ArcGIS Server REST API and be given a sample of how to use it to build a custom legend widget. This is also the first dive into using the Dojo AMD loading system and modularizing your application.

GIS as a tool

Where we are, and our understanding of location, has an impact on our daily lives. Walk around almost any public space and you'll see people staring at their smartphones, updating their statuses, or looking for the closest taco joint. You may have shopped for a house online, and been able to view homes in your area and even see nearby schools. When shopping for a car online, you can usually limit the search to within so many miles of a zip code. Formerly, a paper map book was essential in every vehicle, but today, drivers keep a GPS (Global Positioning System) on the dashboard or have a system that speaks to them, directing them when to turn. If you're following directions on paper, chances are you printed them from an online map. Location has become a key component of the way we get many tasks done. A simple map can be a driving force in delivering information, sometimes in the most subtle ways. ArcGIS, a key subject of this book, is a geographic information system (GIS) platform that allows users to work with maps and geographic information. With it, users can create and use maps, gather and analyze geographic data, and use that data in a variety of applications.

This chapter gives you a quick overview of the key pieces of information in this book:

- The ArcGIS platform
- Why you should consider learning how to add spatial capabilities to your applications
- Benefits of the ArcGIS API for JavaScript
- Dojo Toolkit and how it relates to the ArcGIS API for JavaScript
- Useful GIS concepts

Volumes have been written on the subject of GIS alone, but for our purposes, I'll discuss what GIS means and how location-aware applications impact our daily lives.

1.1   GIS: here, there, everywhere

For years, GIS was something used by academics and government agencies for studies or infrastructure purposes. GIS is "a system designed to capture, store, manipulate, analyze, manage, and present all types of geographical data."[1] GIS is the way we work with spatial information. It's also a technology that's been used mainly in the realm of desktop computers, with large enterprise applications that require extensive training.

The World Wide Web has caused an explosion in most technologies today, including the use of GIS tools. Since the mid-1990s, you've been able to find addresses and get directions from websites like MapQuest. Projects like Google Maps and OpenStreetMap emerged a few years later to bring GIS to the masses, introducing the power of maps to everyday people. Esri, founded in 1969, has grown into a leading company that provides GIS tools and services, including a suite of web mapping tools, which is why you're reading this book. Before we take a closer look at Esri's GIS offerings, let's sample the other tools available.

1.1.1   The GIS tools landscape

You have a number of choices when it comes to developing web mapping applications with JavaScript, including robust open-source options. Some options come in the form of an API, which is an interface for an underlying web service, like maps and directions.

---

[1] "Geographic Information System," Wikipedia, last modified May 24, 2014, http://en.wikipedia.org/wiki/Geographic_information_system.

What exactly is a web service?

The World Wide Web Consortium (W3C) defines a web service as "a standard means of interoperating between different software applications, running on a variety of platforms and/or frameworks."[a]

[a] "Web services Architecture," W3C Web Services Architecture Working Group, last modified Feb 2004, www.w3.org/TR/ws-arch/

Google and MapQuest provide web mapping APIs that are popular for embedding maps and directions into websites. Microsoft offers a Bing mapping API to showcase its mapping data. Various open-source mapping libraries also have much to offer:

- *OpenLayers*—A popular open-source mapping library with a large community of users
- *Leaflet*—A mapping library that has grown in popularity due to its ease of use and focus on performance for mobile browsers
- *Modest Maps*—A super-lightweight mapping library that does a good job of displaying interactive maps

This list is a sampling of open-source options for building web mapping applications, and I encourage you to try them out. The explosion of mapping in the browser has only increased the importance of location for everyday users. Personally, when I'm out running errands, my phone keeps me updated as to how long it'll take me to get home based on my current location and traffic conditions. That's pure location-awareness in action.

GIS plays a large role in many areas of technology. Knowing the location of something can be critical in large asset-management systems that track construction and maintenance information of certain infrastructures, such as water and power. GIS is commonly used in crime analyses to help local law enforcement officials focus their resources. GIS is also used to project population growth in urban areas to help determine future infrastructure needs. GIS is used to assist the public when a disaster strikes—for example, mapping out damage after storms and floods.

Considering the various web mapping APIs available to developers other than the ArcGIS API for JavaScript, such as OpenLayers and Leaflet, you wonder which is the better choice: proprietary or open source. This decision may depend on many factors but usually boils down to preference. Are you working with data stored in an existing ArcGIS database? Are you working with services in an existing ArcGIS Server? Is the entire GIS ecosystem being built from scratch? What is the budget? Are there any regulatory guidelines on vendors? Do you require on-call customer support? There are varying advantages and disadvantages to each choice. A few of these pros and cons are listed in table 1.1.

Table 1.1 Pros and cons of proprietary and open-source web mapping

	Proprietary	Open-source
Cost	Infrastructure can get expensive, but API is cost-free	Infrastructure and API are cost-free
Community support	Available in Esri forums	Quite extensive
Professional support	Available with ArcGIS licensing	Can be purchased from various providers

Like most open-source debates, the question of whether to use a proprietary or open-source web mapping API can get heated. In my experience, it usually boils down to what's currently in place and what you're willing to spend to get something done quickly. This book assumes that you, as a developer, are working with ArcGIS Server or ArcGIS Online services, so it makes sense for you to work with the ArcGIS API for JavaScript. This API isn't an open-source toolkit, but rather was developed by Esri, a leader in GIS technologies. It's a powerful library built to interact with ArcGIS Server.

1.1.2 *Introducing the ArcGIS platform*

ArcGIS is a platform for providing location-based tools and functionality that range from desktop to server and mobile. The ArcGIS API for JavaScript works with ArcGIS Server, a gateway to GIS data that can be shared on the web to provide access to GIS data via web services. I'll discuss these services in more detail in chapter 2, but for now, all you need to know is that the ArcGIS API for JavaScript is designed to interact with those services so you can build powerful web mapping applications.

> **TIP** Before I get into the details of the ArcGIS API for JavaScript, you may want to visit http://esriurl.com/js for a quick overview of the code samples and reference materials. This book doesn't regurgitate the documentation, but the documentation is the source material for the API and will be a key source of information in your exploration of the ArcGIS API for JavaScript.

The ArcGIS API for JavaScript is a natural choice if you're working with ArcGIS Server. The JavaScript API seamlessly translates the information from ArcGIS Server to provide a rich web mapping experience. Figure 1.1 shows how GIS data that previously was accessible only to a few users can now be shared using ArcGIS Server and the ArcGIS API for JavaScript.

The purpose of this book is to introduce you to the basics of the ArcGIS API for JavaScript and how use the API to interact with various ArcGIS services. You'll also look at how to interact directly with ArcGIS Server if you need information that you can't easily use the API for, and you'll learn how to extend the API to build your own tools to meet your needs.

The second half of the book covers how to build a more involved web mapping application that collects data in a field application. The term "field," in this context,

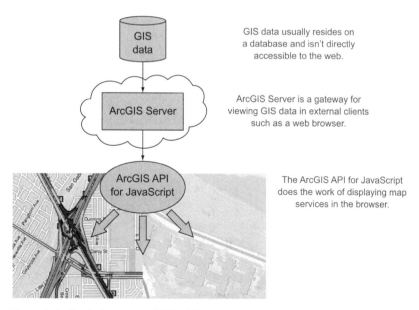

Figure 1.1   Producing maps with ArcGIS API for JavaScript

means "not behind a desk." Field applications present their own unique challenges, which I'll cover in later chapters.

NOTE   I'll cover aspects of how to use ArcGIS Server services with the API, but I won't cover how to install ArcGIS Server (which isn't required for this book), publish services, or create services using ArcGIS for Desktop.

A look ahead

In chapter 4, you'll set up a free ArcGIS developer account so you can create your own services for use in your application. You'll also use free services from ArcGIS Online, a cloud-based version of ArcGIS Server.

For now, let's broaden the discussion to talk more about what spatial applications are and how the internet has changed what you expect from these applications. As developers (beginner or advanced), what does GIS bring to the table and why should you care?

1.1.3   *Why care about spatial applications?*

My first car was small, it was old, and it was rusty, but it was mine, and I was excited to have my own ride to school, something that I think my parents were excited about as well. The first thing my father gave me when I got my car, after a brief yet stern word of caution about being a safe driver, was an awkward and heavy map book. As a kid, I remember sitting in the backseat of the car on long road trips, and my duty was to periodically flip the pages of an identical map book and point out what town was coming up or how many streets we needed to pass before making a right turn. I used to marvel at the detail each page provided, from the winding roads we'd already traveled to the upcoming hills I could look forward to. The map book was a staple in my travels as well as the travels of many others.

These days you may not rely on spiral-bound bricks of paper to navigate the road, but many people do rely on GPS, either on a smartphone or in the car. If you're using a paper map, you probably printed it from a website and folded it up in your pocket for later use.

Navigation isn't the only way our information-consuming society uses spatial information in our daily lives. For years, the retail industry has used your location for targeted advertising. From something as simple as the paper advertisements that fill your mailbox, to an application on your smartphone that can give you a coupon for a nearby restaurant without your asking for it, location can be a key component to targeting an audience in a meaningful way. We constantly share messages, photos, and videos via mobile devices, and each of these bits of information we share carry with them location information. You can even play games on your smartphone that interact with your location, using real-world streets to direct you to victory. When a new fast-food restaurant is built, time has been put into analyzing the benefits of placing that restaurant at that location. A study was probably done to review the demographics of the area (for example, the average household income), proximity to freeways or major highways, average drive-time from major business areas, and more. Similar analyses are also done when new schools are built or new roads are paved. At the end of the day, location matters.

1.1.4 Trends in the GIS industry

Previously, people who worked in the GIS industry needed the skills not only to analyze data but also to employ cartography to display that data. Today, GIS professionals are typically required to have an expanded skillset that allows them to adapt to challenges they face, but they don't need to be versed in all aspects of using GIS. Professionals who prefer to focus on one particular aspect of GIS may not have masterful cartographic skills, rock-star spatial analysis skills, or ninja-level developer skills, but familiarity with all these skillsets is helpful. You may already be working in the GIS field or you may be a student looking forward to cutting your teeth in the job market. Or you may already have experience working with web applications and JavaScript and want to expand your skillset with a web mapping API. Whatever the case, anyone with a skillset in building location-based web applications can find many opportunities.

A cursory review of recent GIS-related job postings reveals that employers are looking for employees who not only can analyze and work with data, but also have programming knowledge. Programming skills could include a language like Python, which has cemented itself in the GIS industry as a staple in automating GIS analysis, thanks to some robust spatial libraries. Skills could also include languages like C# or Java, which are typically used to extend desktop tools or build web services. Employers also need current GIS professionals and developers who can use web technologies to provide quick and efficient access to much of the GIS data that has traditionally been inaccessible to the general public.

The web development aspect of using GIS is an exciting area not only for GIS professionals but also for anyone learning web development with maps. I started working with GIS in early 2002 as a drafting technician recruited into doing GIS technician work to help out with various projects. One of my tasks was manually adjusting hundreds of small boundaries. It was tedious, and I was unfamiliar with the tools, which at that time ranged from somewhat familiar drawing tools to some odd command-line tasks. I was asked to edit script files that added new menus to the software I used, which magically searched a database for related information. I was still green and didn't realize the power of the automation I was working with. Today, a majority of my time is spent doing GIS web development. I attend regular GIS conferences and local events, and over the years I've noticed the growing need for GIS professionals to have a basic understanding of programming to get daily tasks done. I've seen presentations that include not only the analytic details of the way a project was completed but also the customizations that were done via programming tasks that were critical in completing the project. These customizations could be automating tasks or developing a web application to allow stakeholders to collaborate during the project lifecycle.

The goal of this book is to give you a solid working foundation in using the ArcGIS API for JavaScript to build web applications that meet the needs of the task at hand. This could be an application that's used by first responders during a natural disaster or a work-order application to keep track of work that's being done. A web application can be used in an office setting or on mobile devices, making it a flexible platform to work on.

Let's shift our focus to the structure of a GIS web mapping application.

1.2 Understanding the GIS bits

Various components contribute to building a web mapping application. Each one is critical to the process. As shown in figure 1.2, all these components ultimately lead to one thing: a happy user, which means the data is communicated in a clear manner and provides meaning to the user.

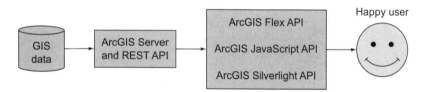

Figure 1.2 The pieces that make up a web mapping application

The GIS data is behind the ArcGIS Server. To get to this data, you communicate with the ArcGIS Server via a collection of URL endpoints. You can communicate with these endpoints through a variety of methods, such as Silverlight and Flex, but this book's focus is on the ArcGIS API for JavaScript. This communication process, combined with your impeccable skills, leads to happy users. This is method of communication is called a REST API, which is discussed in more detail in section 1.2.2.

In this section, I'll introduce you to each of these components of building a web mapping application, starting with the key component: the data.

1.2.1   *The what and the where of GIS data*

Data is the starting point to a successful application. Someone has to compile the data, possibly analyzing and even digitizing (the process of using drawing tools) the

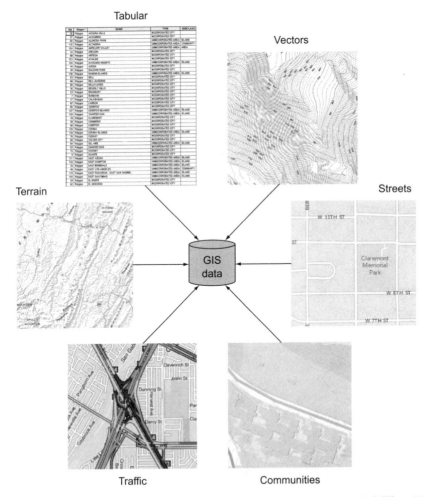

Figure 1.3   ArcGIS Server provides access to GIS data, which is composed of different types of data, such as tabular, vector, terrain, streets, communities, and so on, via services.

data based on external sources. For example, a company or government agency will need to translate old, hand-drawn maps into a digital format, usually parcel or park boundaries. The data often is drawn based on aerial images, such as locations of trees or possible routes to navigate to areas without road access. Infrared aerials frequently are used to find vegetation, which appears in hues of red in an infrared image. This method is used to look at the way areas of vegetation change over a certain period of time. Without data, you'd have nothing to display in a web mapping application.

This data can be stored in a few formats but usually resides in a database. Regardless of format, it's still data, and it's easier to manage a lot of data when it's kept in a database. This allows it to be searched quickly, backed up, and shared easily. To share this data, you could print out paper maps or you could email it back and forth in a digital format. Although these are still valid methods of sharing digital GIS data, users expect to have quicker and easier access to this type of information (see figure 1.3). This is where the need to share this data to the web comes into play.

With a wealth of valuable data to be shared, the next critical component of a web mapping application is a *web server*.

1.2.2 *Serving GIS data: ArcGIS Server and the REST API*

A web server's job, as you may already know, is to serve data from a physical computer out to the World Wide Web so people can view it in their web browsers. An ArcGIS-specific server performs specialized tasks, such as serving aerial imagery, which I'll cover briefly in chapter 2. Sharing data online is done through web services. A web service is a URL (pronounced U-R-L) that returns a web page, an image, or another form of data. This book focuses on data that's accessed via ArcGIS Server services.

ArcGIS Server is enterprise server software that provides a quick method to build web services that serve GIS data. It has more functionality than merely serving data, which I'll cover in later chapters, but all interaction is done through the REST (representational state transfer) API, which is an interface for interacting with the server (see figure 1.4).

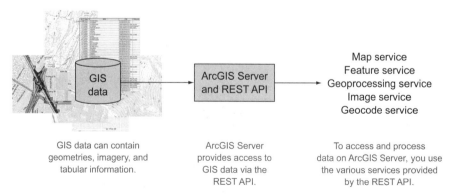

GIS data can contain geometries, imagery, and tabular information.

ArcGIS Server provides access to GIS data via the REST API.

To access and process data on ArcGIS Server, you use the various services provided by the REST API.

Figure 1.4   Data served via ArcGIS Server is made available as various services; each service has a specific purpose.

To properly communicate with the ArcGIS Server REST API, you use a specially designed web API—the next component of a web mapping application.

1.2.3   *Choosing an ArcGIS web API*

The ArcGIS Server REST API is the foundation for all ArcGIS web APIs. A developer has a few choices when deciding to build a web application based on ArcGIS technology:

- ArcGIS API for Flex
- ArcGIS API for Silverlight
- ArcGIS API for JavaScript
- and others

The ArcGIS API for Flex, based on the Flex software development kit (*SDK*), used to be an Adobe product but has been open-sourced in recent years. It's built on top of Flash technology and can be used to build interactive applications. The ArcGIS API for Silverlight uses Microsoft Silverlight to build applications that, similar to the Flex API, can provide fluid and interactive applications.

The drawbacks to both of these APIs are that they require users to have a browser plug-in installed for each of them, and they don't work on the web browsers in mobile devices. This has led many developers to embrace the ArcGIS API for JavaScript. JavaScript runs on all browsers, with minor differences in the way it runs on each browser, and it also provides a fluid and interactive application.

All these web APIs are translators for the ArcGIS REST API, and they make it easy to interact with ArcGIS Server to provide data-rich web mapping applications (see figure 1.5). The web APIs may be built on different technologies, but once you learn one API, it's easy to pick up another one without much trouble.

The ultimate goal of these various components is to make the user of the application happy. Providing an easy-to-use web mapping application that delivers the necessary data for the user to accomplish a task or find the right information without stumbling through the application is the key to a happy user.

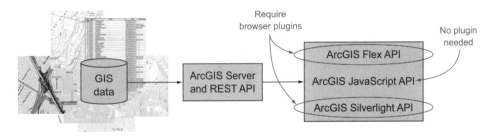

Figure 1.5   The ArcGIS API for JavaScript is the only API that doesn't require a browser plug-in.

Whether you're a seasoned GIS pro looking to enhance your skills with JavaScript or a JavaScript ninja who wants to add GIS web mapping notches to your belt, you'll want to be familiar with a few items before working with the ArcGIS API for JavaScript.

1.3 *Things to know*

No matter your level of competence in either GIS or JavaScript, you should know a few things before working with the ArcGIS API for JavaScript. I'll cover the following topics in detail in chapters 2 and 3, but I want to touch on them briefly in this section to give you an overview of what you'll need to know to work with the ArcGIS API:

- JavaScript stylistics
- GIS concepts

1.3.1 *JavaScript, Dojo Toolkit, and Dijit*

This book is about using JavaScript to build web mapping applications, but you don't need to be a JavaScript master to use this book. I don't explicitly cover what I consider JavaScript best practices when building your applications, but the code I provide is written in a style I think is best suited for the task at hand. For example, sometimes you use a single JavaScript file to build an application; other times, you load up to half a dozen JavaScript files.

DOJO AND AMD LOADING

The *Dojo Toolkit* is a popular JavaScript library that offers many tools for writing JavaScript, in particular for larger applications. The ArcGIS API for JavaScript is based on Dojo, so it's inevitable that you'll also learn Dojo as you begin using the API. Dojo provides an extensive suite of tools that you can use in building your web mapping applications. I'll dig deeper into Dojo tools in chapters 2 and 3, but Dojo's use and how it applies to the ArcGIS API for JavaScript is something you should be aware of.

Another typical JavaScript stylistic choice is the way files are loaded. A common and still acceptable way to load JavaScript files to your web page is to use a <script> tag, as follows:

```
<script src="file1.js"></script>
<script src="file2.js"></script>
<script src="file3.js"></script>
```

Loading JavaScript files in this manner isn't wrong, and you need at least one script tag to load a file. But, as you can imagine, as the application grows and the amount of JavaScript files grow, this method gets unwieldy. Not to mention that there's no guarantee that the JavaScript files will load in the order in which you place them on the page.

The ArcGIS API for JavaScript uses a method called *asynchronous module definition* (AMD), which loads your JavaScript files on an as-needed basis. The reason for using it boils down to the fact that the ArcGIS API for JavaScript is built with the Dojo Toolkit.

Dojo uses AMD to build applications, so AMD loading is another method you'll learn to build your applications. A quick example of AMD loading is shown here:

```
define(['dojo/_base/array'], function(arrayUtil) {
    var sqItems = function(items) {
        return arrayUtil.map(items, function(item) {
            return item * item;
        });
    };
    return sqItems;
});
```

Defines custom module and uses AMD to load other JavaScript files

I'll cover more details of the AMD loader in chapter 3 when you build a custom widget.

USING DIJIT

Dojo has a library called Dijit, which is used to build the JavaScript components that provide an interface in a web application. The interface could be a form to enter information or it could be a calendar date-picker. A process is in place for building these custom components, commonly referred to as *widgets*. Using Dojo, a developer can create custom widgets using the Dijit library's base set of tools, which simplifies the process and makes writing reusable widgets much easier as an application grows. I'll cover custom widgets in chapters 3 and 4.

1.3.2 *Introducing a tad of GIS*

I'm focusing on building web mapping applications using the ArcGIS API for Java-Script, and although knowledge of GIS isn't a requirement to get into this subject, I want to review a few GIS concepts:

- *Interactive maps*—An interactive map serves a specific purpose: a map is there to show you where. Show you where what? Maps communicate location information: it could be streets, neighborhoods, homes for sale, or how much income people make in certain cities, but the information revolves around where this information is displayed. As shown in figure 1.6, when you're looking for a particular answer, sometimes you need to ask, "Where are you?"

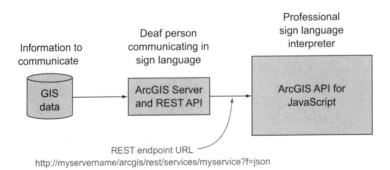

Figure 1.6 A map can communicate many things but often asks a simple question.

- *Maps and layers*—You'll learn about the parts of a map and how to use layers in chapter 2, but for now, all you need to know is that the map is the starting point for relaying information. For example, a point on the map could represent the location of a gas station, a series of lines on the map could show a city's road network, or polygons on the map could display voting areas.
- *GIS data analysis*—GIS helps you answer questions about the information you're working with. How close am I to a certain location? How do I find a house that's closest to schools, shopping centers, and where I work? Using the ArcGIS API for JavaScript, you can do interesting analyses. I won't cover anything too extensive, but the capability is there should you need it, and you'll learn how to access the tools to do so.

1.3.3   *Interacting with the ArcGIS REST API*

The engine that keeps the ArcGIS API for JavaScript running is the ArcGIS REST API, which I discussed in section 1.2.2. I'll cover how to access the ArcGIS REST API to meet needs you might have that aren't provided in the ArcGIS API for JavaScript in chapter 3. What it boils down to is being able to use the ArcGIS REST API to find out more information about the data you're working with. You can think of it as metadata about your services. In this case, metadata includes information about a map service, such as what data is in the service, and whether the data is made up of points, lines, or polygons, or all of the above. Is the map service compatible with your other map services? What is the default look of your map service?

In terms of being able to fill possible gaps in functionality of the ArcGIS API for JavaScript, in chapter 3 you'll build an extension in JavaScript that will display a legend that allows you turn individual layers on and off. This is a handy tool that isn't provided out of the box with the ArcGIS API for JavaScript. These types of custom tools that require you to interact with the ArcGIS REST API aren't always necessary, but when they are, you'll be grateful to have a basic understanding of working with the ArcGIS REST API to cover your bases.

1.4   *Summary*

- In this chapter, I discussed the prevalence of spatial applications in our everyday lives. From how we shop to where we live, location plays a vital role in our society.
- I discussed various options available for building web mapping applications, each with its own merits. In this book, the focus is on the ArcGIS API for JavaScript, which is best suited for working with ArcGIS Server map services.
- Trends in the GIS industry have shown a sharp increase for GIS professionals to have familiarity with a programming language, even if it's to supplement GIS analyses and automate workflows. This opens up the opportunity for non-GIS professionals to dive into building web mapping applications that use the power of GIS data.

- I covered the basics of accessing GIS data through web services, which you can use to build web mapping applications.
- I provided a quick overview of concepts that you'll know by the end of this book, such as JavaScript, the relevant parts of the Dojo Toolkit, the bits of GIS in your web maps, and what to look forward to when working with the ArcGIS REST API.

In chapter 2 you'll learn how to use the ArcGIS API for JavaScript to work with various map services, query data from these services, and filter that data.

Introducing core API concepts

The ArcGIS API for JavaScript is a well-stocked JavaScript library you can use to build mapping applications. In later chapters you'll use advanced features of the API, but in this chapter I'll discuss core features and their uses. We'll begin our introduction to the core functions of the API with a bit of explanation about how things work so you can be better prepared when something doesn't work as expected.

A mapping application requires you to fit together many small pieces, but the ArcGIS API for JavaScript brings all these pieces together for you, which simplifies the process. The ArcGIS API for JavaScript uses a modular approach to building web mapping applications; it loads only the necessary pieces (modules) to perform various tasks. An application that features an onscreen interactive map that you can zoom in on and pan around is remarkably simple to create. Additional functionality, such as providing user feedback or building intelligence into the application, takes more work.

To better prepare you for troubleshooting when something doesn't work the way you expect, my approach in this chapter is to provide more in-depth explanations about how the core API functions work. I'll cover the options that are available when you make a map, as well as the kind of data you'll typically work with. I'll also show you how to query your data to help you use the map to answer questions and display the results on your map. Then I'll finish by covering the advantages of a `FeatureLayer` and how you can use it in your web mapping applications.

Docs are your friends

This isn't a reference book, so I won't cover every method and property in the ArcGIS API for JavaScript. One resource you'll become intimately familiar with while using the API is the documentation, which you can find at https://developers.arcgis.com/en/javascript/. The API reference pages can save you time when you're stuck on how to work with a certain module.

Esri, the company that supplies the ArcGIS API for JavaScript, also provides a collection of samples on its website that do a good job of introducing users to the basics of the API and some tools. I highly recommend these samples and reference pages, which can be found at http://esriurl.com/js, as required reading along with this book.

Now for the moment you've been waiting for: you're going to dive right in and make a bare-bones mapping application. Get ready for it!

2.1   From data to map

A map is a way to visualize data. It could be basic data, such as locations of streets, or more detailed data, such as the location of census tracts. This section covers the following:

- Creating a simple map with ArcGIS API for JavaScript
- Understanding in detail the pieces that make up the map
- Reviewing common map options

TIP   Before jumping in, review appendix A to make sure you have the recommended software installed to run the samples.

First, create an HTML file using your text editor of choice, name it ch2_1.html, and enter the code shown in listing 2.1, saving it in a directory where you can view it from a local web server. Remember that to view applications built with ArcGIS API for JavaScript, the HTML files must use a local web server of your choice. Again, refer to appendix A for more information.

Listing 2.1   A simple ArcGIS JavaScript mapping application

```
<!doctype html>
<html>
  <head>
    <title>ArcGIS Web Development</title>
```

```
        <link rel="stylesheet"
href="//js.arcgis.com/3.11/esri/css/esri.css">

    </head>
    <body>                          ⌐ Displays the map
      <div id="map"></div>    ◁
    </body>
    <script src="//js.arcgis.com/3.11/"></script>
    <script>
      require(['esri/map'], function(Map) {
        var map = new Map('map', {
          basemap: 'streets'
        });
      });
    </script>
</html>
```

Stylesheet is required for map to display correctly

References current version of ArcGIS API for JavaScript

Gets reference to esri/map module

Instantiates new map using provided streets layer

This is the minimum code you need to build a map using the ArcGIS API for JavaScript:

- A reference to the current version of the ArcGIS API for JavaScript.
- A container element, the most common of which is a div element in your HTML.

  A div is a block-level HTML element used for organizing your web page and can be used only within the <body> element of the page.

  The div element that contains the map must have a unique ID, which is associated with one element on your web page. In this case, the ID is map. You could name it Bob as long as you reference the ID correctly, but map is a convenient name for this example.

- A reference to the Esri Cascading Style Sheets (CSS) file, which defines how elements look on the page; the CSS is provided with the API to make sure the map displays correctly.

With these pieces in place, a few lines of JavaScript code are all you need to reference the esri/map module and instantiate a new instance of a map.

DEFINITION I use the term *module* to refer to individual JavaScript components that are defined in the ArcGIS API for JavaScript.

To create the map, you pass the id of the div element as the first argument to the Map constructor. This element is used to draw the map on the screen. Let's take a look at this map in a browser.

2.1.1 *Parts of a basic map*

To view the results of the code in listing 2.1, run a local web server of your choice and view the HTML file in a web browser using one of the server options provided in appendix A—Visual Studio, XAMPP (Apache, MySQL, PHP), or Python:

TIP See appendix A for viable web server options.

- *Visual Studio*—Right-click the HTML file and select View in Browser.
- *XAMPP*—Browse to http://localhost/agswebdev/ch2/ch2_1.html in your browser of choice.
- *Python*—From the command-line tool, navigate to the folder in which you're saving this sample, run the command `python -m SimpleHTTPServer`, and navigate to http://localhost:8000/ch2_1.html in your browser.

No matter which tools you choose, you should see something similar to figure 2.1.

Now that's amazing! A few lines of code and some HTML on your part, and you have a map that you can pan around and zoom in on. That's quite the time-saver for you. Granted, this application doesn't do much, but what do you expect from a couple of lines of code? Let's review what you get with this basic sample. As expected, figure 2.1 is a map. Along with the map, you're provided, by default, the attribution information in the lower-right corner. You'll learn how to disable this attribution information at a later time, but it's a good idea to display it so others know the source of the map information. You also have access to a navigation tool to zoom in and out of the map.

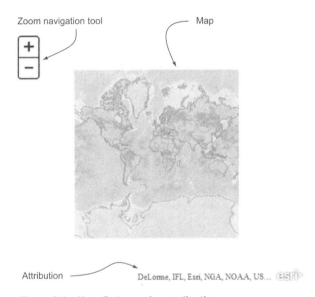

Figure 2.1   Your first mapping application

NAVIGATING THE MAP

I'll talk about where this map data came from and how to change it in section 2.1.2, but first I want to point out how to navigate the map. Table 2.1 summarizes the various navigation techniques.

Table 2.1   Standard map navigation techniques

Technique	Description
Left mouse-click and drag	Allows you to pan around the map
Mouse wheel	Zooms in and out of the map
Zoom navigation tool	API-provided zoom tool
Shift-Left mouse click and drag	Zoom shortcut

Intuitively, you can use your mouse to left-click inside the map and pan it around. You may notice that when you pan left or right, the map keeps going. This is referred to as *wrap-around*, and it allows you to pan the map with a globe-like effect. It's a neat feature if you ever need to work with the map at or near global scale.

To zoom in and out of the map, you can use the mouse wheel. The API also provides a built-in zoom navigation tool located, by default, in the upper-left area of the map. As advertised, clicking the plus (+) button zooms in; clicking the minus (−) button zooms out. One of the quickest zoom shortcuts, though, is to press the Shift key while clicking and holding the left mouse button as you move the mouse cursor over the map. You'll notice a rectangular gray box with a red outline that represents where you'll zoom to. You can see this preview box in figure 2.2.

When using the Shift-Left mouse-click shortcut to zoom to a location on the map, you're defining an *extent*, which the map uses to zoom in on. An extent in a mapping application is composed of a pair of x/y minimum coordinates and a pair of x/y maximum coordinates. An extent can also be referred to as a *bounding box*, because it's a box that defines boundaries on a map. The lower-left coordinates of the bounding box define the minimum coordinates of an extent, and the upper-right coordinates define its maximum coordinates, as shown in figure 2.2.

When discussing map extents, it helps to cover coordinates as well.

UNDERSTANDING MAP COORDINATES

Coordinates vary based on the spatial reference of the map, which I'll discuss when I explain how to use map options, but they typically appear as shown in figure 2.2. The x axis, referred to as the longitude, runs horizontally on the globe, west to east, while

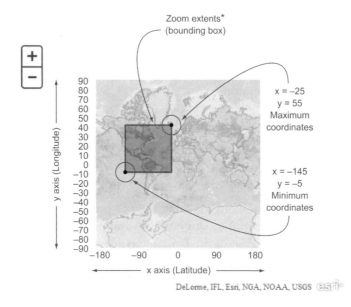

DeLorme, IFL, Esri, NGA, NOAA, USGS

*Actual coordinates of the extent not shown.

Figure 2.2   Zooming with the Shift-Left mouse click shortcut displays the extent coordinates.

the y axis, referred to as the latitude, runs vertically along the globe, north to south. Latitude at 0° and longitude at 0° is the intersection of the equator and the prime meridian. Traversing upward along the latitude yields positive coordinates, but downward yields negative coordinates. The same concept applies to the longitude: if you go west along the longitude, you get negative coordinates, and east produces positive coordinates.

Latitude and longitude terminology

Most people commonly say "x and y" to refer to latitude and longitude, but, as you can see in figure 2.2, "x and y" refers to longitude and latitude.

Don't fret if the terminology becomes confusing. Discerning x and y and latitude and longitude can at times trip up seasoned professionals, even me.

Now let's take another look at the JavaScript in listing 2.1 and review commonly used options that you can pass in as parameters when instantiating a new instance of a map.

2.1.2 *Specifying common map options*

When you created an instance of your new map, you passed it a couple of arguments:

- The id of the element on the page that contains the map
- A JavaScript object with a single value of basemap: 'streets'

The JavaScript object in the second argument contains optional parameters for creating the map. These options control the way the map is displayed when it first starts up, what type of map the user sees when it starts, where you want the map to start from, and more. When it comes to the basemap, common options, in addition to streets, include satellite, hybrid, and gray. As the parameter name suggests, this is a shortcut method to add a basemap to your application. What basemap option you choose is completely dependent on your intentions:

- streets—Provides visible information at the street level; you can see street names, and highways are easily identifiable.
- satellite and hybrid—Provides aerial images; you can see cars on freeways, the tops of buildings, and so on.
- gray—Makes the focus of the map other data, which displays on top of the map.

You don't need to define all the options available for the map, but you should be aware of a handful of common options as you build your application. Table 2.2 lists several of the options that you can use in the parameters to construct a new map in the ArcGIS API for JavaScript. I won't cover all the options available to pass to a map, but I'll discuss the few that are probably used most often, such as basemap, center, and zoom.

TIP I encourage you to review the documentation at https://developers .arcgis.com/javascript/jsapi/map.html#map1 for a full listing and explanation of all the optional parameters.

Table 2.2 Common map options

Option	Description
autoResize	When set to `false`, the map doesn't resize when you resize the browser. I've yet to find a need to set this value to `false`, but you never know.
basemap	Specifies the type of basemap the map uses by default. The options are `hybrid`, `satellite`, `topo`, `gray`, `oceans`, and `national-geographic`.
center	The longitude and latitude coordinates to center the map when it first starts.
LOD (Levels of Detail)	You can specify custom LODs for your map. A level of detail is a combination of the following: • Level—A numeric 2number that identifies the LOD • Scale—For example, 1 inch equals 1 meter • Resolution—The accuracy to which the map is displayed For example, suppose a basemap service has 20 LODs, including the whole world. You can define custom LODs using the scale and resolution of the map service to whittle that down to 10 LODs.
logo	When set to `true`, displays the Esri logo on your map.
nav	When set to `true`, displays pan arrow buttons along the edges of the map to pan in the direction of the arrow. The usefulness of this option depends on the application's design.
scale	Sets the initial scale of the map when it first starts up. To focus on particular areas of the map, combine with the `center` option.
slider	When set to `false`, the map doesn't display navigation tools. Other options are available to define the orientation and position of the slider navigation tools.
zoom	Sets the initial zoom level of the map when it first starts up. The zoom level is equal to the level value specified in an LOD.

The next commonly used option after `basemap` is the `center` option. This is a convenient way to center your map on a specified location when the application first loads. It's typically used in conjunction with the `zoom` option to also set the default zoom level of the map.

When working with the `center` option, note that the center coordinates you provide are in longitude and latitude, respectively, even though that may not be the *spatial reference* of your map. Spatial reference, in simplest terms, is the way a 3D globe of the earth is represented on a 2D map. Latitude and longitude are the most common representations of this transformation. The following code specifies the `basemap`, `center`, and `zoom` options for the map:

```
require(['esri/map'], function(Map) {
  var map = new Map('map', {
```

```
    basemap: 'streets',
    center: [-118.2095, 34.0866],
    zoom: 10
  });
});
```

First value in array is longitude; second is latitude

The map that results from these parameters is shown in figure 2.3.

In figure 2.3, the map centers itself at the specified location and zooms in to the tenth available zoom level. A zoom level of 1 is the full global view of the map in this case; the tenth level, in addition to the coordinates you provided, zooms the map approximately to the Los Angeles County area.

So far, you've digested quite a bit of information about what comprises a map from the basic application you created. Now let's dig deeper into adding layers and what layers to add.

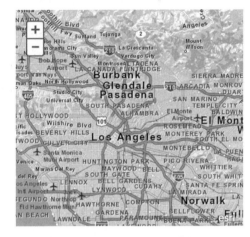

Figure 2.3 Result of providing additional parameters for a new map

2.2 *Understanding layers and accessing data*

Different types of data require different types of mapping layers to represent them. This section covers the following:

- Layer types and how they are used
- Details on vector layers
- How to use the `QueryTask` to display data

What you've seen so far by creating an instance of a map with the `basemap` option is an example of using a *tiled service*. This web mapping service aligns smaller tiled images to display a proper-looking map. This service is one type of layer you can use in your applications. A layer is a representation of geographic data displayed in your map. A simple depiction of the way layers are displayed in a map is shown in figure 2.4.

Different layers that make up a map

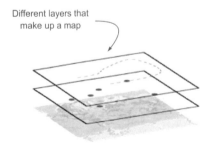

Figure 2.4 Depiction of map layers

The ArcGIS API for JavaScript provides various layer modules, some designed for specific purposes, such as KML (Keyhole Markup Language), XML-based markup (popular with Google Maps), and WMS (Web Map Services), but at the end of the day, the only difference among these services is whether the data they provide is raster- or vector-based. Raster data can be in either PNG or JPG formats; vector uses SVG (Scalable Vector Graphics), VML (Vector Markup Language), or `canvas`.

> **NOTE** Technically, `canvas` is raster-based, so it doesn't draw vector graphics, but instead draws bitmap data. When used to render map graphics in the browser, it would be difficult to tell the difference.

2.2.1 *Layer types for raster-based data*

If the map you see in the web browser is a raster-based image file, it was either created ahead of time on the server or generated on an as-needed basis.

Raster data that was created ahead of time is referred to as *cached* data, because it's already prepared and delivered by the server in small chunks called *tiles*. Data that doesn't change often, such as streets, parcels, and aerial imagery, is cached ahead of time on the server and updated only as needed.

Raster data that's generated on an as-needed basis is called *dynamic*, because the image files are created on the fly. Data that does change often is provided as dynamic data so that users always have the latest version of the data visible to them.

When to use cached or dynamic data is a decision beyond the scope of this book, but it's still important to note what kind of map service you're working with.

Cached data is served as an instance of an `ArcGISTiledMapServiceLayer` inside the ArcGIS API for JavaScript. That's quite the mouthful, but at least it's descriptive. To see a sample of what these tiles look like, let's return to your bare-bones application and use the browser debugging tools in Google Chrome:

1. Press Ctrl-Shift-I (or CMD-Shift-I in Mac OS X) and then click the Network tab to see a list of all network activity in the browser.
2. Scroll the results until you see a listing of files from services.arcgisonline.com.
3. Click the image icon. You can now see a preview of an image file that was downloaded from the server.

This is only one of a few image files that were downloaded, and when tiled together, they display the base data in your map, as shown in figure 2.5.

> **NOTE** You'll become more familiar with the Chrome DevTools as you work more with the ArcGIS API for JavaScript, especially in chapters 4 and 5. The DevTools let you view the raw HTML of the page to inspect individual HTML elements, monitor network traffic in the browser, and view what the JavaScript code is doing in real time. To learn more about Chrome DevTools, visit Code School at http://discover-devtools.codeschool.com.

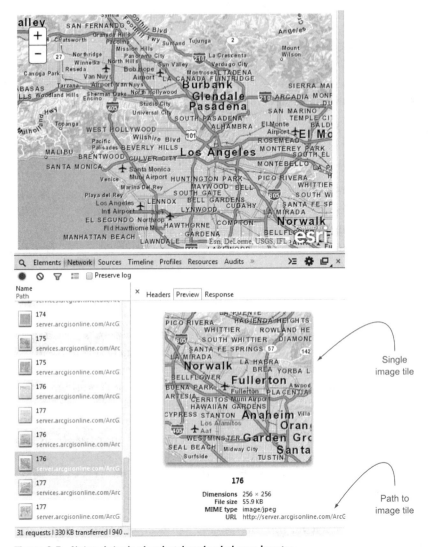

Figure 2.5 **Network tools showing downloaded map images**

Map tiles are typically 256 x 256 pixel images and are organized on the server in a specific structure:

```
http://<service-url>/tile/<level>/<row>/<column>
```

This tiling scheme is determined by the resolution of the data and the number of rows and columns that are zero-based. This means that the origin tile is located at row 0, column 0, and then you traverse right to get the next columns and down to the next rows.

> **NOTE** You can get more details about the ArcGIS Server map cache tiling scheme in the following blog posts from Esri: http://blogs.esri.com/esri/ arcgis/2007/11/07/deconstructing-the-map-cache-tiling-scheme-part-i/ and

http://blogs.esri.com/esri/arcgis/2008/01/31/deconstructing-the-map-cache-tiling-scheme-part-ii-working-with-map-caches-programmatically/.

The current extent of the map displayed in the browser determines which tiles are downloaded. The ArcGIS API for JavaScript sends the map's current extent to the server, and the server determines which map tiles are needed to display the map correctly in the browser. Because individual map tiles are small, they're cached by the browser. If you pan the map to a new location and then pan back to the previous location, these tiles don't need to be downloaded from the server again, and because the browser caches these tiles, they load quickly.

The difference between tiled and dynamic raster data is that dynamic raster data isn't served in tiles. The ArcGIS API for JavaScript sends a request for the current extent of the map displayed to ArcGIS Server, and ArcGIS Server returns a single image of the map that matches that extent. These dynamic images are served as an instance of the `ArcGISDynamicMapServiceLayer` in the API. This method isn't as efficient, but it still serves a purpose in developing mapping applications. One such purpose is to easily display sets of data that change on a regular basis, so it wouldn't be efficient to cache all this data ahead of time. I won't use this layer type in this book, but it's something you should be aware of.

HTML5 graphics

HTML5 is the latest revision of the HTML standard. Most modern browsers support it—or at least support most HTML5 features. I'll cover some of the capabilities of HTML5 in chapter 4, but when it comes to drawing graphics on a map in the ArcGIS API for JavaScript, a couple of HTML5 features are important to note. The first is SVG (Scalable Vector Graphics), which is part of HTML5 but is also a specification of its own. The HTML5 `canvas` element is used to draw graphics, but it doesn't draw vector graphics. Instead, `canvas` draws in bitmap data, which is based on pixels.

2.2.2 Layer types for vector-based data

Vector data as it's used in a web map is a graphical representation of geographic data in the browser. Instead of displaying images of your mapping data, vector data is displayed as graphics using x and y coordinates. Most modern browsers can display vector data using SVG, which is a standard method of displaying scalable graphics on the web. Older versions of Internet Explorer use VML, which is no longer supported in Internet Explorer 10 and above. Graphics also can be drawn using the `canvas` element in HTML5. VML is similar to SVG, but SVG is the current web standard for displaying vector graphics in the browser.

Browser compatibility issues plague web map development as much as any other form of web development. Luckily, the ArcGIS API for JavaScript is designed to handle these types of browser compatibility problems and use the correct vector markup as needed.

> **Ignore that error**
>
> You may notice when running the code samples at home and viewing the console window in the debugging tools of your favorite browser that the following error pops up in the console:
>
> XMLHttpRequest cannot load
>
> http://services.arcgisonline.com/ArcGIS/rest/info?f=json. Origin
>
> http://localhost is not allowed by Access-Control-Allow-Origin.
>
> This error can be safely ignored in your browser. This error means that the web services are coming from a web server that isn't CORS-enabled. *CORS* means *cross-origin resource sharing*. I won't cover CORS in detail, but in a nutshell, it's a browser protocol that allows servers to make requests to each other from different domains. It prevents the browser from executing JavaScript on mydomain.com from yourdomain.com, unless yourdomain.com allows it. Techniques are available to work around this from the source server, but for now, if you see this error, remember that it can be safely ignored.

The core layer that displays vector data in the ArcGIS JavaScript API is the `GraphicsLayer`, which is a container for various locations on the map. Locations are represented by points, lines, or polygons. Let's look at an example to see how this works.

2.2.3 Getting to know the GraphicsLayer

Suppose you want to display a `Graphic` on the map at the location where the mouse was clicked. You first identify the location on the map where the mouse was clicked, and then create a `Graphic` to display on the map. The `Graphic` is a single geographic item that represents something on the map—in this case, a single coordinate on the map.

Listing 2.2 shows how to use the `map.on()` method to add the `Graphic` to the map at the location where the user clicked.

NOTE The code for this section is available in the chapter2 folder of the source code included with the book. See chapter2/2.2.html and chapter2/2.2.js.

Listing 2.2 Adding a `Graphic` to the map

```
map.on('click', function(e) {
        var mapPoint = e.mapPoint,
            symbolSize = 24,                                   // Specifies size of Graphic
            lineColor = new Color([255, 0, 0]),                // Specifies outline color
            fillColor = new Color([255, 255, 0, 0.75]),        // Specifies fill color
            line = new SimpleLineSymbol(SimpleLineSymbol.STYLE_SOLID,
                lineColor, 3),                                 // Creates outline
            sms = new SimpleMarkerSymbol(SimpleMarkerSymbol.STYLE_CIRCLE,
                symbolSize, line, fillColor),                  // Creates SimpleMarkerSymbol to represent graphic on map
            graphic = new Graphic(mapPoint, sms);              // Creates new Graphic
        map.graphics.add(graphic);                             // Adds Graphic to GraphicsLayer in map
    });
```

Let's take a closer look at the `map.on()` method.

IDENTIFYING MOUSE-CLICK LOCATION

You add `map.on()` after the code that defines the map variable and creates the map:

```
...
var map = new Map('map', {
    ...});                                          Creates instance of new map
map.on('click', function(e) {
...                                      Listens for click event
                                         on map  (see listing 2.2)
```

The map instance has the ability to listen for various events, such as when the mouse is clicked on the map. The `map.on()` method executes a function when the designated event happens. In this case, you're waiting for a `click` event. As shown in listing 2.2, when a mouse-click event occurs, the ArcGIS API for JavaScript attaches a `mapPoint` to the event, and the `mapPoint` represents the location on the map that was clicked.

CREATING THE GRAPHIC

You designate a size in pixels for your `Graphic`, and specify what the `Graphic` looks like using other modules from the ArcGIS API for JavaScript. For example, you use the `dojo/_base/Color` module, which uses RGB (Red, Green, Blue) values in an array to assign a color. The fourth value in the RGB array is the transparency level for the color. You don't want the outline to have any transparency, so omit it from the array. You want the fill color to have a 75% transparency, so set that to a value of 0.75.

When you have the outline ready using an instance of the `SimpleLineSymbol`, you then create a `SimpleMarkerSymbol` using the `SimpleLineSymbol` and the `Color` instance you created. Next, create a new `Graphic` using the `MapPoint` geometry and the `SimpleMarkerSymbol`. Geometry can be a point, a line, or a polygon, which are vector geometries, and in listing 2.2 you're using a point.

The fully functional `Graphic` doesn't do much until you add it to the `Graphics-Layer`. The map instance has a default `GraphicsLayer` in the `map.graphics` property. This property is provided so developers can easily add graphics to the map without concerning themselves with adding the `GraphicsLayer` manually. The resulting `Graphic` is shown in figure 2.6.

No matter what type of `Graphic` you plan on adding to a map, complete the following steps:

1 Capture geometry (a point, a line, or a polygon).
2 Define symbology (the way it looks on the map).
3 Create a new `Graphic`.
4 Add the `Graphic` to the map.

These steps may seem involved at first, but, technically, what you've done in this example is a prototype for a data-collection application, which is the type of application you'll create later in the book.

Map graphics

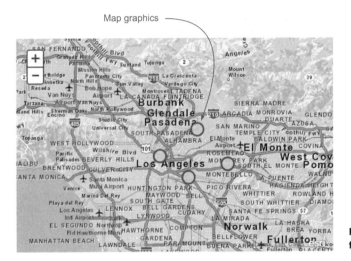

Figure 2.6 Adding `Graphic` features to the map

In previous versions of the ArcGIS API for JavaScript, the `GraphicsLayer` was the only way to add graphics to the map. Typical workflow involved running a query on a map service (I'll cover this section 2.2.4) and adding the results to a `GraphicsLayer`. You can still follow this workflow to display a `Graphic` for the user's current location or the result of an address search, for example. Typically, you use a `GraphicsLayer` to display dynamic or temporary data.

At one point in the development of the ArcGIS JavaScript API, I was provided with a more robust method of working with existing data using the `FeatureLayer`, which I'll cover in greater depth in section 2.3.

2.2.4   Creating graphics with the QueryTask

So far I've covered how to add graphics to the map by clicking locations on the map. This approach is useful in many workflows, but how would you add graphics to a map you're not manually drawing? For example, an external map service may provide maps of river networks, point sources of emissions, or areas in danger of seasonal fires. In this scenario, you can add `Graphic` items to the map with the `QueryTask` module, which queries data in a map service. This allows you to ask the map data questions, and then you can do something with the results you're given—for example, display the answers on a map.

`QueryTask` uses a `Query` object to define the criteria to perform this task. The `Query` object can have a `where` statement, which describes criteria for the query, such as `NAME = Bob`, or it can define a geometry to perform the query, as well as many other options. A query is a way of extracting data from a map service based on a defined set of criteria, such as these examples:

- Find all states that begin with "New."
- Find all the major highways in a particular city.

To demonstrate using `QueryTask`, let's embed several queries in a drop-down menu.

CREATING THE DROP-DOWN MENU

Let's expand on what you've done so far and include a drop-down menu in the HTML page (before the div element that contains the map). The following code uses a select element with option elements inside it to provide the drop-down menu:

```
<body>
<select id="population" name="population">
  <option value="" selected="selected">Select Population</option>
  <option value="2500">2,500</option>
  <option value="5000">5,000</option>
  <option value="7500">7,500</option>
</select>
<div id="map"></div>
</body>
```

When a drop-down item is selected, you use the QueryTask to retrieve the locations of census tracts that correspond to the selected population number (greater than 5,000 people, for example). So now you're adding census tract data to the map.

> **DEFINITION**   According to the U.S. Census Bureau, census tracts are "small, relatively permanent statistical subdivisions of a county."[1]

To make the census data easier to work with on the map, you'll work with a point layer that represents the centers of each census tract in Los Angeles County. This particular layer includes labor statistics that show the population and percentage of people working in each census tract. You can see a sample of what this data looks like in figure 2.7. This is similar to what the data will look like in your application.

Census tract points in Los Angeles County

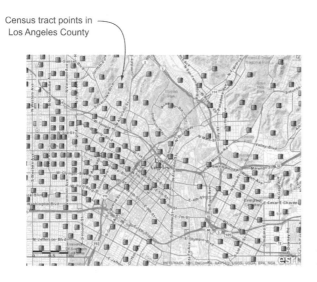

Figure 2.7   Census tracts in Los Angeles County represented as points

---

[1] "American Community Survey," U.S. Census Bureau, www.census.gov/acs/www/data_documentation/custom_tabulation_request_form/geo_def.php.

DISPLAYING THE DROP-DOWN MENU RESULTS ON A MAP

You'll need the following modules to use the drop-down menu to filter your data:

```
require([
  'dojo/dom',
  'dojo/_base/array',
  'dojo/_base/Color',
  'esri/map',
  'esri/tasks/query',
  'esri/tasks/QueryTask',
  'esri/symbols/SimpleMarkerSymbol'
  ], function(
  query, array, Color,
  Map, Query, QueryTask, SimpleMarkerSymbol
) {
...
```

I've already discussed the QueryTask and the Query modules. The SimpleMarker-Symbol module defines the way the census tract points, commonly referred to as markers, appear on the map. The SimpleMarkerSymbol also needs the dojo/_base/Color module to define the color of the census tract points. For simplicity, load a helper module called dojo/_base/array, which has many utility functions for working with arrays. Table 2.3 summarizes the modules.

Table 2.3   Dojo and Esri modules needed for the drop-down filter

Module name	Description
dojo/_base/array	Helper module to work with arrays
dojo/_base/Color	Assigns colors to Graphic
dojo/dom	Helper module to search elements in HTML
esri/map	Creates an instance of a map
esri/tasks/query	Defines parameters to perform searches
esri/symbols/SimpleMarkerSymbol	Defines how a Graphic looks on the map
esri/tasks/QueryTask	Queries a map service

With these modules loaded, you can add this functionality to your application as shown in listing 2.3. You'll complete the following steps:

- Instantiate your map and create a SimpleMarkerSymbol to define the appearance of the results of your QueryTask.
- Create two functions. One is used for the successful completion of a query, and the other is used, in the event of an error, to display the error message in the debug console of the browser.
- When a population number is selected from the drop-down menu, create a new QueryTask pointing to the URL of a map service, which in this case is a service that contains the census tracts as points.

- Create a new Query and define a where statement that searches for census tracts with a population greater than the population currently selected.
- Using the Query, set the returnGeometry option to true, which makes sure that the x and y coordinates of the census tract are returned with the results.
- Use the QueryTask to run an execute command (using the Query you defined) and pass along your success and error-handling functions.

When the QueryTask completes, the result you get is referred to as a FeatureSet, which is a collection of geographic data. It could contain a single point or 1,000 points; it's only a container for this collection of data. A FeatureSet has a few properties, including the following:

- *geometryType*–In this case, it's a point, but it could be a polygon or line in other situations.
- *features*–Contains Graphic features that represent the results of your Query.

The graphics don't have a symbology assigned to them when you first get them, so it's up to you to define it, which is why you made the SimpleMarkerSymbol previously in the application. You can use the array module you loaded to loop over the features, set the symbol of each Graphic to the defined symbology, and then add the Graphic to the map's default GraphicsLayer, as shown in the following listing.

NOTE The source code for this section is available in the chapter2 folder in the files chapter2/2.3.html and chapter2/2.3.js.

Listing 2.3 Add graphics with a QueryTask

```
require([
  'dojo/dom',
  'dojo/on',
  'dojo/_base/array',
  'dojo/_base/Color',
  'esri/map',
  'esri/tasks/query',
  'esri/tasks/QueryTask',
  'esri/symbols/SimpleMarkerSymbol'
], function(
  dom, on, array, Color,
  Map, Query, QueryTask, SimpleMarkerSymbol
) {
    var map = new Map('map', {
        basemap: 'streets',
        autoResize: true,
        center: [-118.2095, 34.0866],
        zoom: 10
    }),
    url = 'http://services.arcgis.com/V6ZHFr6zdgNZuVG0/arcgis/rest/services/'
      +
'la_county_labor_centroid/FeatureServer/0',       ◁  Specifies service to use
    markerSymbol = new SimpleMarkerSymbol(
```

```
    SimpleMarkerSymbol.STYLE_SQUARE, 10,
    null, new Color([50,50,255])
);
```
Manually defines symbology to describe what results look like

```
function onQuerySuccess(featureSet) {
    map.graphics.clear();
    array.forEach(featureSet.features, function(feature) {
        feature.setSymbol(markerSymbol);
        map.graphics.add(feature);
    });
}
```
Sets symbology of how results are displayed

```
function onError(error) {
    console.error('An error ocurred in the query: ', error);
}

on(dom.byId('population'), 'change', function(e) {
    var population = e.target.value;
    if (population.length > 0) {
      var queryTask = new QueryTask(url);
      var query = new Query();
      query.where = 'TOTAL_POP > ' + population;
      query.returnGeometry = true;
      queryTask.execute(query).then(onQuerySuccess, onError);
    }
  });
});
```
Defines where statement

Executes QueryTask using Query; passes it to functions to handle results or error

The result of this application can be seen in figure 2.8.

This small sample covers quite a bit of ground. You're building queries to retrieve data from a map service, you're defining the way those results are going to look, and

Results of QueryTask displayed as graphics on the map

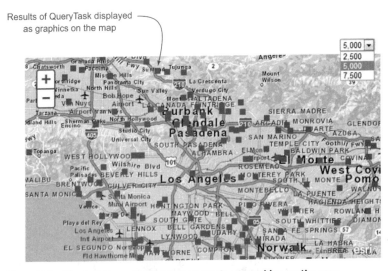

Figure 2.8 Displaying results of a `QueryTask` **as graphics on the map**

you're using Dojo utility modules to accomplish it all. This represents a pattern you'll see often in developing your web mapping applications:

- Perform a query
- Handle query results
- Display results on a map

The `QueryTask` is a commonly used tool in your ArcGIS API for JavaScript toolbox. Before I cover the next powerful tool, the `FeatureLayer`, review table 2.4, which summarizes the key terms I covered in this section.

Table 2.4 Key raster, vector, and `GraphicsLayer` terms

Term	Description
`FeatureSet`	A collection of features returned as a result from performing a query on a map service
`Graphic`	Used to represent vector geometries on the map
`GraphicsLayer`	Layer in the map that contains various `Graphic` items to display data on the map
Map tiles	256 x 256 image tiles used to represent static map data
`QueryTask`	Module provided in the JavaScript API to perform queries on map services
Raster data	Nonvector data represented as an image in the browser
Symbology	How a `Graphic` is displayed on the map, such as by color, size, and opacity
Vector data	Geometries such as points, lines, or polygons displayed on the map

The `FeatureLayer` in the ArcGIS API for JavaScript is a combination of a `GraphicsLayer` and a `QueryTask`.

2.3   *Working with the FeatureLayer*

The `FeatureLayer` was added to the API to provide a more robust method of working with vector data. It provides various methods to display vector data on the map in an efficient manner. You'd use a `GraphicsLayer` to display fire hydrants on a street, but you'd use a `FeatureLayer` to add new fire hydrants to the map.

The `FeatureLayer` is a robust module in the API because it acts as a `GraphicsLayer` for a layer in a map service and also provides editing capabilities, which I'll cover in chapters 4 and 5. Because it also includes a built-in `QueryTask`, it can be used to select items from itself.

For now, let's discuss how the `FeatureLayer` can display data from a single layer in a map service or a feature service. I'll cover a feature service, which is a service that allows you to edit data, more extensively in chapter 4. This section covers many things, so here's a brief overview:

- I'll cover some of the reasons you would use a `FeatureLayer` and what advantages it provides to you as a developer.

- Then I'll discuss how to create a `FeatureLayer` and the various options that are available to you.
- I'll also cover what modes are available for a `FeatureLayer`, as well as how to create a `DefinitionExpression`.
- I'll wrap up the discussion of the `FeatureLayer` by looking at how to perform a spatial query in which you select items in the `FeatureLayer` using a geometry that you define.

2.3.1 Advantages of a FeatureLayer

When you first start working with a `FeatureLayer`, you may wonder why you shouldn't use the `GraphicsLayer` to display data on the map. A `FeatureLayer` is a combination of a `GraphicsLayer` and a `QueryTask`, so what makes it so special? The `FeatureLayer` has optimizations built into it that make displaying large datasets faster and more efficient than trying to manage it on your own with a `GraphicsLayer`.

PERFORMING GENERALIZATIONS

A `FeatureLayer` is designed to request only the data that matters. Browser real estate is measured in pixels. The resolution of a map can be measured by specifying that "one pixel equals [a certain distance on the map]." Depending on the zoom level, this distance could be 100 miles or 100 feet. The `FeatureLayer` sends this information to the map server. The server then determines whether more than one vertex of a line or polygon is displayed in a pixel. If so, it returns a single vertex instead of the dozen or so vertices that might be there. This process is called *generalization*. The browser would be unable to draw the `Graphic` features at any finer detail anyway, so for larger datasets, this makes quite a difference in the download size of the data returned from the server. It can make the difference between returning a 2-megabyte file and a 200-kilobyte file, which you'd definitely notice (see figure 2.9).

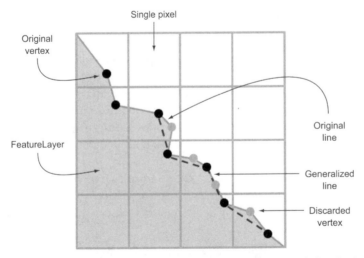

Figure 2.9 How a `FeatureLayer` might be generalized to optimize the data

In figure 2.9 you can see that if a single pixel contains multiple vertices, the server returns only one vertex per pixel.

Changing the default generalization settings

The generalization setting in a `FeatureLayer` is automatic, but you can disable it or set it manually:

To disable generalization—Set the `autoGeneralization` option to `false` in the constructor for a `FeatureLayer`.

To manually set generalization—Specify an offset using `setMaxAllowableOffset` with the `FeatureLayer`.

I haven't run across a case in which I've needed to do this; however, if you're working on a large dataset that still loads slowly with the default options, you can rest easy knowing that these options can be changed.

USING VECTOR TILES

Another great feature you get with `FeatureLayers` is the use of vector tiling. I discussed image map tiles previously (see section 2.2), and vector tiles work in a similar manner. By default, when data is requested to be used in a `FeatureLayer`, it's requested in chunks. These chunks are defined by a virtual grid of the current map extents. So instead of making a single request for all the data currently in the map extents, it makes multiple requests for smaller sections of the map to display all the features. You can see an example of how this might look in figure 2.10.

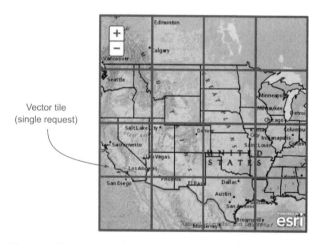

Vector tile (single request)

Figure 2.10 How vector tiles might be requested for a map

Vector tiling is the default behavior of a `FeatureLayer` and is described as "on-demand" mode. A few modes are available for a `FeatureLayer`, and I'll discuss those in section 2.3.3, but with the on-demand mode, the data is requested only as needed.

Another benefit of vector tiling is that the data is cached in the browser, so when panning the map around, if the web application requests a vector tile from the server that was previously provided, the server tells the application to get the data from the cache. This optimization allows the `FeatureLayer` to take advantage of the browser cache to increase performance of the web application.

Now that I've talked about the advantages of a FeatureLayer, let's move on to creating a map with it.

2.3.2 *Creating a FeatureLayer*

To add a FeatureLayer to the map, create a new instance of a FeatureLayer with a source URL and add it to the map:

```
var featureLayer = new FeatureLayer(
  'http://services.arcgis.com/' +
  'V6ZHFr6zdgNZuVG0/arcgis/rest/services' +
  '/la_county_labor_centroid/FeatureServer/0'
);
map.addLayer(featureLayer);
```

With a couple of lines of code, you can load this entire layer of graphics into your map, as shown in figure 2.11.

What you see in figure 2.11 are numerous points displayed as Graphic features on the map. By default, the FeatureLayer renders items on the map as they were designed when the source data was defined; it uses the same symbols used in the desktop software that created the data. In this case, instead of being an SVG element on the map, it's displaying an image for each point on the map internally, using a SimplePictureMarkerSymbol from the ArcGIS API for JavaScript. The SimplePictureMarkerSymbol allows you to use an image instead of an SVG graphic to represent a location on the map.

If you use a debugging tool like the tools built into Google Chrome and inspect the map element, you'll see that the GraphicsLayer is composed of thousands of images using Base64-encoded image data (see figure 2.12). I'll cover Base64-encoded image data in the next chapter.

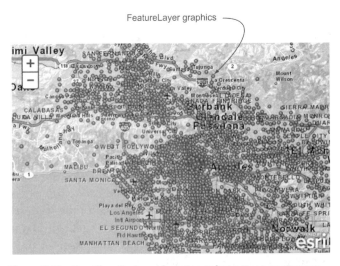

Figure 2.11 **Graphics displayed in a map using a FeatureLayer**

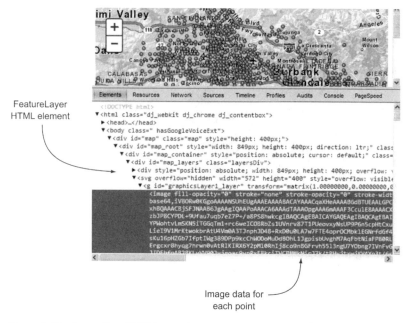

FeatureLayer
HTML element

Image data for
each point

Figure 2.12   Inspecting HTML to see how FeatureLayer provides data

As you can see from the number of features shown in figure 2.12, this is a large amount of data for the map to display. Too much data can significantly impact the performance of your application. In this case, even though this image is fairly small, the browser still uses up memory to draw it on the screen.

2.3.3   *Optimizing application performance*

To manage your application's performance, you can set different modes for the FeatureLayer:

- *MODE_SNAPSHOT*—Retrieves all data from the service and displays it on the map. My suggestion is to use this one sparingly as it can heavily impact map performance. This mode is best suited for a service that provides minimal data, such as a jurisdictional boundary.
- *MODE_ONDEMAND*—Retrieves only data from the service that's in the current extent of the map.
- *MODE_SELECTION*—Retrieves only data from the service when the data is selected using a query.

I won't cover MODE_SNAPSHOT, as it downloads all the data, and you have quick access to it. This could impact the performance of your application if it tries to download a large amount of data. It's best used for smaller bits of data and also prevents the application from retrieving data from the server unnecessarily.

FeatureLayer
graphics limited by
DefinitionExpression

**Figure 2.13
FeatureLayer with
DefinitionExpression
of 'TOTAL_POP > 5000'
applied**

USING A DEFINITIONEXPRESSION

By default, the FeatureLayer uses MODE_ONDEMAND. In the case of this example, this retrieves almost all the data in the feature service, which is why it may not perform well. To make working with large amounts of data in the FeatureLayer more manageable, you'll define a DefinitionExpression—a set of criteria you can define on the FeatureLayer to limit the data that's retrieved.

This particular feature service includes population information for census tracts, so you may want to display only locations with a population greater than 5,000 people. You can do this by setting the DefinitionExpression on the FeatureLayer:

```
featureLayer.setDefinitionExpression('TOTAL_POP > 5000');
```

When you do this, you can see in figure 2.13 that the map displays markedly less data.

The FeatureLayer is still in on-demand mode, but now it limits the amount of data requested by the criteria you set in the DefinitionExpression. This combination can greatly improve performance of your application.

Now you're starting to do something more interesting with your data. By providing a DefinitionExpression, you're asking the data questions and displaying the response. Let's make this application even more interactive.

USING A DYNAMIC DEFINITIONEXPRESSION

Let's add a menu that allows users to filter the data by a specific population range. To create the menu, add a select HTML element with options to your page (found in the chapter 2 folder in the 2.4.html file) as you did with the GraphicsLayer previously:

```
<body>
    <select id="population" name="population">
      <option value="2500" selected="selected">2,500</option>
      <option value="5000">5,000</option>
      <option value="7500">7,500</option>
    </select>
    <div id="map"></div>
  </body>
```

Now that you've modified your HTML page, let's look at the JavaScript (the 2.4.js file of the source code) that makes everything work, as shown in the following listing.

Listing 2.4   JavaScript for simple filter application

```
require([
        'dojo/dom',                          Uses dom module to select
        'dojo/on',                           HTML element by id
        'esri/map',
        'esri/layers/FeatureLayer'
        ], function(dom, on, Map, FeatureLayer) {
    var map = new Map('map', {
        basemap: 'streets',
        autoResize: true,
        center: [-118.2095, 34.0866],
        zoom: 10
    });

    var featureLayer = new FeatureLayer(
        'http://services.arcgis.com/' +
        'V6ZHFr6zdgNZuVG0/arcgis/rest/services/' +
        'la_county_labor_centroid/FeatureServer/0'
    );

    featureLayer.setDefinitionExpression('TOTAL_POP > 2500');

    map.addLayer(featureLayer);
                                                    Listens for change
  on(dom.byId('population'), 'change', function(e) {  event on select menu
    var population = e.target.value;
    var definitionExpression = 'TOTAL_POP > ' + population;
    featureLayer.setDefinitionExpression(definitionExpression);
  });
});
                                             Builds new definition expression based
                                             on newly selected value in drop-down
```

You're now interacting with the map to update the data displayed on the map. This example is starting to look more like a functioning application. The newly updated application is shown in figure 2.14.

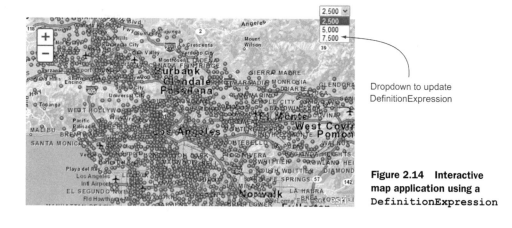

Dropdown to update
DefinitionExpression

Figure 2.14 Interactive map application using a `DefinitionExpression`

Working with the `DefinitionExpression` in a `FeatureLayer` is an elegant yet powerful way to interact with your data. Previously I mentioned that a `FeatureLayer` is a combination of a `GraphicsLayer` and query functionality. It's that built-in query functionality that allows you to interact with the `FeatureLayer` by selecting features, which I'll cover next.

2.3.4 *Selecting items in the FeatureLayer*

Another method of using the `FeatureLayer` is to use it in `MODE_SELECTION`. In `MODE_SELECTION`, you don't set a `DefinitionExpression` because the data that's retrieved from the server is retrieved using the `FeatureLayer.selectFeatures()` method. This works similarly to the `DefinitionExpression`, in which you define a set of criteria to filter your data, but you gain more flexibility. One of the main benefits of using `MODE_SELECTION` is that you can filter the data by a spatial geometry, such as a polygon.

In `MODE_SELECTION`, the `FeatureLayer` doesn't display any data when it first loads. It's up to you to define the criteria to do the selection. In this example we'll draw a polygon on the map and use that polygon to select items in the `FeatureLayer`. The HTML page looks similar to the previous example except that you click a button on the page to activate a drawing tool and begin drawing on the map:

```
...
<body>
    <input name="drawPolygon" type="button" id="drawPolygon" value="Draw"/>
    <div id="map"></div>
</body>
...
```

Your JavaScript (see listing 2.5) introduces a new module in the ArcGIS API for JavaScript, the Draw toolbar, which allows you to draw graphics on your map. The result of a completed drawing is an event that contains the geometry that was drawn on the map. The geometry could be a point, line, or polygon, but the key is that you use this geometry to perform a spatial query on your `FeatureLayer`. A spatial query is a way to filter data by spatial means, such as a polygon.

> **Listing 2.5 JavaScript to perform a `FeatureLayer` selection**

```
require([
        'dojo/dom',
        'dojo/on',
        'esri/map',
        'esri/layers/FeatureLayer',
        'esri/toolbars/draw',
        'esri/tasks/query'
        ], function(dom, on, Map, FeatureLayer, Draw, Query) {
            var map = new Map('map', {
                basemap: 'streets',
```

```
        autoResize: true,
        center: [-118.2095, 34.0866],
        zoom: 10
    }),
    featureLayer = new FeatureLayer(
      'http://services.arcgis.com/' +
      'V6ZHFr6zdgNZuVG0/arcgis/rest/services/' +
      'la_county_labor_centroid/FeatureServer/0',{
            mode: FeatureLayer.MODE_SELECTION
      }
    ),
    drawToolbar = new Draw(map);

    drawToolbar.on('draw-end', function(e){
        drawToolbar.deactivate();
        var query = new Query();
        query.geometry = e.geometry;
        featureLayer.selectFeatures(query);
    });
    map.addLayer(featureLayer);

    on(dom.byId('drawPolygon'), 'click', function() {
        drawToolbar.activate(Draw.POLYGON);
    });

});
```

Instantiates Draw toolbar by providing instance of map

Listens for Draw toolbar to finish drawing and returns an event with geometry

Selects features in FeatureLayer using drawn geometry

The result of this code is shown in figure 2.15.

As shown in figure 2.15, when you query a FeatureLayer using the geometry from the DrawToolbar, it displays only the features that are inside that geometry, which gives this example a lot of power.

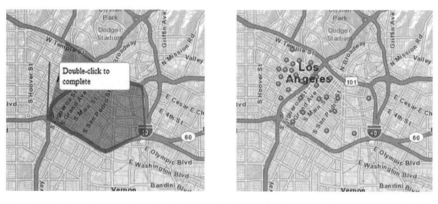

Figure 2.15 Drawing a polygon (at left) to select features in a FeatureLayer (at right)

Table 2.5 summarizes the `FeatureLayer`-related terms that I covered in this section.

Table 2.5   Key `FeatureLayer` terms

Term	Description
`DefinitionExpression`	A set of criteria you can set on a layer to limit the data shown on the map
`FeatureLayer`	Optimized layer that works with vector data on the map
Generalization	A method of optimizing vector data to reduce the amount of data needed to display on the map
Modes	Various modes that you can set on a FeatureLayer to determine how it's used in the map
Vector tiles	An optimized method of requesting vector data as a virtual grid and taking advantage of the browser cache

The ability to filter features in a map based on geometry is one of the most common use cases in developing mapping applications. Imagine that a researcher wants to restrict an analysis to a particular area or that an engineer wants to extract only manholes in a particular service area. Filtering spatial data is a cornerstone of GIS analysis and a feature that proves useful in a web application.

2.4   Summary

- The ArcGIS API for JavaScript is an extensive collection of modules that provide a full suite of tools to build powerful mapping applications. It would be impossible to cover every module in depth without this book becoming a reference manual, but the goal here is to provide information on how to get the pieces to fit together. The topics covered in this chapter provide a solid foundation in understanding how a map is displayed in the browser and the types of data that can be used.
- I covered tiled services and vector graphics in the map, but you could display numerous other types of data, such as a `WMSLayer` (Web Map Services), a `KML-Layer` (XML-based format popular with Google Maps), or a `WebTiledLayer` (generic layer to load nonArcGIS Server tiles), which I didn't cover.
- You learned how to use a `GraphicsLayer` to display data on a map and how to use a `FeatureLayer` to not only display your data but also perform queries on that data.

In chapter 3 you'll become more familiar with how to interact with the ArcGIS Server through the ArcGIS Server REST API.

Working with the 3 *REST API*

Chapter 2 covered examples of building simple mapping applications by using the ArcGIS API for JavaScript. These applications may not have been difficult, but they introduced core functions of the JavaScript API. One of the cool things about the API is that, like many other JavaScript libraries, it abstracts away some of the nitty-gritty work being done behind the curtain. Where does all that fancy mapping data come from? By looking at how the JavaScript API interacts with ArcGIS Server, you'll have a better grasp of what it might take to build your own custom components that may not be provided in the ArcGIS API for JavaScript.

Various components are at play when working with the ArcGIS API for JavaScript, such as how you acquire the data that composes a map. The other key component is the ArcGIS Server REST API. *REST* stands for *Representational State Transfer,* which is a method of communication over the web that uses what is typically called an endpoint. An *endpoint* is a URL used as a reference to get data from ArcGIS Server. An endpoint could look like http://myservername/arcgis/rest/services/myservice?f =json. In this URL example, you'd be asking the REST API to provide information about the map service in JavaScript Object Notation (JSON) format, which I discuss later in this chapter.

To get a better understanding of these components, consider an analogy of having a conversation with a deaf person through an interpreter. My sister is deaf and uses a service that enables her to make a video call to an interpreter through her television, using a webcam that looks like a bright, red, all-seeing eye. The interpreter routes her call to the intended recipient and relays the conversation by interpreting what my sister is saying in sign language to the person on the other end of the line. This method of communication works pretty well for all parties involved. Now, maybe you have sign language experience and could do much of the interpretation work yourself but aren't as efficient at sign language as the professional interpreter. You could get the job done, but not as efficiently. You could think of the ArcGIS Server software as the deaf person; in this case, the information being communicated is GIS data. The Arc-GIS Server REST API is analogous to sign language, being a specific form of communication provided by a URL endpoint. The ArcGIS API for JavaScript would then be the interpreter, relaying the information to us in a more efficient manner than if we tried to do it ourselves. This relationship is shown in figure 3.1.

Figure 3.1 shows the source for all the fancy mapping data that ends up in your applications. To expose this data to a web browser, ArcGIS Server can view the details of the data and relay this data via the REST API in a format that's easily digestible to the outside world. This data is communicated by a URL endpoint. The ArcGIS API for JavaScript is designed to take this structured information and allow us to work with it more easily than if we tried to do it on our own.

Although the ArcGIS API for JavaScript simplifies the process of working with GIS data, sometimes you'll need to work directly with the ArcGIS Server REST API to perform a task that isn't readily available in the API for JavaScript. In this chapter, you're going to use the ArcGIS REST API to build a custom widget, take a closer look at how

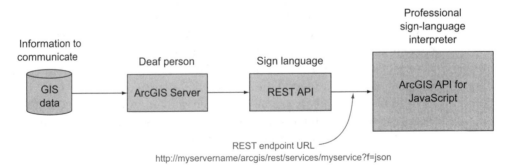

Figure 3.1   Comparing ArcGIS components to sign-language interpretation

to use the Dojo loader, and use a neat utility of ArcGIS Server to perform geometric analyses.

3.1   *Introducing the ArcGIS Server REST API*

So far you've built examples of mapping applications by using the ArcGIS API for JavaScript. The purpose of these examples was to whet your appetite (or wet your feet) with the capabilities of the API. The API is like a giant toolbox at your disposal. It not only displays your geographic information on a map but also allows you to ask the map questions about that information. But what questions do you ask? What's the population in this area? How large is the area? This information has to come from somewhere, and until now, you haven't explored this part of the process in developing an application. The key is to become at least somewhat familiar with the ArcGIS Server REST API so you understand how to use the data in the services you'll work with. In doing so, you'll explore how features of the ArcGIS API for JavaScript work and how to customize these capabilities.

This section covers the following:

- How the ArcGIS REST API relates to the ArcGIS API for JavaScript
- Understanding how to read an ArcGIS Server page
- ArcGIS REST API legend endpoint and retrieving data

3.1.1   *Exploring how the API works*

The ArcGIS Server REST API is the foundation for the ArcGIS API for JavaScript. The technical details of how REST works aren't important for this book, but you should know that, as shown in our example, the REST API is similar to a deaf person communicating in sign language to people who want access to the information. This scenario is how a web server communicates with a browser to deliver that information. In the case of ArcGIS Server, it's how you can access spatial and attribute information from the server. Figure 3.2 illustrates a simplified model of the ArcGIS web stack and what

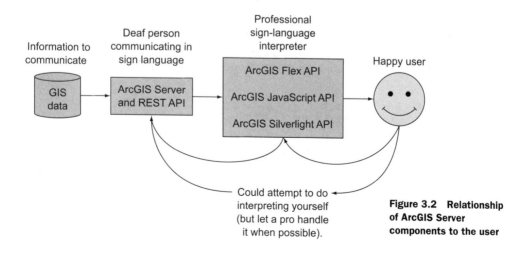

Figure 3.2   Relationship of ArcGIS Server components to the user

functionality is available to you as a developer when communicating with ArcGIS Server. You can be the happy user who is receiving nicely and professionally translated data. Hopefully by now you realize that this book's focus is the ArcGIS API for Java-Script and not the other available APIs, such as Flex or Silverlight, but I'll remind you anyway to keep you on your toes.

The takeaway from figure 3.2 is that these web APIs are speaking the same language to ArcGIS Server via the REST API. So if you ever decide to undertake one of these other APIs in a future project, the basics are the same; you're just working in a different programming language and development environment.

Having a common base to work from with the REST API can be advantageous to developers because you'll know what to expect when working in any API. The workflow you choose depends on the tools you have available, whether the API is JavaScript or Silverlight.

Quick REST rundown

REST uses four basic operations—create, read, update, and delete—referred to as CRUD functions. These functions operate on a few Hypertext Transfer Protocol (HTTP) methods; typically POST, GET, PUT, and DELETE. GET is what you could call a safe method, because it's used only to retrieve information. The other methods potentially make a change. POST usually inserts data via REST, PUT performs updates, and DELETE removes information.

To learn more about these method definitions, refer to the W3C specification at www.w3.org/Protocols/rfc2616/rfc2616-sec9.html.

In theory, you could build your own JavaScript API to interact with the REST API and you'd get the same information, but only after more work on your part. But that doesn't mean it isn't useful to get a better understanding of how to work directly with ArcGIS Server. When you're building your application, you'll need a basic understanding of the data you're working with. When working with ArcGIS Server, you can view details about the data directly in nicely formatted HTML pages. This same data is available in JSON used by the JavaScript API. JSON is a way of transferring data in web applications. It boils down to a set of key/value pairs, as shown in the following example:

```
{
 "name":"Chuck Finley",
 "occupations":["Secret Agent","Entrepreneur","Super Hero"]
}
```

The HTML pages provided with ArcGIS Server services are useful when you want to view details about the information being supplied by the ArcGIS Server REST API. You can view the documentation for the ArcGIS Server REST API at http://resources.arcgis.com/en/help/rest/apiref/index.html.

3.1.2   *Interacting with ArcGIS Server pages*

At the time of this writing, the ArcGIS Server REST API is at version 10.11. Let's take a look at an ArcGIS Server service that provides census information. This is the type of information you need to become familiar with in a web service so you can build an application. The REST API provides HTML pages to give you easy access to web service information, as shown in figure 3.3.

Let's focus on a few items of this web service page:

- The list of Layers is vital because you'll use these layer IDs when deciding which features are visible on the map and which layers you'll want to query or use with the Identify tool covered in chapter 4.
- The Spatial Reference is important because, ideally, you want all your data to be in the same projection (showing how the earth is represented) for performance reasons.
- The REST API page lets you know whether the data in the service is Single Fused Map Cache, meaning that tiles for the map have already been generated ahead

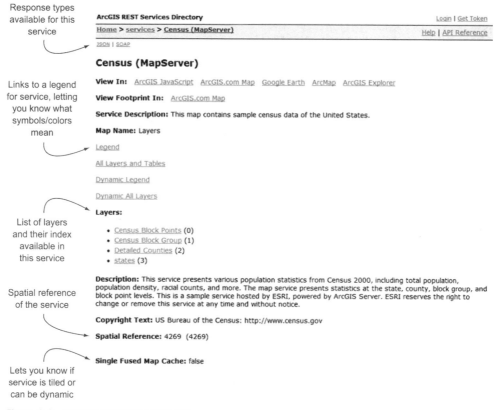

Figure 3.3   Sample ArcGIS Server page

of time and can load quickly as a tiled service. Typically, this is done for aerial imagery or large datasets that don't change often.

- The Legend link is something you'll take a closer look at next to build a custom widget.

A note about legends in web mapping applications

Using a legend in modern web mapping applications can sometimes be considered outdated. In a best-case scenario, your map data is cartographically designed so a legend is unnecessary, and the needs of your users can be met without it. But that's a best-case scenario. At times, data requires a legend to better express the intent of the map and your application.

LEGEND ENDPOINT

The legend widget provided in the ArcGIS API for JavaScript interacts with the legend endpoint of the ArcGIS Server REST API. Remember, an endpoint is an exposed part

```
{
  "layers" : [
    {
      "layerId" : 0,
      "layerName" : "Census Block Points",
      "layerType" : "Feature Layer",
      "minScale" : 99999.9999894534,
      "maxScale" : 0,
      "legend" : [
        {
          "label" : "0 - 61",
          "url" : "6E4168CF",
          "imageData" : "iVBORw0KGgoAAAANSUhEUgAAABsAAAAbBAMAAAB/+ulmAAAACVBMVEUAAABzsv/+//+7q4cPAAAAA3RST",
          "contentType" : "image/png"
        },
        {
          "label" : "62 - 264",
          "url" : "5B9D87CD",
          "imageData" : "iVBORw0KGgoAAAANSUhEUgAAABsAAAAbBAMAAAB/+ulmAAAACVBMVEUAAABzsv/+//+7q4cPAAAAA3RST",
          "contentType" : "image/png"
        },
        {
          "label" : "265 - 759",
          "url" : "B3328260",
          "imageData" : "iVBORw0KGgoAAAANSUhEUgAAABsAAAAbBAMAAAB/+ulmAAAACVBMVEUAAABzsv/+//+7q4cPAAAAA3RST",
          "contentType" : "image/png"
        },
        {
          "label" : "760 - 1900",
          "url" : "1A6645DD",
          "imageData" : "iVBORw0KGgoAAAANSUhEUgAAABsAAAAbBAMAAAB/+ulmAAAACVBMVEUAAABzsv/+//+7q4cPAAAAA3RST",
          "contentType" : "image/png"
        },
        {
          "label" : "1901 - 9409",
          "url" : "1E035412",
          "imageData" : "iVBORw0KGgoAAAANSUhEUgAAABsAAAAbBAMAAAB/+ulmAAAACVBMVEUAAABzsv/+//+7q4cPAAAAA3RST",
          "contentType" : "image/png"
        }
      ]
    },
    {
      "layerId" : 1,
      "layerName" : "Census Block Group",
      "layerType" : "Feature Layer",
      "minScale" : 1000000,
      "maxScale" : 0,
      "legend" : [
        {
          "label" : "",
          "url" : "6E3AC8F2",
          "imageData" : "iVBORw0KGgoAAAANSUhEUgAAACIAAAAbBAMAAADrHECUAAAAB1BMVEWCgoL+//97Fd17AAAAAnRST1P/J",
          "contentType" : "image/png"
        }
      ]
    },
    {
      "layerId" : 3,
      "layerName" : "Coarse Counties",
      "layerType" : "Feature Layer",
      "minScale" : 0,
```

Figure 3.4
JSON representation
of legend endpoint

of your interface in the REST API that's used for communication. The legend endpoint contains information such as the names of items in the map service as well as how those items should be drawn in the map. This data can be represented in HTML format so that a user can easily review the data, or as a JSON representation that you can use with the ArcGIS API for JavaScript to make a custom widget. You can see what the JSON representation of the legend endpoint looks like in figure 3.4.

This widget makes it easy to display symbols and their meanings. The census block points shown in figure 3.5 display the legend as shown in the ArcGIS Server pages and the legend displayed in an application using the out-of-the-box legend widget.

The out-of-the-box legend widget is a time-saver that accomplishes its task nicely. But suppose your application requires you to allow users to turn layer items on and off via a check box next to each legend item. This feature isn't built into the legend widget of the ArcGIS API for JavaScript. You'll need to build a custom solution. To do that, you'll interact directly with the legend endpoint of the ArcGIS Server REST

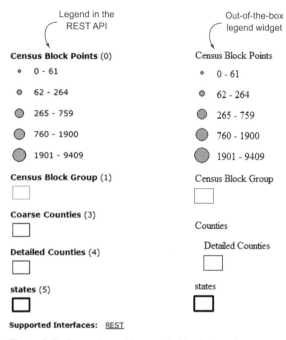

Figure 3.5   Legend graphics created by ArcGIS Server REST API (at left) and by legend widget (at right)

API and dig into the ArcGIS API for JavaScript to get the job done by using the built-in Dojo tools introduced in chapter 2.

Widgets and more

The set of tools and widgets provided by the API are more than enough for a developer to build a suitable application that could meet most needs and requirements. But for those times when you're challenged to meet a requirement that may have you digging through API documentation, scouring obscure blog postings, or reading through an abandoned mailing list for a solution, fret not; remember your tools and take a look in your toolbox. A widget in its simplest form is a chunk of portable code that can be used in any application. When working with the ArcGIS API for JavaScript, widgets usually involve a visual element of the page, such as the legend.

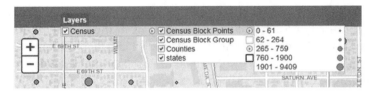

Figure 3.6   Custom legend widget built using Dojo Dijits

3.2   *Building your own widget*

To build your own legend widget with the added capability to turn layers on and off, you'll use the built-in Dijit framework that comes standard as a part of Dojo. A Dijit in Dojo is a visual component, and in this case you'll use the Dijit menu suite of components to make a menu-based legend table of contents. This will enable you to build a nice-looking legend widget, as shown in figure 3.6. The entire code base to build this widget can be a bit involved, but you'll learn the main steps needed to accomplish your goals.

This section covers the following:

- Building the root menu of a legend widget
- Retrieving and using legend details from ArcGIS REST API
- Using methods to display legend items in a widget

NOTE The code for the custom widget is available in the chapter3/legendtoc folder of the source code included with the book.

The purpose of this widget is to display legend information and allow users to turn items on and off in one place. The key to building this custom widget is interacting directly with the legend endpoint of the ArcGIS Server REST API. Accessing the legend endpoint from your application is easy, but building this custom widget requires a few steps.

3.2.1   *Building the legend root menu*

The first step is to build the root menu for a map service to add to the custom legend. To build the root menu, initialize a custom module called `CheckedPopupMenuItem` that displays the root element of a service:

```
startup: function (options) {
...
  serviceMenu = new CheckedPopupMenuItem({
                    label: layer.title,
                    layer: layer,
                    checked: layer.visible,
                    popup: layerMenu,
                    onChange: onServiceChecked
                });
...
```

You initialize a custom `CheckedPopupMenuItem` widget that is composed of a `Checked-MenuItem` and `PopupMenuItem` from the Dijit library. This widget contains a title and a reference to the layer it represents. It will also contain a menu that displays each individual item in the layer as well as the ability to toggle the visibility of the whole service.

3.2.2 *Retrieving legend details*

The next step is to retrieve the detailed legend information about your map service. The key to building this custom widget is interacting directly with the legend endpoint of the ArcGIS Server REST API. Accessing the legend endpoint from your application is easy. You can use the built-in `esri/request` module to call the endpoint and return the results. This function returns a JavaScript promise. A *promise* returns the result of a task, in this case the request sent to the legend endpoint. After you have these results, the next couple of steps are where you need to apply a little bit of elbow grease. You need to send a request to the legend endpoint of the map service and then parse those results to make them useful for your widget:

```
esriRequest({
    url: layer.url + '/legend',                      Obtains legend endpoint
    content: {
        f: 'json'                          Indicates you want result as JSON
    },
    callbackParamName: 'callback'                    Updates menu with
}).then(legendResponseHandler(layer, layerMenu));    legend results
```

You've created a `request` object by using the `esriRequest()` method. This `request` object is referred to as a *promise*. The promise pattern is used for handling asynchronous requests, such as needing to wait for a response from the server for the legend information. You can handle the response of this request by passing a function to `esriRequest().then()` and interacting with the legend results.

The result you get back from the legend endpoint has various pieces of information that will be useful in building your legend widget. I've omitted the `url` and `imageData` results to conserve space and truncated portions of the results to emphasize what a response from a legend endpoint looks like:

```
"legend": [                            Array of items to be shown in legend
    {
        "label": "0 - 61",
        "url": "imageurl",
        "imageData": "imagedatastring",
        "contentType": "image/png",        Base64-encoded
        "height": 20,                      image data string
        "width": 20,
        "values": [                  Array of values represented in legend
          61
        ]
    } ...
```

Name of image for source image URL

3.2.3   *Displaying details in the custom legend widget*

Your goal at this point is to turn these results into list items in your widget. You have a couple of options to display the symbols returned in the legend, mostly available to handle cross-browser capabilities:

- *Image source URL*—You can create a URL to the source image on the server, which uses a standard format to access the source image: http://<hostname>/ arcgis/rest/services/<ServiceName>/MapServer/<layerid>/images/imageurl.
- *Image data*—The other option is to use the provided imageData, which is Base64-encoded image data that enables you to display the image without having to make a round-trip call to the server. This adds a bit of a performance increase. If you intend for your application to be used on a mobile device, the fewer calls to the server, the better.

Figure 3.7 shows a Chrome debug console, comparing the image source URL method and the imageData method.

As shown in figure 3.7, using the image source URL method required sending a single request that took 139 milliseconds to load the image. You may display it ten times, but the browser is smart enough to know that it doesn't need to make ten requests. Compare that to using the imageData method, and you can see that no requests were made to the server. Now, 139 milliseconds may not seem like much, but if lots of images need to be loaded for a legend and a request takes longer than usual,

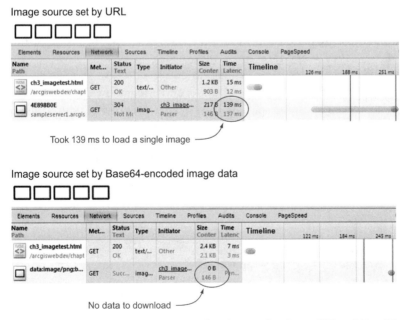

Figure 3.7   Chrome debug console comparing the use of an image URL and Base64-encoded data

those small delays can add up and cause a noticeable difference to someone using the application.

This `imageData` technique isn't supported in older desktop browsers, but to avoid unnecessarily complicating the widget, you'll use `imageData` to display legend symbols. You can do so by adding `data:image/png;base64` to the beginning of the `src` attribute inside an image tag before you add the `imageData` string from the server:

```
<img src="data:image/png;base64,<imageData>" />
```

The next step is to build the subsequent item in your custom legend menu.

3.2.4 *Working with multiple symbols in a feature*

To find out whether any of your legend items have more than one set of symbols, such as the census block points shown previously in figure 3.6, you need to do a little more work. Part of the results you get back from a legend endpoint will include an array of legend symbols for each layer in the map service. You need to loop over the results of this array, which contain information such as the ID of the layer that you'll use in the custom widget:

```
arrayUtils.forEach(layer.layerInfos, function(info) {
...
    var legendMenu = buildLegendMenu(sub_info.legend);        ◁⌐  Builds legend
    lyrMenu.addChild(new CheckedPopupMenuItem({     ◁⌐
        label: sub_info.layerName,                           Adds new menu
        info: info,                                          item with check box
        popup: legendMenu,
        checked: arrayUtils.indexOf(
                    layer.visibleLayers, sub_info.layerId
                ) > -1,                              ◁⌐  Indicates whether check
        onChange: onChecked                              box should be selected
}));
...
```

You use a helper function to build the legend menu items that don't have check boxes but are symbols, like the census block points in figure 3.6:

```
define([
...
  function buildLegendMenu(legend) {
    var legendMenu = new Menu({});                Creates new instance of
    arrayUtils.forEach(legend, function(item) {   custom LegendMenuItem
      legendMenu.addChild(new LegendMenuItem({   ◁⌐
        label: item.label.length > 0 ? item.label : '...',
        legendUrl: 'data:image/png;base64,' + item.imageData     ◁
      }));
    });                                            Uses Base64-encoded
    return legendMenu;                             image data for images
  }
...
```

Another alternative is to simply use the image URL from the legend service and let the browser cache the image to eliminate excessive requests to the server. That could be done by making one small adjustment, as shown in the following snippet:

```
legendMenu.addChild(new LegendMenuItem({
    legendUrl: item.url
}));
```

Both options are viable, and using image data or an image URL is a choice of which method will best suit your situation or need to optimize the number of requests sent to the server.

I hope you take away from this section that you can interact directly with the ArcGIS Server REST API to acquire information that may not be readily available with the Arc-GIS API for JavaScript. This opens a whole new world of possibilities for presenting your data to the user, interacting with that data, and making a pleasant-looking application.

Next you'll learn about using a special service in ArcGIS Server called the geometry service that can be used to perform spatial analyses in your application.

3.3   Working with the geometry service

Numerous types of services are available in ArcGIS Server, most of these representing spatial data, such as aerial imagery, streets, or points of interest. One that is not special data and may prove useful in everyday tasks is the geometry service. The *geometry service* is a suite of utilities provided in ArcGIS Server to perform general types of geometric analysis, such as creating a new feature based on a distance from a given point, or determining where two features intersect.

This section covers the following:

- Overview of the geometry service
- Turning points into buffered areas
- Using the buffer to make selections with the `FeatureLayer`
- Incorporating use of a proxy to make large requests

The geometry service can be useful in developing your applications, and the ArcGIS JavaScript API requires you to specify a geometry service to be used in some widgets before they can be implemented. These include the *measurement widget*, used to do measurements on the map, and the *editor widget*, which uses the geometry service for various tasks while editing. Figure 3.8 provides a sample of what the geometry service can do.

3.3.1   Buffer your heart out

Figure 3.8 shows a small sample of what the geometry service can do, but these operations are a good place for us to start our little adventure. One of the most widely used analyses when working with spatial data is the ever-popular buffer operation. You can imagine a *buffer* working the same as a compass. No, not the kind that tells you what direction you're going in, but the kind that you probably used when you were in grade school to draw awesomely perfect circles. That's what the buffer operation of the geometry service does: it draws circles around a particular point. As you can imagine,

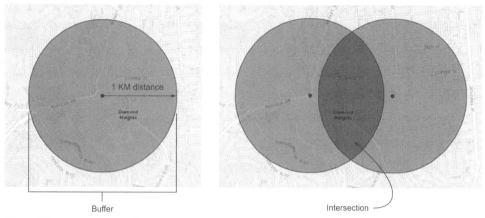

Figure 3.8 Types of tasks the geometry service can do

this could prove to be useful. Have you used an application on your phone to find nearby restaurants or movie theaters? Powering that search is a buffer operation to provide an answer based on your current location. Let's experiment with buffer operations to see how easy it is.

> **NOTE** The source code for this section is available in the chapter3 folder of the source code included with the book. See chapter3/3.2.html and chapter3/3.2.js.

After loading your dependencies in your JavaScript, you create your map and geometry service task, as shown in the following listing. The application you build will create a buffer geometry based on where you click on the map.

Listing 3.1 Using `GeometryService` to buffer a location

```
require([
        ...
], function (
  Map, Graphic, FeatureLayer,
  Draw, GeometryService,
  BufferParameters, Query,
  symbol, dom, on, Color, arrayUtils
) {
  var map = new Map('map', {
      basemap: 'gray',
      center: [-122.4348, 37.7582],
      zoom: 13
  }),
  geometryService = new GeometryService(
      'http://tasks.arcgisonline.com/ArcGIS/rest/services/' +
      'Geometry/GeometryServer'
    ),
  featureLayer = new FeatureLayer(
      'http://sampleserver1.arcgisonline.com/ArcGIS/rest/services/' +
```

Indicates geometry service task provided in ArcGIS JavaScript API

```
    'Demographics/ESRI_Census_USA/MapServer/1',
  {
    mode: FeatureLayer.MODE_SELECTION,
    outFields: ["*"]
  }),
drawTool;
map.addLayer(featureLayer);
map.on('load', function() {
drawTool = new Draw(map);                      Initializes Draw toolbar
on(drawTool, 'draw-end', function(e) {
  drawTool.deactivate();                              Listens for when Draw
  var ptSymbol = new symbol.SimpleMarkerSymbol(       toolbar finishes drawing
    symbol.SimpleMarkerSymbol.STYLE_CIRCLE,
    10,
    null,
    new Color([255,0,0,1])
  ),                                             Initializes BufferParameters
  params = new BufferParameters();               object for geometry service
  map.graphics.add(new Graphic(e.geometry, ptSymbol));
  params.geometries = [e.geometry];
  params.distances = [1];
  params.unit = GeometryService.UNIT_KILOMETER;       Indicates buffer
  params.outSpatialReference = map.spatialReference;   of I kilometer
  geometryService.buffer(params, function(geometries) {

    var fill = new symbol.SimpleFillSymbol(        Uses Buffer method
      symbol.SimpleFillSymbol.STYLE_SOLID,         provided in the
      new symbol.SimpleLineSymbol(                 ArcGIS JavaScript API
        symbol.SimpleLineSymbol.STYLE_SOLID,
        new Color([255,0,0,0.65]), 2
      ),
      new Color([255,0,0,0.35])
    );
    arrayUtils.forEach(geometries, function(geom) {
      map.graphics.add(new Graphic(geom, fill));       Adds buffered
      var query = new Query();                          area to map
      query.geometry = geom;
    });
  });
});
 });
 on(dom.byId('drawPoint'), 'click', function() {
drawTool.activate(Draw.POINT);
 });
});
```

What toolbar?

The Draw toolbar module provided in the ArcGIS JavaScript API isn't a visual toolbar per se, but it provides all the functionality you need to add points, lines, polygons, and more to the map. You could create your own toolbar with this functionality. It is a module designed to interact with the map.

When a button on the page is clicked, you allow the user to draw a point on the map. This can be done by listening for the `drawPoint` button to be clicked and activating the `drawTool` to specifically draw a point:

```
on(dom.byId('drawPoint'), 'click', function() {
  drawTool.activate(Draw.POINT);
});
```

You can then wait for the `drawTool` to send a `draw-end` event that triggers a function that will immediately deactivate the tool so the user can add only one point at a time:

```
drawTool.on('draw-end', function(e) {
    drawTool.deactivate();
...
```

When you click the Point button and then click the map, you see a result similar to figure 3.9.

Look at that amazing buffered area. You've now mastered the ArcGIS JavaScript API in all its glory! All kidding aside, these are the first steps to more-interesting analyses you can do. Maybe you want information about what's inside the buffered area you created. Maybe you're interested in which census blocks are centered inside your buffered area. To do this, you could take advantage of our trusty old `FeatureLayer`.

3.3.2 *Buffer and select*

As you learned in chapter 2, a `FeatureLayer` enables you to add data to the map in different modes. You can use it to add data as needed, so when you first see the map, it downloads only the information in your current view. You can load the data all at once, which helps prevent more HTTP requests to the server during use of your application. This is best suited for small datasets, because anything more than a few hundred features may slow the startup of your application. The mode we're most

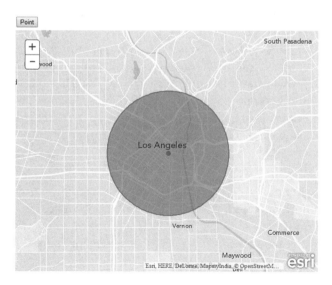

Figure 3.9 The geometry service creates a buffer equal to one kilometer.

interested in at the moment is the ever-popular *selection mode*. When a `FeatureLayer` is first loaded, no features are immediately downloaded from the server. But you can perform queries directly against the `FeatureLayer`, and it'll download and draw those features in the service that match the query. You could use a standard query, where you ask for `ITEM = 'Yes'`, or you could pass in geometry, such as a line or polygon, to perform the selection. Do you see where this is going? You can initialize a new `FeatureLayer` right after you create the `GeometryService`:

```
featureLayer = new FeatureLayer(
  'http://sampleserver1.arcgisonline.com/ArcGIS/rest/services/' +
  'Demographics/ESRI_Census_USA/MapServer/1',
  {
    mode: FeatureLayer.MODE_SELECTION,
    outFields: ["*"]
}),
drawTool;
map.addLayer(featureLayer);
```

Then you add code during the iteration to add the buffered area that will set the geometries of the buffer and make the selection of items in the `FeatureLayer` using the buffers:

```
arrayUtils.forEach(geometries, function (geom) {
    map.graphics.add(new Graphic(geom, fill));
    var query = new Query();
    query.geometry = geom;
    featureLayer.selectFeatures(query, FeatureLayer.SELECTION_NEW);
});
```

If you run this code, something amazing happens! Actually, nothing happens at all. If you check your debug console window in Chrome or Firefox, you'll probably see an error that looks like this:

```
esri.config.defaults.io.proxyUrl is not set
```

TOO MANY CHARACTERS IN URL REQUEST

Oh dear, we've run into the dreaded *proxy issue*. When you pass the geometry of the buffered area to do a spatial query on the `FeatureLayer`, that chunk of information is passed in the URL string, which has a limit of 2,048 characters. That buffered area looks like a nice circle, but it's composed of many smaller line segments. The coordinates at the end and beginning of each line segment are being passed in the URL, and that's a lot of coordinates. You can't pass any more characters than that in a URL; the internet says you can't.

INCORPORATE A PROXY PAGE

But the ArcGIS JavaScript API is smart enough to recognize this, and so it tries to use a proxy page to pass this information as a `POST` request, which isn't subject to the same character limits. In the preceding message, the API is letting you know that you're trying to perform a task that requires a proxy page. Please see appendix C for more details on setting up the proxy page.

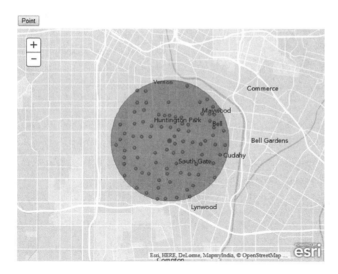

Figure 3.10 `FeatureLayer`
features selected from a buffer

So how do you use a proxy page inside the ArcGIS API for JavaScript? Once you set up the proxy page per the instructions in appendix C (I'll assume you have the proxy in the root of your project), you can add this line of code just before you add the `FeatureLayer` to the map using the `esri/config` module aliased as `esriConfig`:

```
esriConfig.defaults.io.proxyUrl = 'proxy.ashx';
```

> **NOTE** For PHP or JSP, change the file extension as needed. Please review appendix C and its references for more details.

To better see your results, change the color of the buffer area. Run the project again and try adding a buffer; you should see something like figure 3.10.

As you can see, you were able to select only the census block centroids that are inside your buffered area. That's a nifty analysis tool to have at your disposal. For fun, let's add one more small analysis into this workflow.

3.3.3 *Buffer and intersect*

One analysis that you may run into during your time as a GIS professional is finding locations that are suitable for specific needs. Maybe you want to find a home that's within a certain distance from your workplace and your favorite gym. You decide you don't want to move any farther than a couple of kilometers between the two. Now, I don't have home sales data to share with you, so we're going to pretend that the census block centroids you've been working with are homes for sale. Bear with me; the process is what matters, not the data at the moment.

MODIFYING THE EXAMPLE TO PREPARE FOR ADDING INTERSECTION CAPABILITIES

You can perform this analysis by adding a few lines of code to your application. First you initialize an empty array (`geometryArray = []`) to hold your buffer geometries near the top of your application. Then you slightly modify the portion where you loop over the returned buffer geometries. Here's the code:

```
arrayUtils.forEach(geometries, function (geom) {
    geometryArray.push(geom);
    map.graphics.add(new Graphic(geom, fill));
});
if (geometryArray.length > 1) {
    intersectGeometries();
}
```

This snippet adds the buffered geometries to an array. It then checks if the array is not empty and calls another function that will intersect the geometries.

ADDING NEW INTERSECTION FUNCTIONALITY

Then you add a new function that will use the intersection method of your geometry task, as shown in the following listing.

> **NOTE** The code for this section is available in the chapter3 folder of the source code included with the book. See chapter3/3.2.js.

Listing 3.2 Intersecting buffered geometries

```
map.on('load', function() {
...
}
function intersectGeometries() {
  var inputGeomertry = geometryArray[0],
      targetGeometry = geometryArray[1];        ◁── Requires array of geometries
  geometryArray = [];                              and target geometry
  geometryService.intersect(
    [inputGeometry], targetGeometry
  ).then(function (geometries) {               ◁── Performs intersection
    map.graphics.clear();                          and adds result
    var fill = new symbol.SimpleFillSymbol(
      symbol.SimpleFillSymbol.STYLE_SOLID,
      new symbol.SimpleLineSymbol(
        symbol.SimpleLineSymbol.STYLE_SOLID,
        new Color([211, 211, 211, 0.65]), 2
      ),
      new Color([255, 0, 0, 0.15])
    );
    arrayUtils.forEach(geometries, function (geom) {
      map.graphics.add(new Graphic(geom, fill));
    });
  });
}
```

At this point, you return only the intersection of these two areas. You should see something similar to figure 3.11.

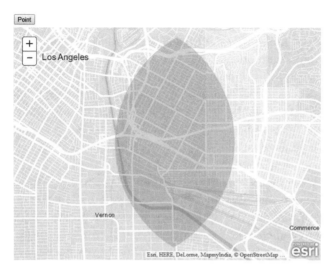

Figure 3.11 The geometry service displays an intersection of two areas.

You can see that the `intersect` method of the geometry service returns a geometry equal to the overlap of the two buffers you added to the map. Now you can use this geometry to perform a selection on your `FeatureLayer` as you did previously and see a result similar to figure 3.12.

The `FeatureLayer` behaves precisely as expected and selects only homes within the intersection of your buffered areas. As I mentioned before, this is the groundwork for multiple types of analysis that you may want to perform in your application. The geometry service is a fantastic tool that helps you perform these types of geometric analyses.

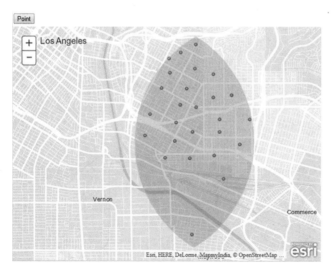

Figure 3.12 Homes for sale in the intersected area

3.4   *Summary*

- This chapter covered how to use the ArcGIS Server REST API directly to build a custom legend table-of-contents widget. In most cases, you won't have to worry about working directly against the ArcGIS Server REST API, as almost everything you need can be accessed via the abstractions provided in the ArcGIS JavaScript API. But it's a good idea to be familiar with the concepts if you're ever required to try to work some magic using the ArcGIS REST API.

- You became more familiar with the Dojo loader, which makes your life easier as an ArcGIS JavaScript developer.

- You dived into the geometry service provided by ArcGIS Server. This is a handy suite of utility functions that offload geometric analyses to the server and can be used in a variety of ways in your application development. We only scratched the surface of the geometry service, and I encourage you to explore its other functions, such as CUT, GENERALIZE, and PROJECT, when you need to work in different coordinate systems.

Congratulations—you've now laid the groundwork to begin working on a full-blown application in chapter 4.

Part 2

Sample Use Case

In the second part of this book you'll build a field collection application for mobile devices. By the end of part 2 you'll learn how to structure your application so that it can grow as needed, build a mobile-friendly data-collection application, and even learn advanced techniques for disconnected editing:

- In chapter 4, you'll set up an ArcGIS Developers account and learn how to use Dojo to build your application.
- In chapter 5, you'll learn how to edit features on the map and use authentication to secure your application, as well as how you can use Local-Storage to enable disconnected editing.
- In chapter 6, you'll focus on building an application for use on a desktop browser, freeing you from some limitations of a mobile environment. You'll also learn how to use OAuth 2.0 with ArcGIS Online and store your credentials to allow users to log in and out. This chapter also covers how you can integrate data collected in the field with some non-spatial data, such as data from a separate web service.
- In chapter 7, you'll be introduced to more advanced subjects and techniques. You'll learn about the ArcGIS WebMap specification and how to use it to configure your map. You'll also learn how to build your entire application from a single JSON file that will configure your widgets for you. This chapter will also describe an alternative to disconnected editing using a library called PouchDB.

Building an application

4

At this point, you've seen a few examples that cover the basics of building a web mapping application by using the ArcGIS API for JavaScript. Some of the samples, like those in chapter 2, were intentionally introductory, to show you how simple it can be to get a web mapping application up and running. In chapter 3, you got more in depth, using parts of the ArcGIS API for JavaScript and Dojo to build a custom legend and table of contents widget, and you even took advantage of communicating directly with the ArcGIS Server REST API to do so. In this chapter, you're going to build what could be a real-world application to deploy to your users or customers. This application will focus on the specific task of collecting data.

67

A popular item these days is a web application capable of being used on mobile devices. A browser-based web application is incredibly convenient for users and developers alike. Users don't need to worry about having the right device, and developers can focus on building a better application without the overhead of building platform-specific versions or having to learn a new programming language. In this section, you'll focus on building a web application that works on most mobile devices. I say *most* because, honestly, so many devices are available that I'm hesitant to say they all work the same, even in a browser environment. Small variances might occur when you tap your finger on an older Android device running the latest Android operating system, versus when you tap your finger on a brand-new Microsoft tablet using Internet Explorer. Nothing is perfect, but the tools in the ArcGIS API for JavaScript handle most compatibility issues for you under the hood, so you won't need to be too concerned about them. We'll discuss more about possible compatibility issues with HTML5 functionality later in the chapter and also in chapter 5.

This chapter covers the type of application you're going to build and its goals. You'll also learn how to register a free ArcGIS developer account so you can publish and edit data in ArcGIS Online. Then you'll learn how to customize what that data looks like in your application, and finally how to incorporate Bootstrap styling into your application and start building what will eventually become a custom edit tool.

4.1   What are you going to build?

I've seen requests come across my inbox and have worked on a handful of applications that all seem to have one recurring theme: people want to collect data. This basic task is so popular that Esri even built a collector application that can be found at http://resources.arcgis.com/en/collector/. You'll build a similar application to this one (see figure 4.1). These types of mobile web mapping applications can vary in terms of bells and whistles, but most are trying to collect information. If they're not collecting information, they're probably verifying it. Because data collection is at the heart of most GIS application building, learning how to build an application that does this from the ground up will teach you many of

Figure 4.1 The application you'll build in this chapter can work on a tablet and phone browsers.

the important skills you'll need for future application development. You'll add functionality to this application in chapter 5, such as the ability to add features to the map and handle a loss of internet connection.

The application in figure 4.1 may look simple at first glance, but it meets some specific requirements:

- Built for use on a tablet, but usable on a phone
- Can collect points at a user-specified location or by user's current location
- Can perform limited editing without an internet connection

Let's cover each of these requirements briefly.

4.1.1 Using a tablet or phone

If you're building an app for general public use, it makes sense to ensure that it's going to work on a phone. You don't see many people walking around with tablets open, working with them. Or maybe you do; I won't judge. The application you're going to build will work on either phones or tablet devices, but let's assume that your prospective users are city employees who have been issued tablets to collect data. That's not to say you can't take what you build and apply it to work on a phone as well, and in many cases, that will require little extra configuration on your part.

4.1.2 Collecting points

You want to provide users with the freedom to add locations to the map along with information. Say, for example, a user sees damage to a utility pole between some homes. The user can't walk directly to the location to collect the point, so you'll provide the ability to navigate a map and add a point with notes on what needs to be fixed. You'll also provide the ability to add a location directly where the user is standing (say, on top of a damaged sidewalk). Chapter 5 covers this capability.

4.1.3 Performing disconnected editing

By far, the number one question anyone asks me when discussing a mobile mapping application, be it a web application or a native mobile application that requires installation, is whether will it work if they lose their internet connection. That's a tricky question, so I mostly say that it depends. You can implement some functionality of HTML5, the latest version of HTML, to minimize the inconvenience of working without an internet connection. But the functionality will be limited, and I'd never fully rely on it. In particular with a web mapping application, if you have no internet connection, you can't download new map tiles to show on the map, or make requests to the server to perform queries on data. You can, however, continue to collect data and save it locally until you have an internet connection, and then push your updates at that time. Chapter 5 covers saving data locally as a solution for disconnected editing.

These are all details covered as you build the application. Before you start writing any code, though, you need to set up a way to store the data that you collect, which you can do using ArcGIS Online.

4.2   *Working with ArcGIS Online*

Unless you work for a large organization or a company that provides GIS consulting services, you probably don't have access to a full ArcGIS Server installation. That's why I've tried to avoid details on the server side of ArcGIS development that aren't necessary to cover the ArcGIS API for JavaScript. Maybe you're wondering how you'll get GIS data that you could edit for your application. That's what's discussed in this section.

This section covers the following:

- Understanding how ArcGIS Online differs from ArcGIS Server
- Registering for a developer account
- Creating a `FeatureService`

If you don't have access to ArcGIS Server, no need to worry, because Esri provides a cloud-based GIS solution you can use to create and consume your own data for a web mapping application. *Cloud-based* indicates that the data resides on servers in a remote location, usually distributed across multiple machines. Using the cloud is a cost-effective way to host and share data and services. In this case, the platform is specifically designed to share GIS data and services. After the data is hosted, it works similarly to the regular ArcGIS Server, as discussed in chapter 3, with a couple of differences you'll learn about shortly. In figure 4.2, you can see that ArcGIS Online can replace ArcGIS Server in this scenario.

4.2.1   *ArcGIS Online vs. ArcGIS Server*

I mentioned that differences exist between ArcGIS Online and ArcGIS Server. In addition to being a cloud-based service, ArcGIS Online differs from ArcGIS Server in that it can't host dynamic map services. As discussed in chapter 2, ArcGIS Online can host raster data, such as aerial imagery or other forms of data that don't often change , such as parcels that can be served as tile services (since they are usually updated on an annual or semiannual basis). It can also host feature services that serve vector data, which are services with a single layer designed to work with a `FeatureLayer`. A `FeatureLayer` is well-suited for editing data and sharing vector data in an efficient manner. This is precisely the type of service you'll create.

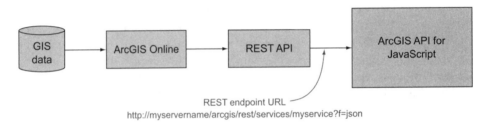

REST endpoint URL
http://myservername/arcgis/rest/services/myservice?f=json

Figure 4.2   ArcGIS Online can be used as a drop-in replacement for ArcGIS Server in some cases.

ArcGIS Online costs

Esri provides developer subscriptions that allow you to use ArcGIS Online to test and build prototype applications and services at no cost. These subscriptions provide a limited number of credits that allow developers to do most of the work they need to do to build test projects. You can upgrade the developer subscription to a paid account at a later time. Full-featured, nondeveloper ArcGIS Online subscription costs can vary based on need and usage. These are called *ArcGIS for Organization accounts*. You'll use the developer subscription for your sample application, which provides everything you'll need.

4.2.2 *Setting up an ArcGIS Online account*

To get your developer subscription up and running, go to the ArcGIS for Developers site at https://developers.arcgis.com/en/. Click the Sign Up for Free link, shown in figure 4.3.

After you click the link, you'll be asked for your name and email address. Fill out this information, and you'll be sent an email to finalize setting up your developer account. You can then log in to the developer page via the link provided in the email. When you first log in, you'll see a page similar to figure 4.4.

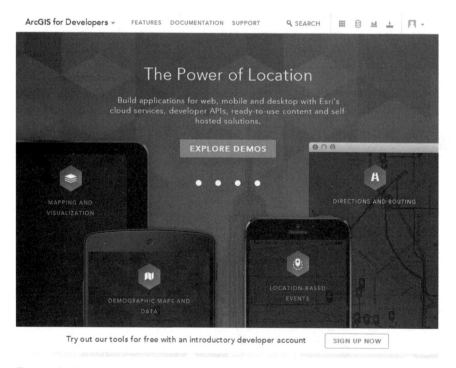

Figure 4.3 The main page for the ArcGIS for Developers site

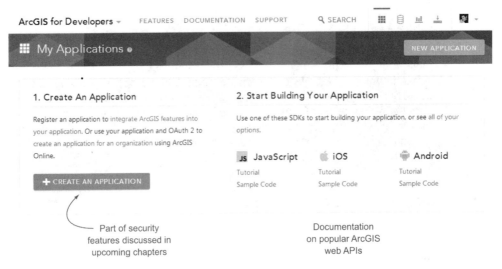

Figure 4.4   The ArcGIS Online developer account page

4.2.3   *Defining a feature service*

Your developer account page provides an option to create an application. You'll return to this page after you get your application started. You'll also find links to documentation on the various web mapping APIs provided by Esri, including the ArcGIS API for JavaScript. At the moment, you want to focus on the Hosted Data link at the top of the page. Click this link to access the page shown in figure 4.5, to create a feature service for collecting data.

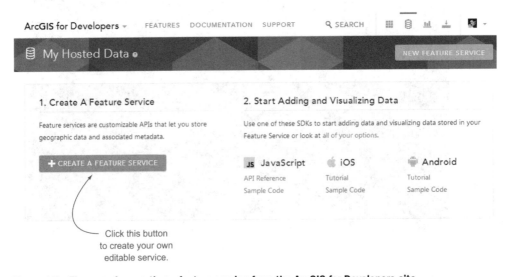

Figure 4.5   The page for creating a feature service from the ArcGIS for Developers site

CHOOSING THE DATA YOU'RE COLLECTING

Before you dive in and start building a feature service, let's think about the kind of information you want to collect. For this application, you're collecting data on various problems that need the attention of your local city: for example, broken street lights and damaged sidewalks. So in this case, you want a type field of some sort. You also want to collect the date of the request you're collecting, so you'll have a date field. That sounds like a good start.

Click the Create a Feature Service button. You're presented with the page shown in figure 4.6.

I've already completed the following information, working from the top down:

- *Title*—Provides the title of your feature service.
- *Description*—Provides a basic description of your service.
- *Geometry Type*—Refers to whether the GIS data is a point, line, or polygon. You'll use points because you're concerned with collecting the location of a request at a single coordinate.
- *Tags*—Allows others to search for services with certain tags on ArcGIS Online, but only if the service is shared with everyone. Someone could search for data

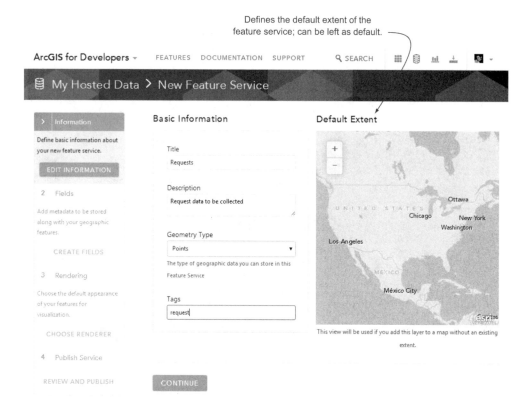

Figure 4.6 Creating a new feature service

that's tagged as *Environmental* or *Water*, for example. You'll tag your service as *request* for testing purposes.

The next step is to add fields to your feature service.

ADDING FIELDS TO YOUR FEATURE SERVICE

Click the Continue button, and you're presented with the screen shown in figure 4.7. As before, I've already filled out the fields you'll use. This page does a good job describing the meaning of each input.

Because ArcGIS Online still resides in a database, you need to abide by field-name constraints. You can't use special characters such as @ or #, and you can't use spaces. What you can do is add a field alias, which is a human-readable label for the data. In this case, you'll have a field name of IssueType, and a field alias of *Issue Type*. Because

Figure 4.7   Defining fields to be used in your feature service

the field name may be descriptive but not exactly user-friendly, you can use the screen-friendly descriptive field alias when the name is displayed in your application. This simplifies your work when you want to edit the data in your application.

One thing we haven't discussed is that you'll identify the data collected by what census tract it's in. This probably isn't something you'd typically collect in a real-world scenario, but it demonstrates how you can assign data by location. Normally, instead of a census tract, you might want to know, for example, what city a request is located in so that workers can be properly assigned. At a larger scale, you might want a city name when collecting data at a county level.

Review table 4.1 for details on defining the fields in your feature service.

Table 4.1   How to define fields in the feature service

Field alias	Field name	Data type	Required
Issue Type	IssueType	String	True
Request Date	RequestDate	Date	True
Census Tract	TractName	String	False
Description	Description	String	False

CHOOSING A RENDERER
After you click Continue on the Define Fields page, you're presented with the option to choose a renderer for your feature service. A *renderer* shows what the features will look like in your application. Feel free to choose whatever you like; you can see what I chose in figure 4.8.

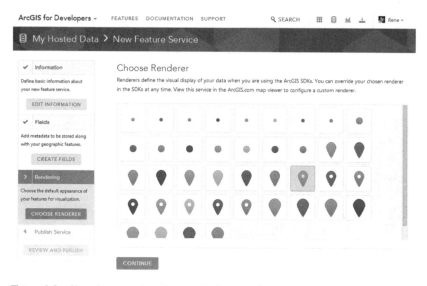

Figure 4.8   Choosing a renderer for your feature service

Review and Publish

Basic Information

Rendering Preview

Title	Requests	
Description	Demo service for use with ArcGIS Web Dev book.	
Geometry Type	Points	
Tags	✎ request	

Field Alias	Field Name	Data Type	
Issue Type	IssueType	string	DETAILS
Request Date	RequestDate	date	DETAILS
Census Tract	TractName	string	DETAILS
Assignee	Assignee	string	DETAILS
Description	Description	string	DETAILS

Figure 4.9   Review the settings of your feature service before you publish it.

Requests

◇ Features (Hosted) by odoenet
Source: Feature Service
Last Modified: September 8, 2013
☆☆☆☆☆ (0 ratings, 14 views)
f Facebook 🐦 Twitter

OPEN ▾   🖼 SHARE   ✏ EDIT   ✖ DELETE   ▣ MOVE ▾   👤 CHANGE OWNER   📈 USAGE

Description

Request data to be collected.

Access and Use Constraints

Layers

Requests ▣
                ◇ Export to Shapefile
                🔁 Export to CSV file
Proper   🖼 Service URL
                🔖 Disable Attachments
Shared wit   🕐 Time Settings
Tags
Credits
Size   1 KB
Extent   Left: -130.73   Right: -60.94
              Top: 59.85   Bottom: 7.46

                                    Click here.

Figure 4.10   ArcGIS Online page for your feature service

You're almost finished setting up your feature service to use in your application. The last page shows an overview of the settings you chose, as shown in figure 4.9. A Rendering Preview window even provides a preview of what you might expect the map to look like. Click the Publish Service button to finish.

4.2.4 *Accessing your ArcGIS Online feature service*

After you publish the service, you're presented with a page that allows you to edit the service details. Click the View in ArcGIS Online button to access the ArcGIS Online page for your feature service. Under the Layers section, click the Requests link, and you'll see the menu shown in figure 4.10. Choose the option Service URL.

Navigating to the service URL opens a page similar to what you saw in chapter 3 when looking at the ArcGIS Server REST API pages. This page, shown in figure 4.11, provides information on this particular service, such as the Geometry Type, and what the default renderer looks like.

At this point, you've defined your feature service on ArcGIS Online by using a free ArcGIS for Developers account. The process is straightforward, and the end result looks similar to the services you were introduced to in chapters 2 and 3. The developer's account is a big benefit for those who may not have access to the full ArcGIS Server and desktop installation required to build the database for the source data of their service and then

ArcGIS REST Services Directory

Home > services > Requests (FeatureServer) > Requests

JSON

Layer: Requests (ID:0)

View In: ArcGIS.com Map ArcGIS Explorer Online

Name: Requests

Display Field:

Type: Feature Layer

Geometry Type: esriGeometryPoint

Description:

Copyright Text:

Min. Scale: 0

Max. Scale: 0

Default Visibility: true

Max Record Count: 10000

Supported query Formats: JSON

Extent:

    XMin: -130.729232616658
    YMin: 7.46341595728869
    XMax: -60.9440763666768
    YMax: 59.8518013865865
    Spatial Reference: 4326

Drawing Info:

    Renderer:
        Simple Renderer:
        Symbol:
            Picture Marker Symbol:

        Label:
        Description:

Figure 4.11 ArcGIS REST page for your ArcGIS Online hosted feature service

publish it as a feature service. All of this can be an involved process, especially for prototyping an application.

4.3 *Building a real-world application*

Now that you've set up an ArcGIS Online account and built a feature service that you can use to collect data, let's start the groundwork for building a mobile application. You're going to cover quite a bit of ground in these next couple of sections, as listed here:

- Organizing your application folder structure
- Building the files and configuring Dojo

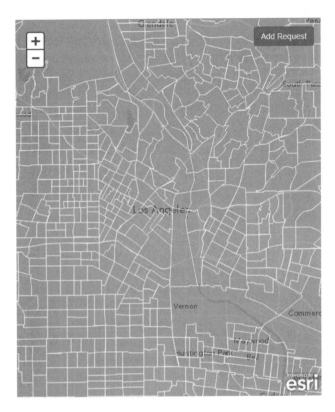

Figure 4.12   Your application will look like this at the end of this chapter.

- Defining required modules to be used in your application
- Building JavaScript classes with Dojo

At the end of this chapter, you'll have an application that looks similar to figure 4.12.

4.3.1   *Setting up Dojo and organizing modules*

When diving into building an application, the last thing you might think of doing is laying out the folder structure of that application. Because the ArcGIS API for JavaScript is built using the Dojo Toolkit with its library of JavaScript tools, you need to take some considerations into account when starting to configure your application.

ORGANIZING YOUR APPLICATION FOLDER STRUCTURE

How developers organize their folder structure varies depending on personal preferences and standards used in development teams. It can be completely subjective from one developer to the next, but I'm going to share with you some best practices to build your applications. This will help keep your modules organized by purpose—widgets separated from your services, and so on—making it much easier to locate the pieces you need. Figure 4.13 shows my recommended folder structure.

I've gone through variations of this folder structure over the years, and it may vary slightly from application to application. When building web applications with the

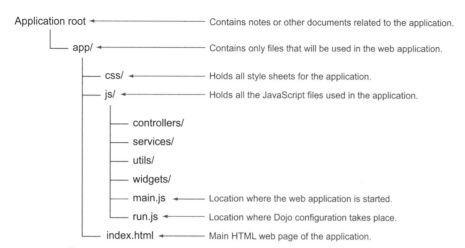

Figure 4.13   Recommended folder structure of an application

ArcGIS API for JavaScript, I've found this works well, because I can keep my modules cleanly organized by purpose. Common modules that interact with outside web services can be kept in the services folder, and any custom widgets I build are kept in the widgets folder. Helper modules that may do basic tasks such as extract data from various GIS layers would be in a utils folder. After you've organized your file folders, you can move on to writing some code.

BUILDING THE FILES AND CONFIGURING DOJO

The first file you'll build is index.html, shown in listing 4.1. This file loads your style sheets, the ArcGIS API for JavaScript, and your run.js file that will get the application started. The index.html file also defines a couple of HTML elements you'll reference in your application.

> **NOTE**   The code for this chapter is available in the chapter4 folder of the source code included with the book.

Listing 4.1   Main index.html file

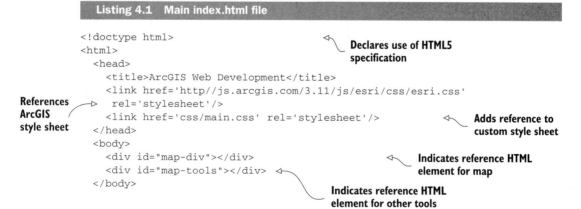

```
<script type="text/javascript" src="http://js.arcgis.com/3.11compact"></
    script>
<script type="text/javascript" src="js/run.js"></script>
</html>
```

**Indicates file for Dojo
configuration and app kickoff**

**Indicates compact build of latest
ArcGIS API for JavaScript**

This index.html file is similar to what you've built in previous chapters for your samples. You're specifying that you want to use the compact build of the ArcGIS API for JavaScript, which is a smaller build of the API, with fewer modules preloaded in the download. It includes most of the commonly used modules for building a web mapping application, and if you need more, it downloads the additional files as needed. I usually start an application by using the compact build, and if the application grows large enough that I'm downloading many additional files, I switch to using the regular build to cut down on network traffic, as discussed in chapter 3.

Before you dive into the JavaScript, I want to point out the main.css style sheet that helps define what your application looks like:

```
#map-div {
  position: absolute;
  top: 0;
  right: 0;
  left: 0;
  bottom: 0;
}
```

If you're unfamiliar with how style sheets work, to style the HTML element with id of map-div, you can reference it as #map-div in your CSS file. To reference an element by class name, reference it by .class-name. In this case, you'd like the map element to take up the whole browser window, so you can provide it a position of absolute, meaning you can now specify that you want it to have 0 space along the top, right, left, and bottom of the browser.

Now you can see how to configure Dojo to work in a modular fashion in your application. The run.js file sets up a regular expression that ensures your modules are loaded correctly. A *regular expression* is a common method in programming for matching strings of text and finding patterns. You'll use a regular expression to help you define the locations of modules. The configuration is shown in the following listing.

Listing 4.2   run.js and configuring Dojo

```
/*global define, require, location*/
/*jshint laxcomma:true*/
(function () {
  'use strict';

  var pathRX = new RegExp(/\/[^\/]+$/)
    , locationPath = location.pathname.replace(pathRX, '');
```

**Indicates global function
objects referenced**

**Sets local JSHint
configuration options**

**Helps catch
coding
problems**

Creates regular expression

**Changes where Dojo looks
for custom modules**

```
        require({                          Passes configuration object
          async: true,                     into first require statement
Loads     aliases: [
modules as   ['text', 'dojo/text']                 Provides aliases for modules
needed    ],
          packages: [{                            Defines packages using
            name: 'controllers',                  modified pathname
            location: locationPath + 'js/controllers'
          }, {
            name: 'services',
            location: locationPath + 'js/services'
          }, {
            name: 'utils',
            location: locationPath + 'js/utils'
          }, {
            name: 'widgets',
            location: locationPath + 'js/widgets'
          }, {
            name: 'app',
            location: locationPath + 'js',
            main: 'main'
          }]
        }, ['app']);        Loads app module
                            after configuration
}) ();
```

Quite a bit is happening in the run.js file in listing 4.2, starting with items that I would designate as good practice but that are entirely optional.

USING LINTING AND STRICT MODE

When writing JavaScript, it's typically considered good practice to use some form of linting on your code. *Linting* is a process that often uses a preprocessing code checker, such as *JSLint* or *JSHint,* to check your code for anything suspicious (for example, accidentally creating global variables mixing the use of single quotes with double quotes). Linting can help filter out possible bugs in your code but mostly provides a nice, warm feeling for writing good code. I use JSHint, but you can use JSLint just as easily, or use nothing at all. You can find online linting tools at www.jshint.com. The following list explains common linting options and strict mode:

- The first line at the top of the file (/*global */) tells the lint tool that you're using specific global variables in this module.
- The second line (/*jshint laxcomma:true*/) lets the linter know that you may be separating your lines with commas at the front as opposed to the end of a line. This is a completely subjective style, but it's how I like to write JavaScript code.
- The next optional line is the 'use strict'; line. Similar to using a lint tool in your code, the 'use strict'; line places the function in strict mode. The function can capture some common JavaScript taboos such as writing to the global namespace (which isn't that bad, but it's good practice to avoid it), and can throw more exceptions when something like that happens.

Where Dojo tries to find file:

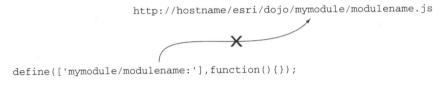

```
http://hostname/esri/dojo/mymodule/modulename.js
```

```
define(['mymodule/modulename:'],function(){});
```

Actual location of file:

```
mymodule/modulename.js
```

Figure 4.14   Demonstrating how Dojo tries to load modules

Again, linting is purely subjective to individual developers. This is the last time I'll show the linting and use strict-mode functionality in the book, but I wanted to point it out because it's used in some of the source code provided with the book. You may need to avoid using strict mode when building custom widgets using the Dijit library, as it can cause issues with some of the core Dijit code. I use it mainly with nonwidget modules.

USING DOJO FROM A NONLOCAL SOURCE

A lot of what's happening inside run.js for the configuration of your application occurs because you don't have access to a local copy of Dojo or the ArcGIS API for JavaScript. The API is provided by a content delivery network (CDN), which means the JavaScript for the API is hosted on another server somewhere. One side effect is that when you create a module by using the define method and provide it a path to a module you want to use, by default the API is going to look on the server for that module. This may seem confusing, but figure 4.14 shows how this might look.

To get around this issue, you can create a regular expression to replace the default hostname with your application's hostname so the API can find the file correctly:

```
var pathRX = new RegExp(/\/[^\/]+$/)
    , locationPath = location.pathname.replace(pathRX, '');
```

You create a regular expression object called pathRX, which finds the application's current pathname in the browser. The pathRX object looks at the URL for the application—for example, let's say the URL is http://myserver/myapp, and the object matches the last portion of that URL as /myapp. In a browser environment, location is an object that can tell you information about the URL, and pathname will find the information for the current URL after the last forward slash (/) in the URL address. In this case, the result is /myapp. You can then use this little hack to define the location of the modules in your configuration. You can do this by defining a package's array in the configuration:

```
{
    name: 'controllers',
    location: locationPath + 'js/controllers'
}
```

You can provide the package a name, such as `controllers`. You then let Dojo know that every time you want to load a module using the path `controllers/modulename`, Dojo should look in the location specified in the package. Because you've defined that location as `/myapp/js/controllers`, Dojo will try to look on the server the application is hosted on rather than the server that provides the ArcGIS API for JavaScript. You can even specify a package with a default file:

```
{
    name: 'app',
    location: locationPath + 'js',
    main: 'main'
}
```

In this case, you create a package called `app`, provide its location, and specify that `app` is a single file in a JavaScript file called main.js. You use this after you've specified the packages by calling the `app` module inside an array: `['app']`. This will load the local js/main.js file after the configuration for Dojo has completed.

Setting up Dojo may seem like an involved process, but this same formula applies in every application you build, so you'll become accustomed to it after a couple of times. It's one of those activities that you perform once, and then you can reuse it with every new application, including the folder structure you already laid out.

Now that you've configured Dojo with the ArcGIS API for JavaScript to properly find custom modules, let's see what happens next inside the main.js file.

4.3.2 Tying the application together

Remember that in your Dojo configuration you defined that the module named `app` would be mapped to the js/main.js file. In the configuration, you're able to launch the js/main.js file by placing `app` in an array as the last argument in the configuration. It looks like this:

```
require({
  ...
  packages: [...]
}, ['app']);
```

The js/main.js file refers to a `controllers/appcontroller` module, which I'll discuss shortly, and to a module called `dojo/domReady`, which is a plug-in for Dojo that says "Don't run the code in this module until the browser has finished loading the page."

Dojo also allows you to provide alias names for a module. In your Dojo configuration, you can alias the `dojo/text` plug-in as `text`. This plug-in loads HTML files as strings. You can execute a plug-in by placing an exclamation mark (`!`) after it to save you a few extra keystrokes. Inside the module, you refer to the instance of the `controllers/appcontroller` as `appCtrl` and call the `init()` method. Pass the method the string `map-div`, which represents the `id` of the HTML element you want the map displayed in, and an object with map parameters. You can see what that looks like in the following listing.

Listing 4.3 main.js–starting the application

```
require([
  'controllers/appcontroller',          Loads application controller
  'dojo/domReady!'
], function (appCtrl) {                  Loads module when page is ready
  appCtrl.init({
    elem: 'map-div',                     Initializes application
    mapOptions: {                        controller with parameters
      basemap: 'gray',
      center: [-118.241,34.0542],
      zoom: 12
    }
  });
});
```

WORKING WITH THE APPLICATION CONTROLLER

So far, you've built your application so the run.js file sets up the Dojo configuration for your application. The main.js file is used to set up any application-level configurations you may want to define ahead of time. This makes it easier for you to change these options in a single file. For example, in listing 4.3, you initialize the application controller with an object that provides the element name to use for the map and some default map options. This is the application configuration. You'll add another item to this configuration object later in the chapter to add more layers to the application. As shown in listing 4.4, the purpose of the controllers/appcontroller.js file is to manage tasks at an application level, meaning it talks to any widgets that get loaded and handles some of the communication in the application (for example, what action the map should take when a widget is closed).

I prefer to handle map actions inside a custom map controller module, which is defined in controllers/mapcontroller.js (see listing 4.5). I've found that keeping this action separate makes maintenance easier. If I need to make changes, I can manage how the map is built in a single module.

Listing 4.4 controllers/appcontroller.js

```
define([
  'controllers/mapcontroller',
], function (MapController) {              Indicates dependency on
  function mapLoaded(map) {                controllers/mapcontroller
    console.debug('map has been loaded', map);
  }
  function init(config) {                  Indicates initialize function
    var mapCtrl = new MapController(config);
    mapCtrl.load().then(mapLoaded);        Loads MapController and
  }                                        waits for load to finish
  return {
    init: init          Exposes initialize function
  };
});
```

Triggered after map loads

Initializes new MapControlle

At this point, the only responsibility the application controller has is to initialize the `mapcontroller` with the configuration file and load it. When it's loaded, you're returned a JavaScript promise like the ones discussed in chapter 3 when building the legend widget. When that load is complete, you send a message to the console to notify you that an action happened.

LOADING THE MAP WITH OPTIONS

We need to cover one last module before you can see the fruits of your labor: the map controller that was mentioned in the preceding section. The `controllers/mapcontroller` loads the map with the specified options and uses a `dojo/Deferred` object to let you know when it's complete. The map controller code is shown in the following listing.

Listing 4.5 controllers/mapcontroller.js

```
define([
    'dojo/_base/declare',          ⟵ Builds classes in Dojo
    'dojo/_base/lang',             ⟵ Provides suite of utility functions
    'dojo/on',
    'dojo/Deferred',               ⟵ Generates JavaScript promises
    'esri/map'
], function (declare, lang, on, Deferred, Map) {   ⟵ Specifies ArcGIS API for JavaScript map module
    return declare(null, {          ⟵ Returns null as first argument
        map: null,
        options: {},

        constructor: function(options) {          ⟵ Calls first function
            this.options = lang.mixin(this.options, options);
        },

        load: function() {          ⟵ Instantiates new map
            var deferred = new Deferred()
              , mapLoaded = lang.hitch(this, function() {
                  deferred.resolve(this.map);
              });

            this.map = new Map(this.options.elem, this.options.mapOptions);
            on.once(this.map, 'load', mapLoaded);          ⟵ Listens once for load event
            return deferred.promise;          ⟵ Returns promise
        }
    });
});
```

Listens to events (annotation for `'dojo/on'`)

Creates new instance of map (annotation for `this.map = new Map(...)`)

USING THE DECLARE MODULE

The map controller may be only a few lines of code, but quite a bit is happening here, including new modules for us to cover. The first is the `dojo/_base/declare` module. The `declare` module is used in Dojo to generate JavaScript classes; you'll become more familiar with it in chapter 5 when you start to build a custom edit widget. You use it to *declare* a new class that this module will provide. Technically, JavaScript doesn't have classes, but `declare` can be used to create class-like constructors. As you can see, it's aptly named. There's no hard rule that states you must use the Dojo modules to generate JavaScript classes; you could use the `prototype` method to add methods to the class. The following snippet is roughly equivalent to what you do with the `declare` module:

```
var MapController = function(options) {
    this.options = options;
};
MapController.prototype.load = function() {};
```

The way I see it, when in Rome, do as the Romans do. You have a multitude of tools available in the Dojo Toolkit provided by the ArcGIS API for JavaScript; you may as well take advantage of them. When using a module built with `declare`, you can instantiate a new instance of that class by calling `new MapController(options)`, and the first method that gets called is the `constructor` method. You typically pass in objects that will contain parameters for this module and then use

```
this.options = lang.mixin(this.options, options)
```

to copy the provided options to the `options` object. This saves the effort of writing the code to loop over the `options` object and copying the properties yourself.

USING THE LANG MODULE

When you call the `load` method, a few things happen.

First you create a new `Deferred` object so you can use the Promises API in this module.

Next you create a new function, but you do so in an interesting way. You use the `dojo/_base/lang` module with a method called `hitch`. The purpose of this method is to *resolve* a deferred instance, meaning to return the result using `map` after it has been loaded. But the `map` is bound to the instance of the `controllers/mapcontroller` module, so the only way to access it is via `this.map`.

Because the function is being used as a handler function to an event on the map, that function doesn't have access to `this.map` of the `mapcontroller`. Does that sound a little confusing? It might, as all this has to do with how the `this` keyword is handled in JavaScript, which is based on the context in which the function was called. In this case, the `mapcontroller` didn't call the `mapLoaded` function, but it was triggered by the `'load'` event of the map, so you need a way to get access to `this.map` inside `map-Loaded`. This is where `lang.hitch` comes in. This utility method binds the `this` keyword inside a function to any object passed as the first argument in `lang.hitch`:

```
mapLoaded = lang.hitch(this, function() {
        deferred.resolve(this.map);
    });
```

The utility method `lang.hitch` returns a function that binds the map controller instance to the function passed to it. This allows it to access `this.map` in the handler. You could also write this without `lang.hitch`:

```
var that = this;
mapLoaded = function() {
  deferred.resolve(that.map);
};
```

Figure 4.15   Result of the first draft of your web application

Doing it this way, you can bind an instance of the map controller to a variable called that and use that in the handler methods. But again, because you have all these tools available, you should use them when you can. It may help you later solve some mind-numbing problem you come across. If you were to launch your application now, you'd see a map in your browser, similar to the one shown in figure 4.15.

Hmm, if you're thinking this looks an awful lot like the first samples you built in chapter 2 that used only a few lines of code compared to the multifile setup you just put together, you're right. But the way you've structured the application now makes it easier to scale as new features are added. You've also worked with more of the Dojo modules. A few more steps are required to get the application looking like our goal for this chapter. In the next section, you'll focus on making the application look good.

4.4   Adding layers and using the renderer

Previously in the chapter, I discussed how you'd capture the census tract number in which a request was placed, so you're going to use a Census Tract map service and modify its appearance to fit the needs of the application.

This section covers the following:

- Using a custom renderer to display data
- Using Bootstrap with ArcGIS API for JavaScript
- Creating a custom widget to help with editing

4.4.1   Adding layers with a module

To accomplish this task, you're going to create another module that creates instances of FeatureLayer to use in the map. The code for the services/mapservices module is shown in the following listing.

Listing 4.6   `services/mapservices` module

```
define([
  'esri/layers/FeatureLayer'                          Creates new
], function(FeatureLayer) {                            FeatureLayer for map

  function loadServices() {                               Creates function to
    var layers = []                                        return array of FeatureLayers
      , censusLayer;
    censusLayer = new FeatureLayer(
      'http://services.arcgis.com/V6ZHFr6zdgNZuVG0/' +
      'arcgis/rest/services/' +
      'CensusLaborDemo/FeatureServer/1'
    );

    layers.push(censusLayer);

    return layers;
  }

  return {
    loadServices: loadServices
  };
});
```

This module is pretty straightforward. Its only responsibility is to generate instances of new `FeatureLayer`s and add them to an array that you can use to add them to the map.

Let's return to the main.js file, where you built the configuration for your application, and modify it, as shown in the following listing.

Listing 4.7   main.js—modified with `services/mapservices`

```
require([
  'controllers/appcontroller',
  'services/mapservices',                          Adds dependency
  'dojo/domReady!'                                   to main.js
], function (appCtrl, mapServices) {

  appCtrl.init({
    elem: 'map-div',
    mapOptions: {
      basemap: 'gray',
      center: [-118.241,34.0542],
      zoom: 12
    },                                               Adds layers property
    layers: mapServices.loadServices()                to configuration file
  });

});
```

You were able to easily modify the main.js file to add an array of layers that are generated by the `services/mapservices.js` module.

Now that you've modified the configuration, modify `controllers/mapcontroller .js` to load the layers in the map, as shown in the next listing.

Listing 4.8 controllers/mapcontroller.js—modified to add layers

```
define([
  ...
], function (declare, lang, on, Deferred, Map) {
  return declare(null, {
    ...
    load: function() {
      var deferred = new Deferred()
        , layersAdded = lang.hitch(this, function() {      Changes name of
          deferred.resolve(this.map);                      handler function
        });

      this.map = new Map(this.options.elem, this.options.mapOptions);

      on.once(this.map, 'layers-add-result', layersAdded);

      this.map.addLayers(this.options.layers);
                                                    Adds layers to map
      return deferred.promise;
    }
  });

});
```

Listens for
layers-add-result
instead of load

All you need to do to the mapcontroller is modify it slightly so that instead of listening for the `'load'` event to occur, you listen for the `'layers-add-result'` event, which fires when the layers you add by using map.addLayers() are loaded. This method takes an array of layers, which coincidentally happens to be what you have in the options of the mapcontroller. Remember, the mapcontroller is passed the configuration object (defined in main.js) and binds those values to its own option

Figure 4.16 Adding the Census Tract map service to the application

property. Because you're no longer listening for the map to load, but for when the added layers are loaded, change the handler's function name from `mapLoaded` to `layersAdded` to better reflect what you're doing.

Refresh the application in the browser to see the Census Tract map service, as shown in figure 4.16.

That's absolutely beautiful, a true measure of cartographic excellence. But now you can't see the streets or the city names on the map. Plus the color scheme of the map is designed to reflect how much of the population is employed in each census tract. That doesn't fit into your plans for using the data, so let's modify it.

4.4.2 *Using the renderer*

When working with map services in the ArcGIS API for JavaScript, you may want to change what the map service looks like. If you're lucky, you could make a phone call to whomever made the service and request the change to be made. But maybe the look of the service is locked in because it's used across multiple applications. No need to worry, as you have the ability to define how you want that service to look. You're going to build a utility module that you can use to define the look of the layer in the map. The following listing shows what this module looks like.

> Listing 4.9 `utils/symbolUtil.js` module

```
define([
  'esri/Color',                          ← Imports esri/Color to define colors
  'esri/symbols/SimpleFillSymbol',                                              ← Defines appearance of polygons
  'esri/symbols/SimpleLineSymbol'
], function(Color, SimpleFillSymbol, SimpleLineSymbol) {                        ← Defines appearance of lines

  return {
    renderSymbol: function() {           ← Returns simple object with utility function
      return new SimpleFillSymbol(
        SimpleFillSymbol.STYLE_SOLID,
        new SimpleLineSymbol(
          SimpleLineSymbol.STYLE_SOLID,
          new Color([255, 255, 255]), 1
        ),
        new Color([128,128,128, 0.5])
      );
    }
  };
});
```

As discussed in chapters 2 and 3, the ArcGIS API for JavaScript provides a handful of modules in the `esri/symbols` namespace to define how features are drawn in the browser. The modules are dependent on the `esri/Color` module to define the colors they use. The `Color` module uses RGB (red, green, blue) to define colors.

> **TIP** To give you an idea of how RGB colors work, an RGB value of `0,0,0` is black, a value of `255,255,255` is white, and a multitude of values and combinations exist between them.

The census tracts in our service are polygons, so you define a `SimpleFillSymbol` that's a solid color to fill them with. You could also make this a hatched symbol, meaning the fill would be multiple lines instead of a solid color. The second argument indicates what you want the outline of the polygon to look like. In this case, you make the outline white by setting the color to `new Color([255,255,255])`, and the third argument defines the color you want the polygon fill to be. You make this a light gray color with a transparency of 50%. Transparency of a color can be set by passing a fourth element in the RGB array to represent the transparency, as shown in the code: `new Color([128,128,128, 0.5])`.

4.4.3 Applying the renderer

After you instantiate the layer for the census tracts, you can use the utility module that helps define what the census tracts in the application should look like. Applying the utility module in the `services/mapservices.js` module makes sense because it's responsible for generating layers for the application. You can see what this modification looks like in the next listing.

> **Listing 4.10 `services/mapservices.js`—modified to apply renderer**

```
define([
  'esri/layers/FeatureLayer',
  'esri/renderers/SimpleRenderer',       ◁── Adds reference to
  'utils/symbolUtil'                           SimpleRenderer
], function(FeatureLayer, SimpleRenderer, symbolUtil) {      and utility module

  function loadServices(config) {
    var layers = []
      , censusLayer,
      , renderer;

    censusLayer = new FeatureLayer(
      'http://services.arcgis.com/V6ZHFr6zdgNZuVG0/' +
      'arcgis/rest/services/' +
      'CensusLaborDemo/FeatureServer/1'
    );
    renderer = new SimpleRenderer(symbolUtil.renderSymbol());    ◁──
    censusLayer.setRenderer(renderer);                Creates new
                                                      SimpleRenderer
    layers.push(censusLayer);                          using utility module

    return layers;
  }

  return {
    loadServices: loadServices
  };
});
```

Applies renderer to feature layer ──▷ (applies to `censusLayer.setRenderer(renderer);`)

You want to change the overall appearance of the Census Tract map service so it doesn't overpower the map in your application. You'll use a `SimpleRenderer`, which

Figure 4.17   The application after altering the appearance of the census tracts layer

will change the appearance of all items in the layer. If you wanted to change the appearance in a more complicated manner (say, by grouping the appearance of census tracts by a certain criteria), you could do that also, but that isn't the purpose of the application.

That's the only change you need to make to change the appearance of the census tracts in the application. You can see what the application looks like now in figure 4.17.

The census tracts no longer overpower the entire map in terms of the coloring scheme, and you can still see city names and streets. As you can see, it's not difficult to alter the appearance of layers used in web mapping applications when the need arises. Feel free to experiment with the color and adjust to your liking. The next step is to get ready to start editing.

4.4.4   *Setting up the editing tools*

You need to build an interface that allows the user to add data to the map. Remember, this is meant to be used on a mobile device, so it would be nice if this tool was as simple to use as possible. The ArcGIS API for JavaScript does come with a neat built-in widget called the `TemplatePicker`, that, similar to the built-in legend Dijit discussed in chapter 3, is provided as an out-of-the-box solution. Figure 4.18 shows what the `TemplatePicker` might look like for your application.

Figure 4.18   Out-of-the-box ArcGIS `TemplatePicker` using your Request feature service

This is a great tool and something I recommend if you're building a larger application targeted more toward users working on desktop computers. You could probably work with it, but remember, you want to focus on simple in terms of usability for the user. So to do this, you're going to flex some of the skills you learned in section 4.3.2 about building classes with `dojo/_base/declare` and the custom widget you built in chapter 3 to build a simple customer editing tool.

BOOTSTRAP CSS: IT'S NOT CHEATING

I'll be frank: I may be able to make a decent-looking map by using the cartographic skills I've picked up over the years, but when it comes to designing a stylish website, I'm not exactly an accomplished designer. To assist in making slick-looking tools, you're going to use a framework that many other web developers use: Bootstrap.

Installing Bootstrap

Go to http://getbootstrap.com/ and download the latest version.

Extract the zip file and find the dist folder in the download.

Copy the css and fonts folders into the root of your application so that the fonts folder is at the same level as the js and css folders (app/css, app/js, app/fonts).

To reference the Bootstrap style sheet in your index.html file, enter the code as shown in the following listing.

> **Listing 4.11 index.html–added Bootstrap style sheet**

```
<!doctype html>
<html>
  <head>
    <title>ArcGIS Web Development</title>
    <link href="css/bootstrap.min.css" rel="stylesheet">     Adds reference to
    <link                                                     Bootstrap style sheet
    href='http://js.arcgis.com/3.113.11/js/esri/css/esri.css'
    rel='stylesheet'
    />
    <link href='css/main.css' rel='stylesheet'/>
  </head>
  …
</html>
```

The Bootstrap style sheet comes in handy not only as you build this application but also when you need to quickly get other applications up and running. I'll give you one tip about using Bootstrap with the ArcGIS API for JavaScriptafter you look at figure 4.19.

Notice anything odd here? After adding the Bootstrap style sheet, the map width is limited to a certain size. If the browser width is larger than that size, you end up with whitespace at the right side of the application. It took me a little debugging to see why

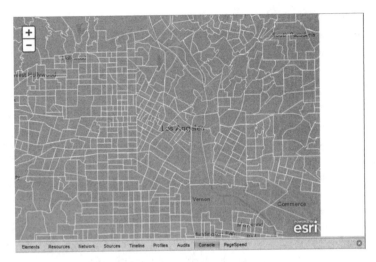

**Figure 4.19
The application after
adding the Bootstrap
style sheet**

this was happening. Using the browser debug tools in Chrome, I figured out that the
HTML element that contains the map has a class called `container`, and Bootstrap has
a specific styling for elements with a class name of `container`. You can see this in figure 4.20.

To correct this, you can modify your own style sheet to override the Bootstrap style
sheet. You can see how that's done in the following snippet for css/main.css:

```
#map-div {
  position: absolute;
  top: 0;
  right: 0;
  left: 0;
  bottom: 0;
}

#map-div .container {
  max-width: 100%;
}
```

Overrides Bootstrap style sheet
for map HTML element

The HTML element that contains the
map has a class name called "container".

```
| Elements | Resources | Network | Sources | Timeline | Profiles | Audits | Console | PageSpeed |
<!DOCTYPE html>                                                          overflow: hidden;
▼<html class="dj_webkit dj_chrome dj_contentbox">                        width: 100%;
  ▶<head>…</head>                                                         height: 100%;
  ▼<body class=" hasGoogleVoiceExt">                                     }
    ▼<div id="map-div" class="map">
      ▼<div id="map-div_root" class="container" style="width: 857px; height:     @media (min-        bootstrap.min.css:9
      530px; direction: ltr;">                                          width: 768px)
        ▶<div id="map-div_container" class="container" style="position:  .container {         bootstrap.min.css:9
        absolute; cursor: default;">…</div>                               max-width: 750px;
        ▶<div class="esriControlsBR">…</div>                            }
        ▶<div class="esriPopup" style="visibility: hidden; z-index:      .container {         bootstrap.min.css:9
                                                                          padding-right: 15px;
```

Bootstrap defines the class "container"
to have a certain width.

Figure 4.20   Chrome debug console to debug style sheet conflicts

The preceding snippet says that for any HTML element that has a class `container` with an id of `map-div`, make the `max-width` equal to 100%. This overrides the Bootstrap style for `container`, but only in your map. This is a small price to pay to have access to the nice styling you get with Bootstrap when building applications.

EVERYONE LIKES BUTTONS

When you think about the process of adding a request to the map, you need to think about the workflow. How do you guide the user in adding a request to the map? Add a request every time the user clicks or touches the map? Maybe, but that could get tough to manage if the user touches it a bunch of times when trying to pan or when cleaning a smudge off the screen. It's tough to get much simpler than adding a button users can push and enabling them to click on the map to add a point where they'd like. So that's what you'll set up: adding a button. This isn't just any button, though. This button will handle the bulk of the editing workflow, so you're going to build this button as a custom widget. Start by creating a template HTML file that contains the HTML for your button:

```
<button type="button" class="btn btn-primary">Add Request</button>
```

This button has class names related to bootstrap styling.

> **NOTE** The code for this section is available in the chapter4 folder of the source code included with the book. See app/js/widgets/edit/editTools .tpl.html.

When working with template HTML files like this one, I prefer to add the tpl extension before the html extension. This is a preference and not a requirement. It helps me remember that I'm working with a template file.

4.4.5 Assigning an action to a button

A button that does nothing or provides no feedback is useless. You want to display feedback to the user that an action is taking place after the button click—for example, by changing the text or the color of the button. To see how this works, let's do both.

With the template file complete, let's build a custom editing widget that tells users to click to start editing and lets them know they're currently editing. The following listing provides the code for this custom widget.

Listing 4.12 `widgets/edit/editTools.js`

```
define([
  'dojo/_base/declare',
  'dojo/_base/lang',
  'dojo/on',
  'dijit/_WidgetBase',
  'dijit/_TemplatedMixin',
  'dojo/dom-class',
  'text!widgets/edit/editTools.tpl.html',
], function(
```

Command converting template to string →

Base class for Dojo widgets

Module enabling widget's template file

Helper module for changing CSS styles of HTML elements

```
      declare, lang,
      on,
      _WidgetBase, _TemplatedMixin,
      domClass, template
  ) {
      return declare([_WidgetBase, _TemplatedMixin], {

          templateString: template,                    String of template
          options: {},                                 HTML file
          editing: false,
          map: null,

          constructor: function(options) {
            this.options = options || {};
            this.map = this.options.map;               Listener added for
          },                                           button click
          postCreate: function() {
            this.own(
              on(this.editNode, 'click', lang.hitch(this, '_addRequest'))
            );
          },
          _addRequest: function() {
            this.editing = !this.editing;              Method used to start editing
            this._toggleEditButton();
          },
          _toggleEditButton: function() {
            if(this.editing) {                         Method to control
              this.editNode.innerHTML = 'Adding Request';  button appearance
            } else {
              this.editNode.innerHTML = 'Add Request';
            }
            domClass.toggle(this.editNode, 'btn-primary btn-success');
          }
      });
  });
```

A lot is happening in the custom widget. Much of this you saw in section 4.3.2, when
you used the dojo/_base/declare module to create custom classes for use in the
application. This time, you're using the declare module to create a new widget that
will also extend a couple of other Dojo Dijits.

USING THE WIDGETBASE MODULE

I won't get into too much detail, but the dijit/_WidgetBase module handles the lifecycle of a widget. This module has all the functions built in that you can access when a
widget is created. The module indicates what happens before the HTML element is
created, what happens after it's created, and what happens when it's removed. Don't
worry too much about this lifecycle process, but for more details, review appendix B.

USING THE TEMPLATEDMIXIN MODULE

The dijit/_TemplatedMixin module is handy when creating widgets that are based on
HTML elements, such as our button. This module allows you to define a template for
your widget and also allows you to add references in the HTML template to methods on

the widget to handle what happens when a button is clicked, for example. You initialize this widget with a set of options that include a reference to the map, but you also pass it a reference to an HTML element where you want this widget to be placed on the page. You start to do some interesting stuff in the two methods defined as _addRequest and _toggleEditButton. The underscores at the beginning of method and property names designate that those methods and properties are intended to be used internally by the class only, so you wouldn't call editTools._addRequest(). Again, this is another subjective preference but is widely used when building Dojo applications.

DOJO DIJIT LIFECYCLE

A few of the methods you're using in the custom widget have to do with the Dojo Dijit lifecycle as defined by dijit/_WidgetBase. You can read more details about this lifecycle in appendix B. The common methods are as follows:

- *Constructor*—Initializes a widget.
- *postCreate*—Runs when the HTML elements of the widget are built but may not be on the page yet. By using this method, you can start attaching event listeners.
- *startup*—Runs after the HTML elements are built and inserted into the page. If you have to do anything involving any style lookups, this is the place to do it.
- *destroy or destroyRecursive*—The destroy method is part of the Dijit lifecycle, but to destroy child widgets, use the destroyRecursive method. Call this method on a widget when it's done being used and is removed from the page (for example, an order form). This cleans up the widget and removes it from memory. You don't typically need to override destroy, as the Dijit will normally clean things up, but if you create a widget inside this module that is not a child widget, you might need to perform the cleanup manually.

WIDGET AND TEMPLATE COMMUNICATION

In the _addRequest method you toggle whether the tool is currently editing. This will come in handy if you ever need to check whether an edit session is already occurring (hint: we'll do that right now). Then you call the _toggleEditButton method. This method does exactly what it says it does. It checks whether the widget is currently editing and sets the text of the button to reflect what's happening by using the this.editNode.innerHTML property. The innerHTML property of HTML elements allows you to change the values inside them, using plain text or more HTML elements. Then you can use the domClass module provided with Dojo to toggle a couple of class names on this.editNode. What domClass.toggle does is add the class name supplied if the HTML element doesn't already have it, but if it does have it, it will remove it. In Bootstrap styling, btn-primary styles the button blue, and btn-success styles the button green.

But what is the this.editNode that we keep referring to? You can use some Dojo magic with the assistance of the dijit/_TempaltedMixin by adding attributes to your HTML template file that allow you to access HTML elements in the template from your code. You can even tell the template to call methods in the widget directly. You can see what this looks like by looking at your modified template:

```
<button type="button" class="btn btn-primary btn-edit"
  data-dojo-attach-point='editNode'Add Request</button>
```

In this template, you've provided an attribute called `data-dojo-attach-point` with a name of `editNode`. This enables you to reference this node in your widget by using the `this.editNode` property. That's a nifty feature. You then use `this.editNode` to listen for click events in widgets/edit/editTools.js and call the `_addRequest` method. All you need to do is instantiate the module inside the application. You do that in the application controller, as shown in the next listing.

Listing 4.13   `controllers/appcontroller.js`—added edit widget

```
define([
  'controllers/mapcontroller',
  'widgets/edit/editTools'            Adds reference to
], function (MapController, EditTools) {    custom edit widget

  function mapLoaded(map) {
    var editTools = new EditTools({      Instantiates widget with
      map: map                           options and reference node
    }, 'map-tools');
  }
  ...
});
```

When you instantiate a new `EditTools`, you'll also provide it a reference to the map so the `EditTools` can have access to the map when you start the edit functionality. You'll also provide `EditTools` a reference to the id of an HTML element you already have in index.html called `map-tools`. You need to do one last thing for everything to come together: edit the main.css style sheet, as shown in the following listing.

Listing 4.14   `css/main.css`

```
#map-div {
  position: absolute;
  top: 0;
  right: 0;
  left: 0;
  bottom: 0;
}

#map-div .container {
  max-width: 100%;
}
                                    Adds style for map-tools
#map-tools {                        at upper right
  position: absolute;
  top: 1em;
  right: 1em;
}
```

Figure 4.21 **The Add Request toggle button changes based on user action**

With all of this in place, if you launch the application, you should see a screen similar to what was shown in figure 4.12. If you click the Add Request button a few times, the text label and the color of the button toggle. Figure 4.21 illustrates.

This is a simple but effective method of providing feedback to the user that something is happening in the application. Users like feedback from the applications and web pages they use.

4.5 Summary

- This chapter covered quite a bit of material, and you haven't even started writing the code to do the edits using HTML5 features yet. You now know how to acquire a free ArcGIS developer's account and set up your own feature services. This is a valuable resource for developers because you no longer need to have access to a full ArcGIS Server installation to publish or even edit data. This will prove invaluable in the next chapter. You also set up an ArcGIS Online account and published a feature service in ArcGIS Online.

- You should be huffing and puffing by now, as you just covered a slew of material about not only ArcGIS API for JavaScript modules but also important Dojo modules used for creating classes and widgets. You used promises in your modules, `dojo/_base/declare` to build your modules, and `dojo/_base/lang` to handle JavaScript scope.

- You customized a `FeatureLayer` with a custom renderer, styled your map with CSS and Bootstrap, and enabled a widget and its template to communicate with each other.

- Previous chapters covered building basic samples and even building a custom widget, but this chapter went into much more detail about how to configure Dojo for your application and dived into the details of how Dojo classes and widgets are built. You didn't get to edit data yet, but you did lay some major groundwork for yourself.

You now have a good base to finish building out the application with the required editing functionality to collect new requests, as you'll do in chapter 5.

Developing a custom
data-collection application

5

This chapter covers

- Using out-of-the-box edit tools
- Creating custom edit tools
- Performing basic authentication for your application
- Using HTML5 features
- Enabling disconnected editing

By now you should have a fairly good grasp of how to write modular JavaScript by using the ArcGIS API for JavaScript. In chapter 4, you used core Dojo modules to build the base for what will become a custom edit widget in this chapter. Here, you'll learn how to use the default Editor widget provided with the ArcGIS API for JavaScript, and how you can add, delete, and even update map locations. You'll look at basic authentication so only authorized users can apply edits to your data. Because your goal is for this application to be used on mobile devices, you'll learn how to accomplish these edits when you lose an internet connection, which can happen far too often on these devices.

When ArcGIS web mapping was in its infancy, there weren't any capabilities in terms of editing your data online. Every now and then at a conference or a small gathering of GIS professionals, you may have heard how they hacked together some editing capabilities into their web mapping applications. Today, we have a rich suite of tools in the ArcGIS web APIs to accomplish these tasks. The editing capabilities aren't anywhere near what can be found on desktop software, but for general use they've become commonplace among many web mapping applications. Especially with the penetration of mobile devices into everyday use, almost anyone can create data with a web mapping application, such as submitting up-to-date traffic conditions, reporting emergency repairs to a local municipality, or submitting requests for a new stop sign in your neighborhood. The OpenStreetMap project is an entire dataset created by contributions from everyday users. Anyone can contribute to the mapping project to ensure that the street you live on is properly aligned on the map or that your local library is shown. It's a perfect example of how editing mapping data on the web can lead to a quality set of data. For more information on the OpenStreetMap project, visit www.openstreetmap.org.

You'll cover a lot of ground in this chapter, so let's quickly look at what you're going to accomplish:

- Use the free ArcGIS developer account feature service.
- Modify what you built in chapter 4 to use the out-of-the-box editing tools.
- Introduce the Identity Manager for secured map services.
- Use the `TemplatePicker` and default `Editor` widgets.
- Remove the default tools to build a custom edit tool.
- Refine the custom edit tool to simplify the data collection process.
- Figure out what to do when the application loses an internet connection.

In this chapter, you won't get into the detail level of adding new streets to a base map like the OpenStreetMap project, but you'll add the capability for a user to submit a new request via the mapping application. This request can be used to report a broken street light, among other things. Let's start with basic editing capabilities.

5.1   *Performing default web map editing*

The ability to edit or create data in a web mapping application has tremendous benefits. The ability to use aerial imagery and GPS coordinates with a mobile device while walking around outside and performing a task as simple as verifying the location of fire hydrants or water meters is extremely powerful. There is no replacement for having a surveyor verify locations from a known benchmark, but many times you only need locations or coordinates that are good enough to get the job done. Esri, the company providing the ArcGIS API for JavaScript, recognized this need some time ago and began providing the tooling in ArcGIS Server and ArcGIS Online, along with their suite of web APIs, to allow users to perform these editing tasks.

To create and edit data with the ArcGIS API for JavaScript, you'll use the feature service you created with your ArcGIS for Developers account via ArcGIS Online. A *feature service* is specifically designed to serve vector data and allows for the editing of that data. Chapter 2 covered the types of data available for use in web mapping applications. In chapter 4, you created a feature service; in this chapter, you'll use a `FeatureLayer` to

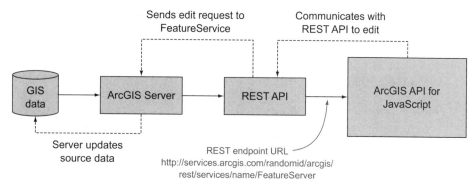

Figure 5.1 Workflow of editing data with a feature service

access this feature service, as you did to access census data in chapter 4. This time, you'll use it to edit data. The workflow for this editing of data is shown in figure 5.1. The Arc-GIS API for JavaScript requests data from ArcGIS Online, which sends an edit request to the server, which in turn updates the source data and returns that newly edited data to the browser.

As you can see, this workflow is straightforward. The default editing widget provided by the ArcGIS API for JavaScript can make the implementation of this in your application simple as well. In chapter 4, you built an application you'll finish in this chapter by using a custom editing tool. Before you do that, though, we'll look at

Figure 5.2
Side-by-side comparison
of the application using
custom (left) and
default (right) edit tools

what's available in the ArcGIS API for JavaScript so you'll know what's in your toolbox. Figure 5.2, shown on the previous page, compares the out-of-the-box editing tools that the ArcGIS JavaScript API offers and the custom tool you'll build in this chapter.

Before you can move on with editing your data or look at the default or custom edit widgets, you need the URL to the feature service you created in chapter 4.

5.1.1   Finding feature service information

Log in to your account at https://developers.arcgis.com and click the Hosted Data link at the top of the page. You'll end up on the My Hosted Data page, shown in figure 5.3, which lists all the services that you created using your developer account.

Figure 5.3   List of hosted data in ArcGIS developer account

Next, click the Requests service that you created in chapter 4. This opens a page showing Service Details, but for now, click the Layers menu option at the left, as shown in figure 5.4.

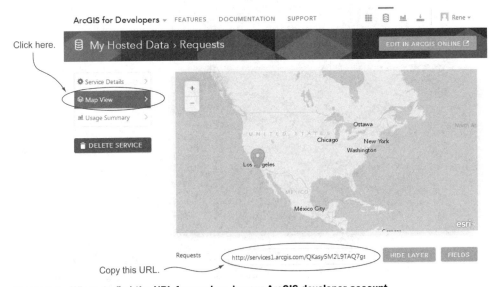

Figure 5.4   Where to find the URL for services in your ArcGIS developer account

Clicking the Layers menu opens a simple map that will eventually show the data you collect. Under the map is a text box that contains the URL for your feature service you'll be editing. Copy this URL, and keep it somewhere you can find it, as you'll use it to get your editing application up and running.

5.1.2 *Adding your feature service to the map*

Two widgets in the ArcGIS API for JavaScript are designed to be used together to get a simple editing application up and running quickly: the `TemplatePicker` and the `Editor`. The `TemplatePicker` displays the names of editable features and their symbols, similar to a legend. It does little except allow you to click and unclick the symbol for a feature. Not too impressive. But when combined with the `Editor` widget, it can be used to activate editing on a selected feature in the `TemplatePicker` and create new features. All of a sudden, it's been given a whole new purpose in life.

More tools available

The `TemplatePicker` and `Editor` widgets aren't the only tools available for editing. You can add edit tools to the `TemplatePicker` when used with the `Editor` widget to provide more editing options, such as moving features, rotating them, or changing their shape. This book doesn't cover this added functionality of the `TemplatePicker`. But when you build your custom edit tool in this chapter and implement editing in the desktop application built in the next chapter, you'll have a better understanding of how to accomplish these tasks.

To use the `TemplatePicker`, modify the code you wrote in chapter 4 as follows:

- Remove your custom module from controllers/appcontroller.js.
- Add a reference to your editable feature service in services/mapservices.js.

In addition, I'll introduce you to the `IdentityManager` to help you work with secured map services, and I'll cover the default edit widget modules provided by the ArcGIS API for JavaScript.

> **NOTE** The code for this section is available in the chapter5/part1 folder of the source code included with the book.

ADD THE EDITABLE FEATURELAYER TO THE MAP

Let's start by deleting the `EditTools` widget from the `mapLoaded` function in your controllers/appcontroller.js file. Your `mapLoaded` function is now empty:

```
function mapLoaded(map) {
}
```

Next, modify your services/mapservices.js file to add your editable feature service and make it available to add to your map. You're going to use your editable service to create a new FeatureLayer and add it to the array that your map can use to display it. Let's look at the following listing to see your new services/mapservices.js file.

Listing 5.1 services/mapservices.js–modified to add your editable feature service

```
define([
    ...
], function(FeatureLayer, SimpleRenderer, symbolUtil) {
    var CENSUS_URL =
        'http://services.arcgis.com/V6ZHFr6zdgNZuVG0/' +
        'arcgis/rest/services/CensusLaborDemo/FeatureServer/1'
        , REQUEST_URL =
            'http://services1.arcgis.com/QKasy5M2L9TAQ7gs/' +
            'arcgis/rest/services/Requests/FeatureServer/0';      ◁— Adds URL of
                                                                     feature service

    function _loadServices(config) {
    var layers = []
            , censusLayer = new FeatureLayer(CENSUS_URL, {
              id: 'Census'
            })
            , requestLayer = new FeatureLayer(REQUEST_URL, {
              id: 'Requests',
              mode: FeatureLayer.MODE_ONDEMAND,
              outFields: ['*']
            })
            , renderer = new SimpleRenderer(symbolUtil.renderSymbol());
        censusLayer.setRenderer(renderer);
        layers.push(censusLayer);
        layers.push(requestLayer);          ◁— Adds FeatureLayer
        return layers;                          to array
    }
    return {
        loadServices: _loadServices
    };
});
```

Creates new FeatureLayer using URL

You add the URL of your feature service as a variable called REQUEST_URL to your file. The use of uppercase for the URL variables is a way to denote to us as developers that these variables are constant and aren't intended to be changed. Then you create a new FeatureLayer by using this URL as well as some options.

Chapter 2 covered the details of a FeatureLayer, but one new option introduced here is outFields. By specifying outFields as ['*'], you're asking the server to return all the fields associated with your data. You could limit the fields returned by specifying them here as ['IssueType', 'Description'], but in this case, you ask for all of them. Also note that you're now providing an id in your options, which makes it much easier to find this layer later when you start using your edit tools. Because you add requestLayer to the array of layers, you don't have to do anything else to the new layer to the map. If you now run your application, you won't see your Add Request button anymore because you removed it, and you won't see any data from your feature service because it should be empty still—but trust me, it's there. Or is it?

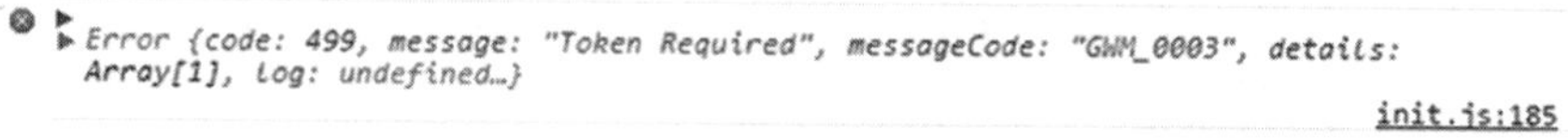

```
Error {code: 499, message: "Token Required", messageCode: "GWM_0003", details:
Array[1], log: undefined...}
```
                                                                    init.js:185

Figure 5.5 Error message after adding the feature service to the application

AUTHENTICATION WITH IDENTITY MANAGER

When you try to run the application at this point, you may not notice any errors in the browser. But if you open the debugging tools for your browser, you'll probably notice a strange error. For example, in the Chrome debugging tools, you'll see an error with a message *Token Required*, as shown in figure 5.5.

Well, that can't be good! Because the services you create by using your free ArcGIS developer account are secured, they require authentication before you can access them. To implement a simple authentication implementation based on username and password, you'll use the Identity Manager module provided in the ArcGIS API for JavaScript. The Identity Manager automatically looks for this error and pops up a dialog box prompting you to log in to your developer account to access and use the service. Use the username and password you created for your ArcGIS developer account for IdentityManager.

Adding the Identity Manager to your application is a three-step process:

1 Modify the dependencies for your controllers/appcontroller.js file as follows to add a reference to the IdentityManager:

```
define([
  'controllers/mapcontroller',
  'esri/IdentityManager'
], function (MapController) {
  ...
```

2 Add the appropriate style sheet reference and a class name to your application HTML in the index.html file:

```
<html>
  ...
    <link
    rel="stylesheet"
href="http://js.arcgis.com/3.11/dijit/themes/nihilo/nihilo.css
    ">
    <link
      href='http://js.arcgis.com/3.11/esri/css/esri.css'
      rel='stylesheet'
    />
    <link href='css/main.css' rel='stylesheet'/>
  </head>
  <body class="nihilo">
    ...
  </body>
  ...
</html>
```

Adds reference to nihilo stylesheet

Adds nihilo class to page

Adding this style sheet, and adding the class name to the body of the page applies the Dijit Nihilo theme to the `IdentityManager` dialog box.

> **NOTE** A handful of other themes are available, but I prefer to work with the Nihilo style because it seems the least flashy. You can read more about the Dojo themes available at http://dojotoolkit.org/reference-guide/1.9/dijit/themes.html.

Voilà: you have an instant authentication tool for the application. When you refresh the browser, you should be greeted with a prompt to sign in to your ArcGIS Online account, as shown in figure 5.6.

Notice that you didn't have to initialize the Identity Manager in your code or interact with it in any way. It's specifically designed to recognize that you're trying to access a secured ArcGIS Online service and handles the authentication process for you. Chapter 6 covers other options for authentication using the provided proxy page that are quite interesting as well.

Figure 5.6   Sign-in prompt when using Identity Manager

Are you using the compact build?

If you noticed that you were prompted with the Sign In dialog box without having to manually add a reference to the Identity Manager, you're probably accessing the full ArcGIS API for JavaScript library through the URL http://js.arcgis.com/3.7. When using that URL, the standard API is downloaded and ready for use, including many of the Dijit modules available for the API.

Because you're building an application intended for mobile devices, I usually recommend using the compact build with the URL http://js.arcgis.com/3.7compact. The compact build loads only the bare minimum of modules to get an application running. It's up to the developer to add modules as needed, which is why in the example you had to add a reference to the Identity Manager. It's standard practice that applications targeted for mobile devices use the compact build, and applications targeted for desktop browsers use the standard build.

5.1.3　*Adding the TemplatePicker and default Editor widgets*

Now that you have the Identity Manager in place and can access your feature service, let's begin adding the default editing widgets to your application. To ensure that the `TemplatePicker` shows up on the page, add an HTML `div` element for the `Template-Picker` to reference and display on the page. Modify the index.html file as shown here:

```
<html>      ...
  <body class="nihilo">
    <div id="map-div"></div>
    <div id="template-div"></div
  </body>
  ...
</html>
```

You want to style this HTML element so it displays correctly in your application. To position it at the top right of the browser, add a style reference for `#template-div` in your css/main.css file:

```
#template-div {
  position: absolute;
  top: 50px;
  right: 5px;
}
```

That's it for styling and positioning; you can now move on to writing code. You want to initialize a new `TemplatePicker` with some options. A `TemplatePicker` needs to know the following:

- The `featureLayers` it's supposed to display
- The number of columns and rows it should have
- The `id` of the HTML element that you want it to display in

Modify your controllers/appcontroller.js file to set the options for number of rows and columns, as shown in the following listing.

> **Listing 5.2　controllers/appcontroller.js–adding the TemplatePicker**

```
define([
  'dojo/_base/array',
  'controllers/mapcontroller',
```

```
    'esri/dijit/editing/TemplatePicker',                    ⟵ Adds dependency
    'esri/IdentityManager'                                    for TemplatePicker
], function (array, MapController, TemplatePicker {

  function mapLoaded(map) {
    var requestLayer
      , layers = []
      , templatePicker;                                     ⟵ Finds Requests layer
    requestLayer = map.getLayer('Requests');
    layers.push(requestLayer);
    templatePicker = new TemplatePicker({
      featureLayers: layers,
      rows: 'auto',
      columns: 1                                            Initializes and starts
    }, 'template-div');                                  ⟵ TemplatePicker
    templatePicker.startup();
  }
  ...
});
```

FIND A LAYER BY ITS ID

Recall that in listing 5.1, when you added your feature service as a FeatureLayer to the application, you assigned it an ID. You did this so you could easily find this layer for later use in your application, as in this instance. The method map.getLayer() finds a layer in the map by its ID. If no ID is specified when the layer is created, it's assigned a generic ID that you won't know. So because you gave your layer an ID of 'Requests,' it now lets you quickly find it in a single line.

> ### Don't know the ID? No problem
>
> The map has an array property called layerIds that contains the IDs of the layers in the map. The standard way of getting the layers from the map when you don't know the ID is as follows:
>
> ```
> var layers = array.map(map.layerIds, function(layerId) {
>         return map.getLayer(layerId);
> });
> ```
>
> You use the Dojo array utility to loop over each ID in the map's layerIds property, and then find the layers by using the ID and storing the layers in an array.

You add your FeatureLayer to an array that's then used as part of the options of the TemplatePicker. Set the number of rows to 'auto', and the columns to 1. If you added more layers, the TemplatePicker would still be one column, but the rows will grow as needed. You also pass as the second argument the ID of the HTML element that you added to the index.html file previously.

Now that you have all the style sheets and code in place, if you refresh the application, you should see the TemplatePicker shown in figure 5.7.

Hey, that looks cool! The TemplatePicker displays the symbols for your feature service defined in your ArcGIS developer account, as well as the ID of the layer. It even

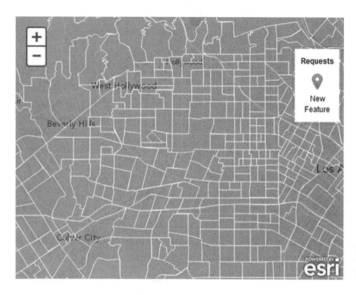

Figure 5.7
TemplatePicker displayed
in your application

reads New Feature, which indicates that clicking it will let you add new features to the map. Right now, though, if you click that button, it only changes colors, indicating it's selected. Next, you'll wire this up to the Editor widget to make it useful.

ADD THE EDITOR

The Editor is a useful built-in widget when paired with the TemplatePicker. It needs only a few bits of information to get the ball rolling. You need to create an array referred to as layerInfos, which will specify which layers are editable with the Editor widget. Then you provide it the map that the layers are in and give it a reference to the TemplatePicker and you're good to go. The updated controllers/appcontroller.js file is shown in the following listing.

Listing 5.3   controllers/appcontroller.js–added Editor widget

```
define([
    ...
    'esri/dijit/editing/Editor',            Adds reference to
    'esri/dijit/editing/TemplatePicker',    Editor widget
    ...
], function (
  array,
  MapController,
  EditTools, Edit, Editor, TemplatePicker
) {

    function mapLoaded(map) {
      ...
      templatePicker.startup();                           Specifies
      var layerInfos = array.map(layers, function(layer) {  featureLayers
            return {                                        to edit
                featureLayer: layer
```

```
        };
    });                                    ⌐ Creates settings object
    var settings = {                       ◁
        map: map,
        templatePicker: templatePicker,
        layerInfos: layerInfos
    };                                        Initializes Editor widget
    var params = { settings: settings };    ⌐ with parameters
    var editorWidget = new Editor(params);  ◁
}
...
});
```

One thing you may notice when you initialize the Editor widget is that you don't use the typical startup() method of standard Dojo Dijits, as you do with the Template-Picker. In most cases, you use the startup() method only if the widget needs to perform some tasks related to position or styling. In this case, you didn't provide a reference to an HTML element to the Editor, so there's no need for it to perform these tasks. If you wanted to use the default Editor toolbar, you could provide a reference to an HTML element, which is covered in the next chapter.

Now if you run your application and click the New Feature button of the TemplatePicker, you can click the map to add a new point and fill out attribute information. You should see a point and editable attribute window, as shown in figure 5.8.

Figure 5.8 The Editor widget combined with TemplatePicker allows adding new features to the map.

Now you can quickly and easily add new features to the map. The window that pops up allows you to provide attribute information for each feature that you add and even to delete the feature. You also have the capability to add attachments to your request. For example, suppose you took a picture of a broken street light. You could attach that picture to the request to provide additional details. Using the `Editor` widget with the `TemplatePicker` is a powerful tool set in web map editing and may be your default choice if you're asked to put something together in a hurry.

I've found that the process of creating a request can be simplified even further for the end user. It requires more work on the developer's side, but the end result works well on mobile devices. Plus it's always more fun when you get to build a custom tool as you'll do next.

5.2 *Building a custom edit tool*

You've seen how the default edit tools in the ArcGIS API for JavaScript work and can be used quickly in your custom application. There's nothing inherently wrong with the default tools, and if I were in a crunch to get something working quickly, they'd be my first choice. But they do have limitations. Let's say, for example, that you want to autopopulate the Census Tract field based on the location of the request. Or what if you lose your internet connection while adding a request to the map? To deal with these kinds of scenarios, you need to build a custom edit tool.

In chapter 4, you built the base for an application that lets you add a request with a single click of a button. Previously in this chapter, you put that aside to use the default edit tools. But now you're going to remove the default edit tools and bring back your custom edit tool, so you can build an application that looks like figure 5.9.

Figure 5.9   This custom edit tool looks incredibly simple.

NOTE The code for this section is available in the chapter5/part2 folder of the source code included with the book. Unless otherwise stated, code listings are located in the chapter5/part2/app/js folder.

To get started, remove the references to the `TemplatePicker` and `Editor` widgets in your controllers/appcontroller.js file and put back the reference to your custom widgets/edit/editTools.js file. Leave the reference to the Identity Manager in place because you're still loading your secured feature service. You should have a file that looks like the following listing.

Listing 5.4 controllers/appcontroller.js–adding your custom edit tool

```
define([
    'controllers/mapcontroller',
    'widgets/edit/editTools',          Adds reference to
    'esri/IdentityManager'             custom edit too
    ], function (MapController, EditTools) {
    function mapLoaded(map) {
      var editTools = new EditTools({      Initializes custom
          map: map                          edit too
      }, 'map-tools');
    }
    function _init(config) {
      var mapCtrl = new MapController(config);
      mapCtrl.load().then(mapLoaded);
    }
    return {
      init: _init
    };
});
```

This should look familiar, as it's where you left off in chapter 4. Now you're going to focus on the edit tool.

5.2.1 Working with the custom edit functionality

Let's step back for a second and think about the workflow for adding a request to the map:

1 *Initiating a request*—Click the Add Request button. This action triggers a function so that when the map is clicked, you create a point at that location and it displays.
2 *Generating the request*—Apply edits to `FeatureLayer` referenced in the map.
3 *Adding the request*—Display the new feature on the map.

Let's start with the button-click step.

LISTEN FOR THE MAP CLICK EVENT

You already have a function set up in the custom edit tool to change the text and color of the Add Request button when it's clicked, so you can trigger a function to listen for a map click in that function by using the `dojo/on` module introduced in chapter 4, specifically in listing 4.12. This module is designed not only to work with application events, such as mouse clicks, but also to pause and resume listening for these events, which comes in handy if users change their minds and decide not to add a request. The following listing shows how this is done.

Listing 5.5 widgets/edit/editTools.js–using `dojo/on` to listen for map clicks

```
define([
   ...
], function(
declare, lang, on,
_WidgetBase, _TemplatedMixin,
domClass, template
) {
   return declare([_WidgetBase, _TemplatedMixin], {
      templateString: template,
      options: {},
      editing: false,
      map: null,
       handler: null,
      constructor: function(options) {
        this.options = options || {};
        this.map = this.options.map;
      },
      postCreate: function() {
        this.handler = on.pausable(
          this.map, 'click', lang.hitch(this, '_addPoint')
        );
        this.handler.pause();
        this.own(
          this.handler,
          on(this.editNode, 'click', lang.hitch(this, '_addRequest'))
        );
      },      ...
      _addRequest: function() {
        this._toggleEditButton();
      },
        ...
      _addPoint: function(e) {
        console.log(e);
        this._toggleEditButton();
      },
      _toggleEditButton: function() {
        this.editing = !this.editing;
        if(this.editing) {
          this.editNode.innerHTML = 'Adding Request';
          this.handler.resume();
        } else {
          this.editNode.innerHTML = 'Add Request';
          this.handler.pause();
        }
        domClass.toggle(this.editNode, 'btn-primary btn-success');
      }
   });
});
```

Adds pausable handler for click event

Immediately pauses handler

Adds point to map

Pauses handler when not adding request

Resumes handler when adding request

As shown at the end of the code listing, I prefer to create pausable handlers inside the widget's postCreate function because this is where most other event handlers will be added since the DOM elements will be available. Remember from chapter 4 that post-Create is part of the Dojo Dijit lifecycle, and is triggered after the widget's HTML template is rendered as a DOM node, but before it inserted to the page. You then immediately pause the handler because you don't want to start listening for map click events until the user has clicked the Edit button. You'll use the _toggleEditButton method that toggles the current state of the Edit button to also toggle the handler for the map clicks.

Then in the _addPoint method, when the map has been clicked, you call the _toggleEditButton method to pause the map click handler again. For now, you've added console.log() to the _addPoint method, so you can analyze what the map click event looks like.

> **TIP** You can also get more details about the map click event at the following link to the documentation: https://developers.arcgis.com/en/javascript/jsapi/map-amd.html#click.

Although the documentation provides information about the event, when developing an application, I prefer to look at the actual returned event. You never know what kind of useful information you might find. (Hint: You'll get extra information from this event later in the chapter!)

Run the application, click Add Request, and then click anywhere on the map. You should see a debug message in your browser's debug window. Expand the message and scroll down until you see mapPoint, as shown in figure 5.10.

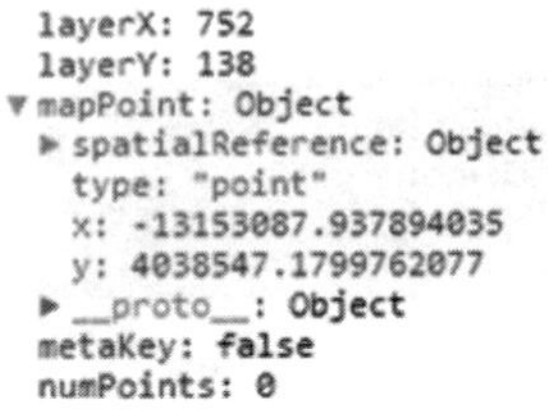

This is perfect! The mapPoint in the returned map click event gives you the location you clicked on the map. This is exactly what you can use to create a new request. Now you can move on to the next step, which is generating a new request using your feature service.

```
layerX: 752
layerY: 138
▼ mapPoint: Object
  ▶ spatialReference: Object
    type: "point"
    x: -13153087.937894035
    y: 4038547.1799762077
  ▶ __proto__: Object
  metaKey: false
  numPoints: 0
```

Figure 5.10   Browser debug window showing a mapPoint in the map click event

GETTING A LAYER REFERENCE

You still need to complete a couple of steps before diving in to adding a request with your custom edit tool. To apply the update, you first need to get a reference to the Requests layer. In section 5.1, you learned that by giving the FeatureLayer for the requests an ID, you could easily find the layer when needed at a later time. You can do the same thing in your custom edit tool by assigning the layer to a property on your tool. Add one line of code in the constructor:

```
constructor: function(options) {
    this.options = options || {};
    this.map = this.options.map;
    this.requestLayer = this.map.getLayer('Requests');
},
```

This snippet adds the `Requests` layer to the widget. You'll also update the services/ mapservices.js file so your census `FeatureLayer` returns all its attribute fields:

```
censusLayer = new FeatureLayer(
  'http://services.arcgis.com/V6ZHFr6zdgNZuVG0/' +
  'arcgis/rest/services/CensusLaborDemo/FeatureServer/1', {
    id: 'Census',
    outFields: ['*']
})
```

This snippet designates that the `FeatureLayer` should return all the available fields with its results.

Now that you have the `FeatureLayer` for the Requests feature service as a property on your widget, you can access it when you need it.

AUTOPOPULATE THE FIELDS

You want to autopopulate two fields for a request: the `RequestDate` field and the `CensusTract` field. The `RequestDate` is easy because you'll apply the current date, but how exactly do you find the census tract for the location of your request? You could perform a query on the Census Tract service using the current location. You performed a similar analysis in chapter 2 when you were first introduced to the `Query-Task` module.

Fortunately, you already added the Census Tract service to your application in chapter 4, so you can access that information directly. Not only that, but recall that I suggested looking at the map's click event that gets returned to see whether it provides anything useful you could use at some point. Well, you happen to be in luck. If you look at the event in more detail, you'll find it has a `Graphic` object attached to it, and if you expand that object, you'll find that it has the census tract information you're looking for, as shown in figure 5.11.

```
evenci nase:  v
  fromElement: null
▼ graphic: Object
    _count: 1
  ► _extent: Object
  ► _graphicsLayer: Object
  ► _offsets: Array[1]
  ► _shape: Object
  ▼ attributes: Object
      COUNTYFP: "037"
      GEOID: "06037203300"
      LABOR_PCT: 0.45960502693
      NAME: "2033"
      NAMELSAD: "Census Tract 2033"
      OBJECTID: 352
      POP_LABOR: 768
      STATEFP: "06"
      TOTAL_POP: 1671
      TRACTCE: "203300"
    ► __proto__: Object
  ► geometry: Object
    infoTemplate: undefined
    symbol: undefined
  ► __proto__: Object
► initEvent: function initEvent() { [native code] }
► initMouseEvent: function initMouseEvent() { [native code] }
```

Figure 5.11 Graphic object returned with a map click event

A nice surprise with a click of the map

The `FeatureLayer` is composed of multiple graphics; the `Graphic` at the location you clicked on the map is attached to the map's click event. If you had another `Feature-Layer` in the map, such as city boundaries, and those city boundaries overlaid the census tracts, you would get the city boundary `Graphic`. It all depends on what `Graphic` is on top. This is an undocumented feature of the map click event, so it may change in future releases. But when I find little features like this, I like to milk them when I can.

You can capture the `Graphic` object from the map's click event. By doing so, you don't have to do any special queries to a map service to find the census tract number; you need only add the new request.

USE THE FEATURELAYER APPLYEDITS METHOD

To add a request, use the `FeatureLayer`'s `applyEdits` method. The documentation for this method can be found at https://developers.arcgis.com/en/javascript/jsapi/featurelayer-amd.html#applyedits. The method takes three arguments that you're currently concerned with—three arrays: one for adding new features, one for updating existing features, and one for deleting features. For the time being, you're concerned only with adding new features, which involves the following steps:

1 Set up attributes.
2 Create a `Graphic`.
3 Add the `Graphic` to an array and pass the array to the `applyEdits` method of your request's FeatureLayer.

You have the geometry and the information to create the attributes needed to generate a new request, so you're ready to use the `applyEdits` method of your Feature-Layer. Modify the `_addPoint` method in the widgets/edit/editTools.js file so it creates a `Graphic`, and then create the attributes for the `Graphic` and add that `Graphic` to your request FeatureLayer. You can see what this looks like in the following listing.

Listing 5.6 widgets/edit/editTools.js–modified `_addPoint` method

```
_addPoint: function(e) {
    var mapPt = e.mapPoint              Gets mapPoint
      , census = e.graphic              from click event
      , attributes = {}
      , graphic;                                          Assigns issue type
    attributes.IssueType = 'New Request';
    attributes.RequestDate = new Date().getTime();        Sets request date
    attributes.CensusTract = census.attributes.NAME;
    graphic = new Graphic(mapPt, null, attributes);       Creates new Graphic
     this.requestLayer.applyEdits([graphic]).then(lang.hitch(this,
    function() {
       this._toggleEditButton();
       alert('Request submitted');     Adds new Graphic
    }));
  }
```

Gets census Graphic from click event

Uses name from census Graphic

You added only a few lines of code to the `_addPoint` method, but a lot is happening here, so let's look at each step in detail:

1 Set up attributes.

The first thing you do is get the `mapPoint` and the `Graphic` for the census tract, which was returned with the map's click event.

You then create an empty `attributes` object to attach these properties to. For now, you set `IssueType` to `'New Request'` (you'll return to it later) so you can focus on adding the point.

Next, you assign a date to the `RequestDate` property. You set this as a `Date` field in your feature service when you created it in chapter 4. This date must be provided in milliseconds (for more details on why, see the "JavaScript date" sidebar).

As I mentioned previously, you can use the `Graphic` of the census tract attached to the map's click event to get the census `NAME` field and assign that to your attributes.

JavaScript date

One thing that usually trips people up when editing dates with the ArcGIS API for JavaScript is how to properly set a date field. You can't just send `new Date()`. The ArcGIS Server and ArcGIS Online REST API expect the time in milliseconds, specifically in coordinated universal time (UTC). You do this with `new Date().getTime()` for older browsers or `Date.now()` in modern browsers. More information about these methods can be found at https://developer.mozilla.org/en-US/docs/Web/JavaScript/Reference/Global_Objects/Date/getTime and https://developer.mozilla.org/en-US/docs/Web/JavaScript/Reference/Global_Objects/Date/now.

---

2 Create a `Graphic`.

After you have the attributes and the `mapPoint` geometry, you have enough information to create a `Graphic`. A `Graphic` has three parameters in its constructor that you're concerned with: the geometry, the symbols, and the attributes. You can replace the symbols with a `null` value and then supply the other values you created in step 1.

3 Apply the edits.

Next you send the `Graphic` object inside an array using the request layer's `applyEdits` method. This method returns a deferred object that you worked with in chapter 4, which means you can place a function in the `then()` method to do something when the edit is done. In this case, you toggle the Edit button to its normal state and show an alert that the request was submitted.

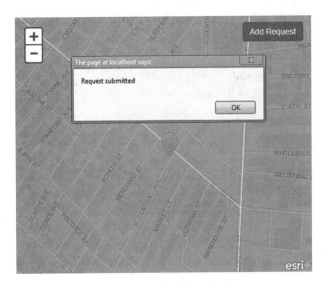

Figure 5.12 This alert lets you know the request was added successfully.

Run the application and add a new request to the map. You should see the request added to the map and the prompt that lets you know the submission was successful, as shown in figure 5.12.

Congratulations! You just submitted your first request with your custom edit tool. If you refresh the map, you should see the request shown where you added it. You need to handle a couple of details before you can say this is complete, including how to provide a description of the request, and one possible way to designate the issue type of the request you're submitting.

5.2.2 *Refining the custom edit tool*

One thing that's missing from your custom edit tool is the ability to add a description in your Description field. You could accomplish this in various ways. One of the simplest ways to populate this data is with a prompt.

USE THE NATIVE JAVASCRIPT PROMPT

You can use a built-in JavaScript function called `prompt`, which asks the user to enter information and returns whatever is entered. You can accomplish this by adding a couple of lines of code to the `_addPoint` method in the widgets/edit/editTools.js file to display a prompt asking for the description of the request. The following listing shows the modified code.

> **Listing 5.7 widgets/edit/editTools.js–added prompt to get description**

```
_addPoint: function(e) {
    var mapPt = e.mapPoint
        , census = e.graphic
        , attributes = {}
        , graphic
```

```
, description;
description = prompt('Description of request');
attributes.IssueType = 'New Request';
attributes.RequestDate = new Date().getTime();
attributes.CensusTract = census.attributes.NAME;
attributes.Description = description;
graphic = new Graphic(mapPt, null, attributes);
this.requestLayer.applyEdits([graphic])
  .then(lang.hitch(this, function() {
    this._toggleEditButton();
    alert('Request submitted');
  }));
}
```

Uses native JavaScript prompt to get description

Assigns description to request for submitting new request

That was easy to do. Now, when you run the application and try adding a new request, you'll see the prompt asking for the description, as shown in figure 5.13.

The best part about using the native JavaScript prompt is that it looks good on any device it's used on, including iOS and Android devices. The next step is to figure out how to best populate the Issue Type field of your data.

DEFINE AN ISSUE TYPE

To populate the Issue Type field in your data, you could use another `prompt`, but the goal of this application is simplicity. You want the user to have to type as little as possible. In most scenarios, only a few types of issues would be submitted. For this application, let's limit it to four types:

- Street light
- Graffiti
- Pothole
- Other

Figure 5.13 This native JavaScript prompt asks for a description of the request.

Now that you have a defined set of issue types, you can adjust how you're adding the request to the map.

UPDATING THE UI

You're going to make changes to your template HTML file for the widgets/edit/edit-Tools.js file. Instead of showing just a single Add Request button, you'll show a button for each type of request. When a user clicks a button for one Issue Type, the others should be disabled so they can no longer be clicked until the current request is done. You can do this by changing the class names of each button as needed. The class name defines which button is active and which buttons are disabled.

First, let's update the widgets/edit/editTools.tpl.html template file to include a button for each issue type:

```
<div>
  <button type="button"
    class="btn btn-primary btn-edit"
   data-type="streetlight">Street Light</button>          Adds data-type attribute,
  <button type="button"                                    btn-edit class
    class="btn btn-primary btn-edit"
    data-type="graffiti">Graffiti</button>
  <button type="button"
    class="btn btn-primary btn-edit"
    data-type="pothole">Pothole</button>
  <button type="button"
    class="btn btn-primary btn-edit"
    data-type="other">Other</button>
</div>
```

You now have four buttons to add requests in your application. One new thing you've done is add a `data-type` attribute to each button that matches the Issue Type you'll save with your request. *Data attributes* are part of the HTML5 specification and allow you to add arbitrary pieces of information to HTML elements.

You also added a `btn-edit` class to each button, which helps manage adding and removing classes to the element as well as disabling buttons when adding a new request. You can then use this template in the widgets/edit/editTools.js file to assign the Issue Type to a request. You can see the updated widgets/edit/editTools.js in the next listing.

> **Listing 5.8   widgets/edit/editTools.js–modified to handle issue type**

```
define([
...
'dojo/dom-attr',              Adds dojo/dom-attr
...                           to module
], function(
  declare, lang, on, domAttr,
  _WidgetBase, _TemplatedMixin,
  domAttr, Graphic, template
) {
    return declare([_WidgetBase, _TemplatedMixin], {
```

```
        ...
        postCreate: function() {
            this.handler = on.pausable(
              this.map, 'click', lang.hitch(this, '_addPoint')
            );
            this.handler.pause();
            this.own(
              on(
                this.domNode,
                '.btn-edit:click',
                lang.hitch(this, '_toggleEditButton'))
            );                                              ⟵  Listens for
        },                                                      click events
        ...
        _addPoint: function(e) {
            var mapPt = e.mapPoint
              , census = e.graphic
              , attributes = {}
              , graphic
              , description;
            description = prompt('Description of request');
            attributes.IssueType = this.requesttype;
            attributes.RequestDate = new Date().getTime();
            attributes.CensusTract = census.attributes.NAME;
            attributes.Description = description;
            graphic = new Graphic(mapPt, null, attributes);
            this.requestLayer.applyEdits([graphic])
              .then(lang.hitch(this, function() {
                this._toggleEditButton();
                alert('Request submitted');
              }));
        },
        _toggleEditButton: function(e) {              Sets request type
            this.editing = !this.editing;        ⟋    to empty string
            this.requesttype = '';          ⟋
            if (e) {
                this.requesttype = domAttr.get(e.target, 'data-type');
Assigns type ⟋     domClass.toggle(e.target, 'btn-primary btn-success');
            }
            if(this.editing) {                          ⟵  Handles
              query('.btn-primary', this.domNode)            enabling/disabling
                    .removeClass('btn-primary')              buttons
                    .attr('disabled', 'disabled');
              this.handler.resume();
            } else {
              query('.btn-edit', this.domNode)
                    .removeClass('btn-success')
                    .addClass('btn-primary')
                    .removeAttr('disabled');
              this.handler.pause();
            }
        }
    });
});
```

This may look like a big change, but the core of what's happening is still the same. You added a couple of Dojo modules to simplify the process. The `dojo/query` module is used to select elements on the page based on ID or class name. It's an incredibly handy tool.

LISTEN FOR BUTTON EVENTS

Instead of listening for click events on a single button, you can listen for click events for all buttons in a particular node with a `btn-edit` class:

```
on(this.domNode, '.btn-edit:click', lang.hitch(this, this._toggleEditButton))
```

When a button is clicked, it calls `this._toggleEditButton`. By doing so, it passes a click event to that function, similar to how you processed the map's click event previously. You can check whether an event was passed into this function, and if so, you know it was from a button click, so you want to make the current button active and disable the others. To do this, toggle the class names as you did before on the target event:

```
if (e) {
this.requesttype = domAttr.get(e.target, 'data-type');
    domClass.toggle(e.target, 'btn-primary btn-success')
}
```

This removes the `btn-primary` class from the button that was clicked and adds the `btn-success` class to it, thus changing the button's color from blue to green. But now you can take advantage of toggling the look of the button to disable the other buttons so they can't be clicked while adding a request.

The `dojo/dom-attr` module that you aliased as `domAttr` in your module is a helper module that lets you pull the value of any attribute on an HTML element. In this case, you want to get the `data-type` attribute from the button that you're using to initiate a request. Passing bits of data from an HTML element to your JavaScript is a neat trick. Because you removed the `btn-primary` class from the button used to start the request, you can disable the other buttons, which still have the `btn-primary` class attached to them. If the user is currently editing, you disable these other buttons:

```
query('.btn-primary', this.domNode)     ⤺ Finds elements with
.removeClass('btn-primary')                btn-primary class
.attr('disabled', 'disabled');          ⤺ Removes btn-primary class
                                        ⤺ Adds disabled attribute
```

This is a neat piece of code, because you can use the `dojo/query` module to chain all these commands together to accomplish what you need to do, which is disable these buttons. When the user is finished editing, the next few lines of code put everything back to normal:

```
query('.btn-edit', this.domNode)        ⤺ Finds elements
    .removeClass('btn-success')            with btn-edit class
    .addClass('btn-primary')            ⤺ Removes btn-success class
    .removeAttr('disabled');            ⤺ Removes disabled attribute
                                           to enable buttons
```

Adds normal btn-primary class

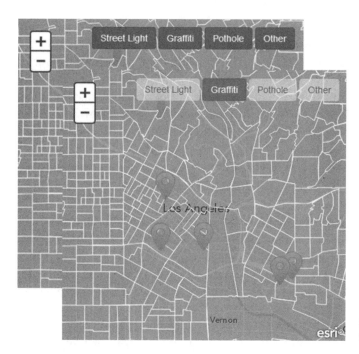

Figure 5.14 The application when adding a request

Again, you can use the `dojo/query` module to accomplish updating the styles of the button by chaining methods together. You remove the `btn-success` class from any button and add the `btn-primary` class back. Don't worry about adding extra class names; Dojo is smart enough to know whether an HTML element already has a class name and won't add extras to it. You then remove the `disabled` attribute from everything to return all elements back to normal. You can see what this looks like in figure 5.14.

Now when you click any of these buttons, the appropriate Issue Type is saved with your feature, and the only thing the user has to fill out is the Description. That's minimal typing for the user, and makes it much more likely to be used. You're almost finished with your mobile-focused application. The only thing you have to worry about is what happens if the user loses an internet connection.

5.3 Enabling disconnected editing

When working with mobile devices, it's a fact of life that you can't always rely on having an internet connection. Various things could interfere, such as tall highway barriers, buildings, or a lack of cell phone towers. Normally, this would be a minimal concern; after all, you're building web apps, and so when no internet connection is available, the application won't work. But when you're working with editing data and someone expects something to just work, you need to take this loss of internet connection into consideration. I'll also let you in on a dirty secret about disconnected editing: there's no perfect solution.

5.3.1   Local storage

Just because no perfect solution exists doesn't mean there isn't a doable solution. *Local storage* is part of the HTML5 specification and is a way to store data locally in key/ value pairs. You can take advantage of this to store requests locally as needed and implement a way to push those updates when an internet connection is available. It can also be used when you have no internet connection; you can store an item with a value of "hello" and a key of 99. You retrieve the data by using the key. The following is an example:

```
localStorage.setItem("99", "hello");          Stores hello with key of 99
localStorage.getItem("99");                   Uses key to retrieves hello
```

It's a simple API to get used to. One thing to remember is that local storage can reliably store only string values. So you can't just save a JavaScript object; you'll need to store a string version of the object, using a module like dojo/json to serialize it to a string.

You can store your data in a couple of ways. The ArcGIS for Developers site suggests storing all the data to local storage (https://developers.arcgis.com/en/ javascript/jssamples/exp_localstorage.html). This may be useful in some situations, such as storing census data locally for use anytime. But again, you need to be careful about your storage limits with local storage.

Limitations

Local storage can reliably hold only about 5 MB of data. Esri has an example worth looking at in the ArcGIS JavaScript samples that uses local storage to save tiled data locally to the browser (https://developers.arcgis.com/en/javascript/jssamples/ exp_webstorage.html). This is a great intro to see how local storage can be used in web applications. Because this module is storing image data locally, local storage can fill up quickly, so it's up to the developer to come up with a scheme to clear local storage as needed. In this case, you're using local storage to store new requests locally as needed and to implement a way to push those updates when an internet connection is established.

What you're going to do is save data locally only when an edit fails. This lets you save all your edits and sync them at once when ready. You'll handle this by wrapping the method that applies the edits in another module; that handles storing the data locally when an edit fails, thus making an assumption that you have no internet connection.

WHEN ARE WE DISCONNECTED?

For some time now, browsers have had a simple way to tell whether they're online or offline. The property window.navigator.onLine returns true when online, and false when offline. But it's probably not what you think it is. This value doesn't check whether you have an internet connection; it checks only whether the browser is working in offline mode. Internet Explorer and Firefox have an offline mode, but not Chrome. So how can you check for a working internet connection? You'd have to make a request that looks something like this by using Dojo:

```
var req = request('//' +
  location.pathname, {                    The preventCache option
    preventCache: true                    appends a timestamp to the URL
}
req.then(
    function() {                 Function called
    },                           when successful
    function() {                            Function called
    }                                       when it fails
);
```

So you can make a request to the current host with a timestamp parameter. This prevents calling a cached URL. Using the deferred results, the first function handles the success of the call, and the second handles the error of the call. You could check for this every time you want to save a request, but it gets tricky to test using `localhost`, and won't always throw an error when you expect. So, keep it as simple as you can, and save the data to local storage when an error occurs trying to save a request.

SAVE DATA TO LOCAL STORAGE

You'll create a new module called `widgets/edit/editService.js` to handle all this for you.

> **NOTE** The code for this section is available in the chapter5/part3 folder of the source code included with the book. All JavaScript files are located in the chapter5/part3/app/js folder.

Let's look at all the code for the wrapper and step through it for clarity. The widgets/edit/editService.js file calls the `applyEdits` method on our `FeatureLayer`, and if it fails, saves the data locally. It also has a method to send all the data when you have an internet connection available. This is shown in the following listing.

> **Listing 5.9 widgets/edit/editService.js–saves to local storage**

```
define([
    'dojo/_base/declare',
    'dojo/_base/lang',
    'dojo/Deferred',
    'dojo/json',
    'esri/graphic'
], function(declare, lang, Deferred, dojoJson, Graphic) {
    return declare(null, {
        layer: null,
        hasLocal: false,
        constructor: function(options) {
            this.options = options || {};
            this.layer = options.layer;
            this._sync = [];                       Checks local storage
```

```
            this.check();
        },                                          Checks for features
        check: function() {                         in local storage
            for (var name in localStorage) {
                if (name.indexOf('request') > -1) {
                    this.hasLocal = true;
                }
            }
        },                                          Pushes features in
        sync: function() {                          local storage as big edit
            var keys = [];
            for (var key in localStorage) {
                if (key.indexOf('request') > -1) {
                    keys.push(key);
                    var item = localStorage.getItem(key);
                    var graphic = new Graphic(dojoJson.parse(item));
                    this._sync.push(graphic);
                }
            }
            if (this._sync.length > 0) {
                this.layer.applyEdits(this._sync)
                    .then(
                        lang.hitch(this, function() {
                            this._sync.length = 0;
                            this.hasLocal = false;
                            for (var i = 0, key; (key = keys[i]); i++) {
                                localStorage.removeItem(key);
                            }
                        }),
                        lang.hitch(this, function() {
                            this._sync.length = 0;
                        })
                    );
            }
        },                                          Adds data to feature layer
        add: function(adds) {
            var deferred = new Deferred()
                , req;
            req = this.layer.applyEdits(adds);
            req.then(                               If edit successful, resolves
                function() {                        deferred object
                    deferred.resolve();
                },
                lang.hitch(this,
                function() {
                    for (var i = 0, item; (item = adds[i]); i++) {
                        try {
                            var id = Math.floor(1 + Math.random() * 1000);
                            var requestItem =
                                localStorage.getItem('request-' + id);
                            if (!requestItem) {
                                localStorage.setItem('request-' +
                                    id,
                                    dojoJson.stringify(item.toJson()));
                            }
                        }
```

If data in local
storage, saves
to server

Stores edits locally

```
                        this.check();
                    } catch (error) {
                        alert('Problem adding request to local storage. Storage
    might be full');
                    }
                }
                deferred.reject(adds);
            })                    );
            return deferred.promise;                    Returns deferred promise
        }
    });
});
```

This module is handling quite a bit for you:

1   Check whether data is available to save.

    When the module first loads, it checks local storage and sets a variable called
    hasLocal to true or false if there is data to be saved. This value can then be
    checked to see whether you have values to save.

2   Save data locally when an edit fails.

    When you add data to your FeatureLayer and it fails, you save those edits to
    local storage with a random key, but prefix the key with request-; in case you
    decide to save other types of data locally. This will help you tell the data apart.
    This is more of a precautionary measure than anything else. A Graphic object
    has the ability to convert to a plain object that can be serialized to JSON for stor-
    age using the dojo/json module. Check to make sure that the key doesn't
    already exist.

3   Provide a way to sync local data.

    You also provide a sync method that iterates over local storage, finds locally
    saved requests, parses them as JSON, and creates new graphics to send to the
    server. If successful, it then removes the items from local storage to make room
    for more. To get this to work, you need to modify a couple of other files.

MODIFY EDIT TOOLS

You want a way to run the sync method in your wrapper module when needed. Add a
new button to your template of edit tool buttons in widgets/edit/editTools.tpl.html:

```
<button type="button"
  class="btn btn-warning btn-sync"
  data-type="sync">Sync</button>
```

You give this button a class name of btn-sync so you can listen for click events on it. In
the constructor for widgets/edit/editTools.js, you initialize the edit service and pass it
the request FeatureLayer in the parameters:

```
        this.editService = new EditService({
          layer: this.requestLayer
        });
```

Then in the `postCreate` method, you add a handler for click events on your Sync button:

```
this.own(
  on(
   this.domNode,
   '.btn-edit:click',
   lang.hitch(this, '_toggleEditButton')
  ),
  on(
    this.domNode,
    '.btn-sync:click',
    lang.hitch(this, '_syncLocal')
  )
);
```

Binds click of Sync button to local method

That `_syncLocal` method checks whether data is saved locally and then calls the `sync` method of your wrapper module:

```
_syncLocal: function() {
  if (this.editService.hasLocal) {
      this.editService.sync();
  }
}
```

That all seems easy enough. If you run the application now, you should see your Sync button added to the page, as shown in figure 5.15, and you can start testing.

This doesn't look that different from what you had earlier, and that's sort of the point. Ideally, the user doesn't need to be concerned about how the tool is working, so aside from the extra Sync button, nothing is new.

Figure 5.15   Add the Sync button to sync local storage data with the server.

TEST SAVING TO LOCAL STORAGE

Determining whether widgets/edit/editService.js is saving data locally can be tricky. As of right now, you can use your application as before, and it behaves the same. To test disconnected editing, you need to, well, disconnect.

Before you attempt to disable your Wi-Fi or unplug your Ethernet cable, both of which are viable options, let's try a different approach that involves using a fake proxy. I recommend using Google Chrome for the bulk of debugging web applications, and Chrome uses Internet Explorer connection settings. This will only work in a Windows environment.

Open the Chrome Settings page and click the Show Advanced Settings link. To open the Connections tab of your Internet Properties, click the Change Proxy Settings button, as shown in figure 5.16.

Network

Google Chrome is using your computer's system proxy settings to connect to the network.

| Change proxy settings... |

Figure 5.16   Proxy settings in Google Chrome

Click the LAN Settings button. Under the Proxy Server settings, enter the local address with a fake port, as shown in figure 5.17.

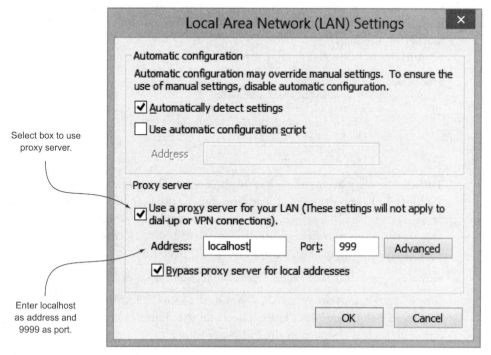

Figure 5.17   Setting up a fake proxy to test disconnected use

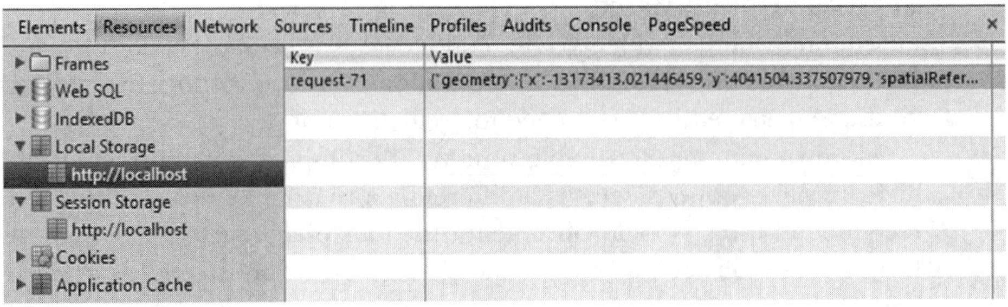

Figure 5.18 The feature is saved to local storage.

This isn't a pretty way to test for disconnected editing, but it works and keeps you from having to unplug/disable the Wi-Fi each time you want to test it. But before doing this on your application, let's zoom to a location on the map and set up a fake proxy. Add a new request to the map, and you should be alerted that a request has been saved locally. Awesome! You can check this in the Google Chrome debug tools under the Resources tab, as shown in figure 5.18.

If you remove the fake proxy at this point and click the Sync button, your feature will display on the map. If you check local storage now, it should be empty. Now you need to display the data that's being saved.

DISPLAY LOCALLY SAVED DATA

Currently, the application doesn't indicate visually on the map that you added the point when it's saved locally. Let's add a function to utils/symbolUtil.js that adds a marker on the map.

Add the following code after the `renderSymbol` function:

```
simpleMarker: function() {
        return new SimpleMarkerSymbol(
          SimpleMarkerSymbol.STYLE_SQUARE, 12, new SimpleLineSymbol(
            SimpleLineSymbol.STYLE_SOLID, new Color([255, 0, 0]), 1),
            new Color([0, 255, 0, 1])
        );
    }
```

This creates a square marker that displays on the map when a feature is saved locally. This lets users know they're still adding data to the map, even if it isn't instantly saved to the server. Create a reference to this module in your widgets/edit/editTools.js file, and use it when you first create the `Graphic` for your edit. Previously, you left the `symbology` argument as `null`, but now you'll pass the `simpleMarker()` method:

```
graphic = new Graphic(mapPt, symbolUtil.simpleMarker(), attributes);
```

Now when you add the `Graphic`, if you have to save it locally, you'll add the feature to the map's default graphics layer. The code that handles adding requests to widgets/edit/editTools.js is shown in the following listing.

Listing 5.10 widgets/edit/editTools.js–adding requests

```
...
this.editService.add([graphic]).then(
  lang.hitch(this, function() {
    this._toggleEditButton();
    alert('Request submitted');
  }),
  lang.hitch(this, function() {
    this._toggleEditButton();
    this.map.graphics.add(graphic);
    alert('Request saved locally');
  })
);
...
```

If connected, proceed as normal

Function to call if adding features to server fails

Add Graphic to map

Now when you add a feature to local storage, you see it on the map, as shown in figure 5.19.

You've implemented a mechanism to assist users when no internet connection is available for the application. You may be asking "Why not store the features in memory and not worry about local storage?" That could be an option, but ideally you want a solution that persists if the user closes the browser, which an in-memory solution can't do.

REVIEW STEPS TO SAVING DATA LOCALLY

Taking a step back, setting all this up is a matter of a few steps:

1 Check whether you can save features to the feature service as normal; if not, save data locally.
2 Display locally saved data on the map.

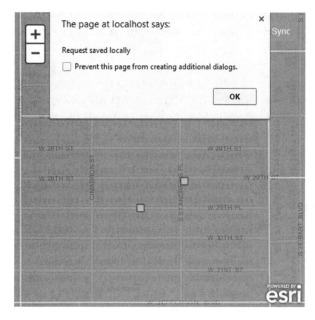

Figure 5.19 The features are added as graphics when added to local storage.

3   Provide a way for the user to send that locally saved data when an internet connection is available.

5.3.2   *Caveats*

You may have realized that this mechanism isn't true disconnected editing, as you need an internet connection to even start the application. It's the nature of writing a web application; it has to have an internet connection when it starts to download required files and data as needed. What you've implemented is more of a fallback system that assists users when they lose an internet connection on their mobile devices. For example, without an internet connection, the user can't see the underlying image tiles of the street data. The necessary census data features may not have been downloaded. You can't provide a perfect solution, but what you can do is provide a stopgap until the connection is restored.

That isn't to say you can't inch closer to providing a more advanced solution to disconnected editing. In chapter 7, you'll use the application cache, a way to tell the browser to cache all the files needed to run the application and keep them stored in the browser, and you'll implement other methods of storing data locally by using third-party tools.

5.3.3   *Other storage options*

Local storage is probably the simplest way to store data locally in the browser, but it's not the only way. *IndexedDB* is the preferred HTML5 storage API for more-complex data. It's SQL-like (Structured Query Language) for the browser. Previously, Web SQL was the preferred way of storing complex data structures, but it was deprecated in 2010. The problem is that mobile browsers still use it and don't currently support IndexedDB, aside from Internet Explorer 11. This is a problem for us, as mobile browsers are our target. You'll learn how to work with this situation in chapter 7.

5.4   *Summary*

- You covered quite a bit about editing in this chapter. You first learned how to use the default widgets provided with the ArcGIS API for JavaScript to perform edits. Then you learned how to build your own custom edit tools that make it even easier for end users to submit new requests with minimal typing on their part. This is incredibly beneficial, and now you have a better idea of how the edit functionalities of the API work.

- You also learned a method to handle disconnected editing when the application loses an internet connection. You learned how to store the data locally when no connection is available and to push the data out to the feature service when the internet connection is restored. This valuable methodology lays the groundwork for even more-advanced usages of local data storage.

In chapter 6, you'll build a desktop browser-based application that uses the data submitted with the mobile application.

Building a desktop browser application

This chapter covers

- Building a browser-based web application for the desktop
- Implementing security, tokens, and OAuth 2.0
- Saving security credentials
- Working with more out-of-the-box widgets
- Editing collected data
- Linking collected data with other data

Chapter 5 covered the details of custom editing and using the built-in capabilities of the ArcGIS JavaScript API to build an easy-to-use mobile editing application. The focus was on designing the application to run on mobile devices efficiently. Yet there is still a need for browser-based web applications for use in a desktop environment. Rather than investing in a desktop GIS application, such as ArcMap, which requires additional licenses for each user and comes with features that many users don't need, you can create a focused web application that meets the specific needs of users. Implementing a web application designed for the desktop also saves time and money otherwise spent training people to use a new GIS application.

In this chapter, we consider the needs and goals of a desktop browser application built with the ArcGIS API for JavaScript. You'll use some new Dijits that we haven't yet discussed, and we'll cover how to make updates or corrections to the data that was collected in the field.

Let's start with the goals of the application, which we'll name the RequestViewer.

6.1   The project ahead

Mobile data-collecting applications are fun to build. They present interesting challenges, as you saw in chapter 5 when dealing with disconnected editing, and encourage you to think in simple terms about design, such as implementing a single button-click to collect data. They also provide a practical exercise because data collection is a common use of mobile web-mapping applications. This chapter takes you a step further to look at what happens to the data after it's been collected in a field application and analyzed in a desktop environment. After all, you should assume that users are collecting data for a reason.

6.1.1   Goals of the RequestViewer

Continuing the municipal services scenario, suppose that the data collected in the field is assigned to specific employees for further investigation, such as determining what work needs to be done to repair a pothole, or verifying the location of a request. Given these requirements, the RequestViewer application must provide users with the following capabilities:

- To choose a location collected in the field
- To assign a location to an employee from a list of employees
- To edit the data that was collected

    For example, the user may want to change the location or type of request to more closely match the description of the request. Maybe the user wants to clarify the description or update the location of a report for a pothole.

6.1.2   Freedom of the desktop browser

You took care when building the application in chapter 5 to make sure it worked as efficiently as possible because it's intended to run in a mobile browser. Care had to go into making sure data could be stored locally in case of a lost internet connection. You had to design a simpler user interface that wouldn't clutter a small display. All in all, working on a mobile-based application required extra care.

Although you don't necessarily have the same restrictions when working on a browser-based web application for the desktop, neither do you have carte blanche to throw every widget in the ArcGIS JavaScript API into the RequestViewer. For example, don't put ArcMap in the browser, which is mocked up in figure 6.1. This is an example of something you should not do! This wall of buttons and menus can be overwhelming for your average user. If users need all this functionality, they may need to use a bona fide installation of ArcMap to do their work.

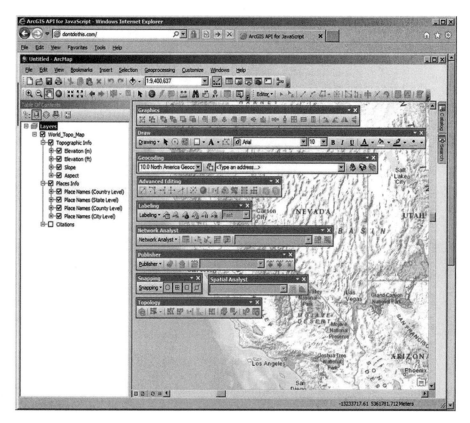

Figure 6.1 Providing desktop GIS software (literally) in the browser overwhelms users and should be avoided.

You should still take care to make sure the RequestViewer runs well, but you don't need to work under the threat of losing an internet connection or let tiny, pocket-sized displays constrain your application. You can take advantage of Dijits from the ArcGIS JavaScript API, which don't lend themselves to a mobile application but work fine in a desktop browser.

In chapter 5, you spent time building a custom `Editor` widget to better meet the needs of a mobile data-collecting web application. Similarly, when building the RequestViewer, it's important to assess the users' needs. For example, suppose you determine that users need to be able to search for data and add new features. You can tailor the application to make these tasks easy to complete, and if you can implement these tasks with out-of-the-box tools, you can also save yourself development time.

> **NOTE** The code for this application is available in the chapter6/part1 folder of the source code included with the book.

Now that we've defined our goals and requirements for the RequestViewer, let's start writing code.

6.2   *Setting up and configuring the RequestViewer*

As in previous chapters, to get the application off the ground, you first define the HTML structure and the basic JavaScript files. Let's start with index.html.

6.2.1   *Creating index.html*

The HTML for the RequestViewer application is similar to what you used in chapter 5. As shown in the following listing, it contains the structure for the application and references for the required style sheets and JavaScript files. This standard HTML structure can be used to get most projects started.

> **Listing 6.1   index.html—main HTML for your application**

```
<!doctype html>
<html>
  <head>
    <title>RequestViewer</title>
    <link href="css/bootstrap.min.css" rel="stylesheet">
    <link
      rel="stylesheet"
      href="http://js.arcgis.com/3.11/
      dojo/dijit/themes/nihilo/nihilo.css">
    <link
      rel='stylesheet'
      href='http://js.arcgis.com/3.11/esri/css/esri.css'/>
    <link href='css/main.css' rel='stylesheet'/>
  </head>
  <body class="nihilo">
    <div id="map-div"></div>                 ◁——— Main div element for map
  </body>
  <script src="http://js.arcgis.com/3.11"></script>  ◁ Full version of the ArcGIS
  <script src="js/run.js"></script>              API for JavaScript
</html>
```

You've seen the content of this HTML file in previous chapters. One difference in this case is that you use the full version of the ArcGIS API for JavaScript rather than the compact version. As a result, you have access to many of the widgets in the API without having to manually load them in your modules. You saw how this works in chapter 5 (see section 5.1.2); when using the compact build of the API, you had to load the Identity Manager manually.

Next, let's take a look at the run.js file.

6.2.2   *Configuring run.js*

This file sets up your application. As shown in the following listing, its configuration lets Dojo know where the files to build the application are located.

> **Listing 6.2   js/run.js—set up DojoConfig**

```
(function () {                                          Uses regular
  var pathRX = new RegExp(/\/[^\/]+$/)              ◁ expression to
    , locationPath = location.pathname.replace(pathRX, '');   help load files
```

```
require({
  async: true,
  packages: [{
    name: 'controllers',
    location: locationPath + '/js/controllers'
  }, {
    name: 'services',
    location: locationPath + '/js/services'
  }, {
    name: 'utils',
    location: locationPath + '/js/utils'
  }, {
    name: 'app',
    location: locationPath + '/js',
    main: 'main'
  }]
}, ['app']);        ⤺  Sets up Dojo configuration

})();
```

Again, this is what you used in chapter 5, aside from omitting the folders you aren't using. This is a standard way of setting up the Dojo part of the ArcGIS API for JavaScript to use your own custom-built modules.

Let's take a quick look at the base main.js file of the application.

6.2.3   Starting the RequestViewer

This file defines the options for the map, loads the layers to be used, and starts up the application. This is the same file you used in chapter 5 and is shown in the following listing.

Listing 6.3   js/main.js—entry point to application

```
require([
  'controllers/appcontroller',
  'services/mapservices',
  'dojo/domReady!'
], function (AppCtrl, mapServices) {
  'use strict';
  var appCtrl = new AppCtrl({
    elem: 'map-div',
    mapOptions: {
      basemap: 'streets',
      center: [-118.241, 34.0542],
      zoom: 12
    },                                       Loads map services
    layers: mapServices.loadServices()   ⤺  for application
  });
  appCtrl.load();    ⤺  Initializes application contro
});
```

In this application, you use the streets basemap to provide more detail on your map. The next piece we'll look at is mapServices.js, again the same file you used in chapter 5.

6.2.4 Defining map services

This file, shown in the following listing, defines the various map services to be loaded into the application. This module loads a census layer, which acts as a service request area, and also loads the requests that were created in the application you built in chapter 5.

Listing 6.4 js/services/mapservices.js—helper to load services

```
define([
  'esri/layers/FeatureLayer',
  'esri/renderers/SimpleRenderer',
  'utils/symbolUtil'
], function(FeatureLayer, SimpleRenderer, symbolUtil) {

  function _loadServices(config) {
    var layers = []
      , censusLayer = new FeatureLayer(
          'http://services.arcgis.com/'+
          'V6ZHFr6zdgNZuVG0/arcgis/rest/services/'+
          'CensusLaborDemo/FeatureServer/1', {
            id: 'Census'
      })
      , requestLayer = new FeatureLayer(
          'http://services1.arcgis.com/'+
          'QKasy5M2L9TAQ7gs/arcgis/rest/services/'+
          'Requests/FeatureServer/0', {
            id: 'Requests',
            mode: FeatureLayer.MODE_ONDEMAND,
            outFields: ['*']
      })
      , renderer = new SimpleRenderer(symbolUtil.renderSymbol());
    censusLayer.setRenderer(renderer);
    layers.push(censusLayer);
    layers.push(requestLayer);

    return layers;                    ◁──  Returns an array of map services
  }                                        to be used in application
  return {
    loadServices: _loadServices
  };
});
```

You can use the same mapservices.js file you used in chapter 5. You will want to replace the URLs for the map services in this example to use your own map services from your free ArcGIS Developer account.

Let's look at the appcontroller.js file.

6.2.5 Setting up the application controller

You're going to start with a simplified appcontroller.js, shown in the following listing, to handle creating the map. Later in this chapter, you'll use this file to handle loading other modules for the application.

Listing 6.5 js/controllers/appcontroller.js—application controller for application

```
define([
  'dojo/_base/declare',
  'esri/map'
], function (
  declare,
  Map
  ) {

  return declare(null, {
    map: null,
    options: {},

    constructor: function (options) {
      this.options = options;
    },

    load: function () {
      this.map = new Map(this.options.elem, this.options.mapOptions);
      this.map.addLayers(this.options.layers);
    }
  });
});
```

Creates new map →

Adds layers to application ←

If you run the application, you should see a map that looks similar to figure 6.2.

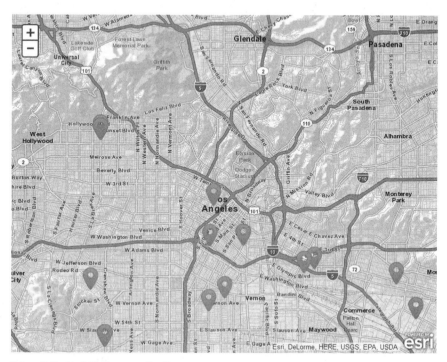

Figure 6.2 No-frills base application

You'll be prompted for your username and password to access your ArcGIS Online service, so have that information ready. Having to enter this information in your application repeatedly gets tedious, so refer to appendix C for information on setting up a proxy page.

After you set up the proxy page, refresh the browser for your application. You should no longer be prompted by the Identity Manager to log in, and your services should work as expected. The proxy page is a handy tool to use in a variety of scenarios. It's also a great way to work when developing with secured services so you don't have to log in each time.

Suppose you have a requirement to provide a level of security in your application, but you want something more robust than the Identity Manager to do it. Let's see how OAuth 2.0 can help.

Choose your security option

The ArcGIS API for JavaScript provides a couple of ways to handle working with secured services:

- The Identity Manager and the OAuth 2.0 protocol require users to log in to use and view the application.
- The proxy page method allows users to access the application and services directly without the need to log in repeatedly.

It boils down to a matter of preference in the route you decide to use. Personally, I like to use the proxy method during development and either the Identity Manager or OAuth 2.0 once deployed to production. All options are viable.

6.3   *Setting up authentication with OAuth 2.0*

A recent addition to ArcGIS Online is the use of OAuth 2.0 to allow access to your applications and services. An open standard for authorization, OAuth allows you to use third parties to access secured resources without having to share credentials. The advantage here is that users can log in using their ArcGIS Online accounts and be redirected back to your application. Your secured services use a token generated by ArcGIS Online, so you don't have to set up individual users to allow access. This allows you to have application-level logins versus individual user-level logins.

The Esri documentation provides a couple of good OAuth samples (https://developers.arcgis.com/en/javascript/jssamples/portal_oauth_inline.html).

6.3.1   *Using your developer account to create an application*

In chapter 4 you set up your ArcGIS developer account, and you created the Requests feature service for use in your application; but you didn't explore the features available from the My Applications page, specifically the security features.

Log in to your ArcGIS developer account and click the Applications link. You'll see a screen similar to figure 6.3 that shows the steps to create an application.

Figure 6.3　My Applications page of ArcGIS developer account

Click the Create an Application button to register an application, as shown in figure 6.4.

Working your way through the text boxes on the Register New Application page is straightforward:

- *Name*—You can give your application any name you'd like; I named mine RequestViewer.
- *Tags*—These are optional but work much the same way as you saw in chapter 4; they help users find your application in search results.
- *Redirect URI*—This information is important. Remember, with OAuth 2.0, users can log in using their ArcGIS Online accounts. Once they log in, this Redirect

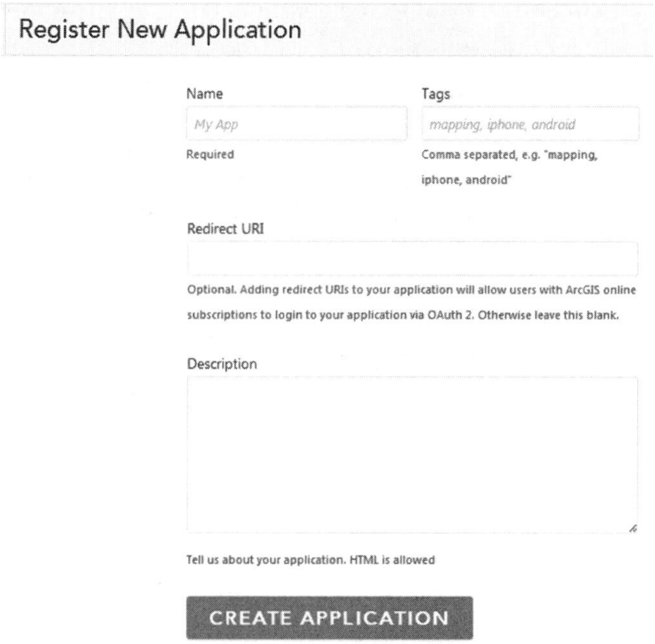

Register New Application

Name

My App

Required

Tags

mapping, iphone, android

Comma separated, e.g. "mapping, iphone, android"

Redirect URI

Optional. Adding redirect URIs to your application will allow users with ArcGIS online subscriptions to login to your application via OAuth 2. Otherwise leave this blank.

Description

Tell us about your application. HTML is allowed

CREATE APPLICATION

Figure 6.4　Page to create a new application

URI redirects the user back to your application with the proper credentials to access the secured services. For development, this is probably `localhost`, but you can update it at a later time for deployment, so don't be afraid to use whatever URL you need at the moment.

- *Description*—You can provide a description for your application so if you share your application via ArcGIS Online, others can understand the purpose of your application.

Once you click Create Application, navigate to the Application Details page. To view the Client ID and Client Secret, click the API Access link at the left. You should see the OAuth Credentials page as shown in figure 6.5 (my details are hidden). The Client Secret is used for server-based applications, but because this is a browser-based web application for the desktop, you need only the Client ID.

Be sure to keep the Client ID and the Client Secret used for authentication purposes hidden in your application. If a malicious user gains access to these, they can access billable services on your ArcGIS Online account, which could result in unwanted charges on the account. This caveat implies that you should store these credentials in a server environment that accesses the credentials for the application and provides them back to the client.

> **TIP** Implementing the server-side component is beyond the scope of this book, but it's something you should be aware of when working with authentication. See the Esri resource-proxy project for a solution (https://github.com/Esri/resource-proxy/) and appendix C for more details.

You now have the credentials you need to use OAuth 2.0 in your application, so let's modify the code to incorporate OAuth 2.0 in the sign-in process for the application.

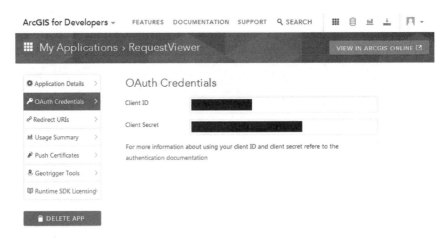

Figure 6.5   OAuth credentials of the RequestViewer application

6.3.2   *Updating main.js*

As I mentioned, to set up the credentials and make requests, you'll use the `esri/arcgis/OAuthInfo` module in combination with the `esri/IdentityManager` module that Esri provides. This Identity Manager makes a request to use OAuth 2.0 to get the credentials for the application using the credentials provided in the `OAuthInfo` module, and then assigns those credentials to the Identity Manager so the application can access secured services. The updated js/main.js file, shown in listing 6.6, now uses the following workflow:

- Check whether user is signed in.
- If signed in, begin application as normal.
- If not signed in, begin the sign-in process.
- Once signed in, begin application as normal.

NOTE   The code for this section is available in the chapter6/part2 folder of the source code included with the book.

Listing 6.6   js/main.js—use OAuth 2.0

```
require([
  'esri/arcgis/OAuthInfo',
  'esri/IdentityManager',
  'controllers/appcontroller',
  'services/mapservices',
  'dojo/domReady!'
], function (
  OAuthInfo, esriId,
  AppCtrl,
  mapServices
) {
  'use strict';

  function startApplication() {                 // Starts application as normal
    var appCtrl = new AppCtrl({
      elem: 'map-div',
      mapOptions: {
        basemap: 'streets',
        center: [-118.241, 34.0542],
        zoom: 12
      },
      layers: mapServices.loadServices()
    });
    appCtrl.load();
  }

  var info = new OAuthInfo({                     // Initializes ArcGISOAuthInfo
    appId: 'zppZ53G093yZV7tG',
    portal: 'http://www.arcgis.com',
    expiration: (14 * 24 * 60),
    popup: false
  });
```

```
esriId.registerOAuthInfos([info]);              ⟵  Register OAuthInfos with
                                                    the Identity Manager
esriId.checkSignInStatus(info.portalUrl)
  .then(startApplication)
  .otherwise(
    function() {
      esriId.getCredential(info.portalUrl)      ⟵  If not signed in, gets the credentials
      .then(startApplication);                      to sign in, then starts application
    }
  );
});
```

Checks if signed in; if so, starts application

When you run the application, you should now be redirected to an arcgis.com page and asked to sign in with your ArcGIS Online credentials; in this case, enter your Arc-GIS developer account information (see figure 6.6).

Once signed in, you're redirected back to the application running on your local machine, and the secured services should work as normal. This is similar to using the Identity Manager, as in chapter 5, but you've offloaded the sign-in process to ArcGIS Online.

When using OAuth 2.0, you may have noticed that users must log in on each page refresh. It would be a neat feature to allow users to stay logged in until they sign out. Let's implement this functionality next.

6.3.3 Saving credentials

If I were a user of an application that required me to log in every time I reloaded the page, I would get annoyed after a while. There could be security reasons for keeping this behavior, but let's look at how to persist a user login on page reloads.

Figure 6.6 ArcGIS sign-in page for RequestViewer application

NOTE The code for this section is available in the chapter6/part3 folder of the source code included with the book.

ADDING A NAVIGATION BAR

To allow users to log in and also log out, let's update the index.html file to add a navigation bar with a Sign In link. Take a look at the following listing to see the updated file.

Listing 6.7 index.html—add Sign In link

```
...
<body class="nihilo">
  <div class="navbar navbar-default">          ◁  Adds Bootstrap-style
    <ul class="nav navbar-nav">                   navigation bar
      <li>
        <a id="signin-elem" href="#">Sign In</a>   ◁  Adds Sign In link
      </li>                                            to navigation bar
    </ul>
  </div>
  <div id="map-div"></div>
</body>
...
```

Note that you're taking advantage of Bootstrap styling because the style sheet is already referenced in your index.html file (see chapter 4). This makes the Sign In link easy to create. So that the navigation bar doesn't interfere with the map, adjust the CSS to reposition the map 50 pixels from the top of the page in the css/main.css file:

```
#map-div {
  position: absolute;
  top: 50px;
  right: 0;
  left: 0;
  bottom: 0;
}
```

If you refresh the browser and log in, a navigation bar now appears at the top of the page with a Sign In link, as shown in figure 6.7. You'll add the Sign Out link later in the chapter.

You're using the Identity-Manager and OAuthInfo modules to log in to your application using OAuth 2.0. This utility does a good job of helping users to sign in, but once signed in, you need another utility module to save users' credentials.

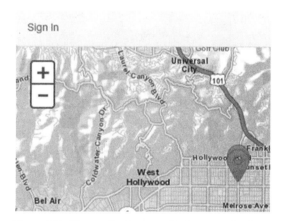

Figure 6.7 The application now displays a navigation bar with one link.

CREATING THE CREDENTIALS UTILITY MODULE

This utility module is inspired by a sample from the documentation for the ArcGIS API for JavaScript. It performs the same function as the original sample but uses the Identity Manager directly.

> **NOTE**   To review the documentation sample, see https://developers.arcgis .com/javascript/jssamples/widget_identitymanager_client_side.html.

The code for the module is shown in the following listing. Key steps are labeled in the code and explained in detail after the listing.

Listing 6.8   js/utils/securityUtil.js—module to handle credentials

```
define([
  'dojo/Deferred',
  'dojo/json',
  'esri/kernel',
  'dojo/cookie'
], function(
  Deferred, dojoJSON,
  kernel, cookie
) {
                                        Defines key to
                                        store credentials
  var key = 'esri_js_creds'

    , hasLocal = window.localStorage !== null          Checks if localStorage
      || typeof(window.localStorage) !== 'undefined';  available

  function loadCredentials() {
    var credJson
      , deferred;

    deferred = new Deferred();

    if (hasLocal) {
      credJson = window.localStorage.getItem(key);
    } else {
      credJson = cookie(key);                           Loads credentials
    }

    if (credJson) {
      kernel.id.initialize(dojoJSON.parse(credJson));
      deferred.resolve(true);
    } else {
      deferred.resolve(false);
    }

    return deferred.promise;
  }
```

```
function saveCredentials() {
  var deferred = new Deferred();

  if (kernel.id.credentials.length === 0) {
    deferred.resolve(false);
  }

  var credId = dojoJSON.stringify(kernel.id.toJson());

  if (hasLocal) {
    window.localStorage.setItem(key, credId);
    deferred.resolve(true);
  } else {
    cookie(key, credId, { expires: 1 });
    deferred.resolve(true);
  }

  return deferred.promise;
}
```
Saves credentials

```
function removeCredentials() {
  var deferred = new Deferred();
  if (hasLocal) {
    window.localStorage.removeItem(key);
    deferred.resolve(true);
  } else {
    cookie(key, null, { expires: -1 });
    deferred.resolve(true);
  }
  return deferred.promise;
}
```
Removes credentials

```
return {
  loadCredentials: loadCredentials,
  saveCredentials: saveCredentials,
  removeCredentials: removeCredentials
};
```
Returns object to reveal available methods

```
});
```

The module accomplishes quite a bit, so let's step through it for clarity:

1 Define a key to store the credentials for your application.

2 Check if localStorage is available.

The module attempts to use localStorage if available as a default storage mechanism, but if localStorage isn't available, it uses a browser cookie to store the credentials. A cookie can hold tiny pieces of information related to your browsing history, including any credentials to secure websites. I'm showing this method of using a cookie to store credentials because ArcGIS Online tokens are only valid for about two weeks, but cookie storage is not the most secure method of storing such credentials. Use this method with caution.

3 Load credentials.

The `loadCredentials` function attempts to load any credentials from `localStorage` or a cookie. If no credentials are available, it returns a Dojo promise and resolves that promise with a value of `false`. It does this by checking the `esri/kernel` module for credentials information.

4 Save current credentials.

The `saveCredentials` function saves the current credentials for one day by converting the credentials to JSON and storing them appropriately.

5 Delete credentials, if needed.

Because you can save the credentials, the module also allows you to remove them. Using the `dojo/cookie` module, you can remove a cookie by passing an object with an `expires` value of `-1`.

6 Expose functions outside the module.

Finally, the module returns a plain JavaScript object that exposes these functions to the outside world.

As you can see, this module makes extensive use of the `dojo/Deferred` module to return promises for each function. You'll see how that works next when you update the js/main.js file.

COMBINING THE CREDENTIALS UTILITY WITH OAUTH 2.0

You're still using Oauth 2.0 to sign in to the application, but you're also now saving the associated credentials when the browser reloads. You can see what the updated js/main.js file looks like, with key steps labeled, in the following listing.

Listing 6.9 js/main.js—save credentials locally

```
require([
  'esri/config',
  'dojo/dom',
  'dojo/on',
  'esri/arcgis/OAuthInfo',
  'esri/IdentityManager',

  'utils/securityUtil',
  'controllers/appcontroller',
  'services/mapservices',
  'dojo/domReady!'
], function (
  esriConfig,
  dom, on,
  OAuthInfo, esriId, securityUtil,        Loads credentials
  AppCtrl,                                utility module
  mapServices
) {

  esriConfig.defaults.io.proxyUrl = '/app/proxy.ashx';
```

```
var info = new OAuthInfo({
  appId: 'zppZ53G093yZV7tG',
  portal: 'http://www.arcgis.com',
  expiration: (14 * 24 * 60),
  popup: false
});

esriId.registerOAuthInfos([info]);

function startApplication() {

  dom.byId('signin-elem').innerHTML = 'Sign Out';

  var appCtrl = new AppCtrl({
    elem: 'map-div',
    mapOptions: {
      basemap: 'streets',
      center: [-118.241, 34.0542],
      zoom: 12
    },
    layers: mapServices.loadServices()
  });
  appCtrl.load();
}

function clearApplication() {
  securityUtil.removeCredentials();
  esriId.destroyCredentials();
  location.reload();
}

esriId.checkSignInStatus(info.portalUrl)
  .then(function() {
    securityUtil.saveCredentials().then(startApplication);
  })
  .otherwise(
    function() {
      securityUtil.loadCredentials().then(function(success) {
        if (success) {
          startApplication();
        }
      });
    }
  );

on(dom.byId('signin-elem'), 'click', function(e) {
  e.preventDefault();
  if (e.target.innerHTML === 'Sign In') {
    esriId.getCredential(info.portalUrl)
      .then(startApplication);
  } else {
    clearApplication();
  }
});
});
```

Loads credentials utility module

Changes Sign In link when user signs in

Removes credentials, signs user out, and reloads the page

Saves credentials and starts application

Loads credentials and starts application

Listens for click event when user signs in or out

A few new security-related features are implemented in this file. The steps are detailed here:

1   Load the `securityUtil` module that will save OAuth 2.0 credentials.

2   To allow the user to also sign out, change the text of the link from Sign In to Sign Out when the user signs in and the application starts.

3   The `clearApplication()` function removes the credentials from the browser and signs the user out, which reloads the page.

4   `IdentityManager` checks whether the user has returned from the ArcGIS Online sign-in page. If so, it saves the credentials locally and starts the application.

5   If the browser isn't redirecting from the ArcGIS Online sign-in page, it checks the local credentials and loads them. If loading the credentials is successful, it then starts the application.

6   Use `dojo/on` to listen for when the Sign In link is clicked and check whether the value of the link is `Sign In`.

    If so, when clicked, the application uses `IdentityManager` to sign in the user and start the application. If the user is already logged in, you assume that the user wants to log out, so you remove the local credentials and reload the page using the `clearApplication()` function.

Now when you refresh the page, you're presented with the navigation bar and the Sign In link with no map. When you click Sign In, you're directed to the ArcGIS Online page, as before, where you sign in and then get redirected back to the application. The application should behave as before, but when you refresh the page, you're no longer prompted to sign in; the application, along with the secured services, loads as expected. When you're done, click the Sign Out link, and the page returns to its original state with the Sign In link and no map.

This handy module you built now manages user credentials for your application, which should make the user happier. With the base of your application built and a way to access secured services in place, let's move on and add more functionality.

6.4   *Building the user interface*

With authentication complete, you can begin to add capabilities to your application. To show the power you get out of the box from the API, let's add two standard ArcGIS API for JavaScript widgets:

-   `Measurement` widget
-   `BasemapToggle` widget

6.4.1   *Working with the Measurement widget*

One of the widgets that I use on a regular basis is the `Measurement` widget. It does exactly what you think it does: it measures length and area and can even be used to determine a coordinate on the screen. I wouldn't necessarily use this widget in a mobile-focused web application because I don't think it's the best fit for the screen

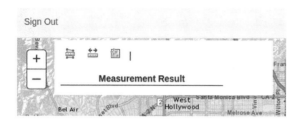

Figure 6.8 Adding the Measurement widget to the application provides tools to measure area, length, and coordinates of a location.

real-estate it uses up, but for a desktop browser application, it works great. When added to your application, the Measurement widget looks similar to figure 6.8.

To get the Measurement widget into your application, modify the following files:

- index.html
- main.css
- appcontroller.js

ADDING AND DISPLAYING THE MEASUREMENT WIDGET

First, add a div element to the index.html file to hold the widget. You can add this element after the element for the map:

```
<div id="map-div"></div>
<div id="measurement-div"></div>
```

Next, add the following CSS to the style sheet (css/main.css):

```
#measurement-div {
  position: absolute;
  background-color: #fff;
  z-index: 1;
  left: 65px;
  top: 55px;
  width: 300px;
  height: 200px;
  padding: 10px 80px 10px 10px;
}
```

This CSS makes the background color for the element white and positions the element on the page in a convenient location.

NOTE The code for this application is available in the chapter6/part4 folder of the source code included with the book.

With the visual elements in place to hold the Measurement widget and display it, you only need to modify the js/controllers/appcontroller module to add the widget to the application, as shown in the following listing.

Listing 6.10 js/controllers/appcontroller.js—add Measurement widget

```
define([
  'dojo/_base/declare',
  'dojo/_base/lang',
  'dojo/on',
```

Adds references to required modules

```
    'esri/map',
    'esri/tasks/GeometryService',
    'esri/config',
    'esri/dijit/Measurement'
], function (
  declare, lang, on,
  Map,
  GeometryService,
  esriConfig,
  Measurement
) {

  var url = 'http://tasks.arcgisonline.com' +
    '/ArcGIS/rest/services/Geometry/GeometryServer';

  return declare(null, {
    map: null,
    options: {},

    constructor: function (options) {
      this.options = options;
      esriConfig.defaults.geometryService =
        new GeometryService(url);
    },

    load: function () {
      this.map = new Map(
        this.options.elem,
        this.options.mapOptions
      );
      on(this.map, 'load', lang.hitch(this, 'onMapLoad'));     Waits for the
      this.map.addLayers(this.options.layers);                 map to load
    },

    onMapLoad: function() {                        When the map loads, builds
      this.measurement = new Measurement({        the Measurement widget
        map: this.map
      }, 'measurement-div');
      this.measurement.startup();
    }
  });
});
```

The key steps are detailed here:

1   Add references to newly required modules for the Measurement widget.
    Add the dojo/on module to listen for the map to finish loading. The esri/
    tasks/GeometryService module is required by the Measurement widget so it
    can perform the calculations needed to display results on the map. To set the
    URL for the new GeometryService, use the esri/config module.

2   When the application starts, add a listener using the dojo/on module, which lis-
    tens for the map to load.

3 When the map loads, create the `Measurement` widget by giving the widget a reference to the loaded map and the ID of the `div` element to use for the widget container.

Because the widget references an HTML element, use the `startup()` method of the widget so the widget can render in the browser.

Refresh the page to see what was shown previously in figure 6.8.

USING THE MEASUREMENT WIDGET

If you begin clicking the icons of the `Measurement` widget, you'll see that you can measure areas on the page and measure distances. When checking for coordinates, the widget even displays the latitude and longitude of the mouse cursor. Examples of what the `Measurement` widget can do are shown in figure 6.9.

As you can see, the `Measurement` widget is a useful tool. Users tell me that one of their most common tasks for this widget is getting the coordinate of a location such as a street intersection. In the case of this application, a user may want to determine roughly how far away a request is from the street. It has numerous possible use cases.

You positioned the `Measurement` widget in a location on the page that's convenient with respect to other elements such as the map and header. During use, the widget grows in width to accommodate the drop-down menu of measurement units, and it also grows in height, downward, to accommodate displaying the results. Realistically, the upper-left corner of the page is the only area that provides the widget with the room it needs during use. But you may not want the widget to be visible at all times. Wouldn't it be neat if you could hide or show the widget with a button click? That's exactly what you'll do next.

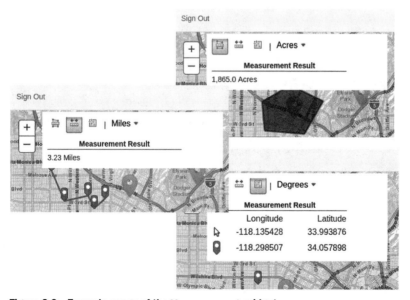

Figure 6.9 Example usage of the `Measurement` widget

TOGGLING VISIBILITY OF THE MEASUREMENT WIDGET

First, update the index.html file with a new anchor tag in a list item in the navigation bar HTML element (see listing 6.7). Add the link below the Sign In link:

```
<li>
  <a id="signin-elem" href="#">Sign In</a>
</li>
<li>
  <a id="measurement-toggle" href="#">Measure</a>
</li>
```

Next, add code to the `controllers/appcontroller` module to handle what happens when the Measure link is clicked. The updated module is shown in the following listing.

Listing 6.11   js/controllers/appcontroller.js—toggle `Measurement` widget

```
define([
    ...                          ⟵ Adds new modules to file
  'dojo/dom',
    ...
  'esri/domUtils',
  'esri/dijit/Measurement'
], function (
  declare, lang,
  dom, on,
  Map,
  GeometryService,
  esriConfig,
  domUtils,
  Measurement
) {
    ...
  return declare(null, {
      ...
    load: function () {
      this.map = new Map(
        this.options.elem,
        this.options.mapOptions
      );

      on(this.map, 'load', lang.hitch(this, 'onMapLoad'));
      on(                                                          
        dom.byId('measurement-toggle'),
        'click',
        lang.hitch(this, 'toggleMeasurement')
      );
      this.map.addLayers(this.options.layers);
    },
      ...
    toggleMeasurement: function(e) {
      e.preventDefault();
      domUtils.toggle(this.measurement.domNode);
    }
  });
});
```

Binds the toggle button's click event to a method

Toggles the visibility of the widget

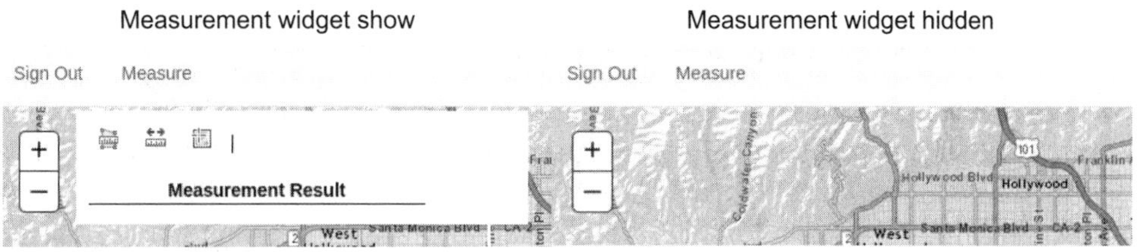

Measurement widget show   Measurement widget hidden

Sign Out   Measure   Sign Out   Measure

Figure 6.10 Clicking Measure in the navigation bar toggles visibility of the `Measurement` widget.

The key steps are detailed here:

1 Add new modules to the controller:

The first is the `dojo/dom` module, which enables HTML document object model (DOM) functionality, such as finding an element by the element ID.

The second is the `esri/domUtils` module. You typically don't see this module in many samples, as this module is largely used internally in the ArcGIS API for JavaScript, but it comes in handy when toggling the visibility of HTML elements.

2 Use the `dojo/dom` module to find the `measurement-toggle` anchor element and bind the `click` event to the `toggleMeasurement` method on the controller.

3 When the anchor is clicked, use the `esri/domUtils` module to easily toggle the visibility of the `Measurement` widget by referencing the `domNode` of the widget. The `domNode` is a reference to the HTML element that contains the widget.

When you click the Measure link, it now toggles the visibility of the `Measurement` widget as shown in figure 6.10.

If required, you could hide the `Measurement` widget when the application starts up as well. Add one line of code to the end of the `onMapLoad()` method of the `controllers/appcontroller` module:

```
domUtils.hide(dom.byId('measurement-div'));
```

With that single line of code, the `Measurement` widget is now hidden when the application starts.

Adding out-of-the-box widgets of the ArcGIS JavaScript API is straightforward. Next, you'll add a widget that allows you to toggle between two basemaps of the application.

6.4.2 *Working with the BasemapToggle widget*

Sometimes users want the application to display a different basemap—maybe a street view to get a general idea of an area, and then an aerial imagery view to see more detail, such as how many buildings are in a location, or how much open space there is. That's where a tool like the `BasemapToggle` widget comes in handy.

The steps to add the `BasemapToggle` widget to the application are similar to adding the `Measurement` widget. Note that because you've already added a widget, the base is already there, so for this widget, you only need to add the reference, pass it options, and add a DOM element to bind it to.

NOTE   The code for this application is available in the chapter6/part5 folder of the source code included with the book.

DEFINING THE WIDGET

Modify the `controllers/appcontroller` module to add the widget as shown in the next listing.

Listing 6.12 js/controllers/appcontroller.js—add `BasemapToggle` widget

```
define([
  ...
  'esri/dijit/Measurement',
  'esri/dijit/BasemapToggle'        ◁── Adds widget to module
], function (
  ...
  Measurement, BasemapToggle
) {
  ...
  return declare(null, {
    ...
    onMapLoad: function() {
      ...
      this.basemaps = new BasemapToggle({     ◁── Initializes and starts
        map: this.map,                             up widget
        basemap: 'hybrid'
      }, 'basemap-div');
      this.basemaps.startup();
    },
    ...
  });
});
```

Add a reference to the `BasemapToggle` module in the `controllers/appcontroller` module, and then, almost identically to how you initialized the `Measurement` widget, pass it a reference to the map, and this time provide it a basemap type you want to toggle. As before, call the `startup` method to render it on the page.

ADDING THE HTML

You also need to add an HTML element to index.html to display the `BasemapToggle` widget:

```
<div id="map-div"></div>
<div id="measurement-div"></div>
<div id="basemap-div"></div>
```

STYLING AND POSITIONING THE WIDGET

Then add some CSS to css/main.css to position the widget correctly on the page:

```
#basemap-div {
  position: absolute;
  top: 55px;
  right: 5px;
  z-index: 1;
}
```

With everything in place, if you refresh the browser, you should see the `BasemapToggle` widget. To change the basemap of the map on the application, click the widget (see figure 6.11).

That was simple to accomplish. In fact, adding out-of-the box widgets to an application follows the same standard steps:

Figure 6.11 **To toggle between the Hybrid and Streets basemaps, click the `BasemapToggle` widget.**

1 Add an HTML element to hold the widget.
2 Style and position the widget.
3 Pass one or more options.
4 Run the `startup` method to render the widget on the page.

NOTE You'll explore a possible way to take advantage of this pattern in chapter 7 when you work with dynamically loading widgets.

Next, let's enhance the application with an editing feature that allows users to move the location of a request. You'll also learn how to use a nonspatial web service to update the GIS data.

6.5 Editing requests

Imagine a user is looking at the application and finds that the location of a request needs to be changed. Maybe the user meant to add the request at a different cross street or the description specifically states a location other than the location where the request was added. This is a common scenario, and the ArcGIS API for JavaScript makes this task painless. This section covers the following:

- Setting up and configuring the `Edit` toolbar
- Setting up the `AttributeInspector` widget
- Linking GIS data to nonspatial services

6.5.1 Editing a request's location

You previously worked with the `Edit` toolbar in chapter 5 to add features to the map (and you used a series of buttons rather than a visual toolbar). This time, you'll use it to edit the location of a request.

Generally, to implement edit functionality, you add the `Edit` toolbar, listen for when the layer is double-clicked, and activate/deactivate the `Edit` toolbar. This functionality lets users double-click the layer to activate the `Edit` toolbar, right-click the selected request to drag and drop it to a different location, and double-click the layer a second time to save the edits and deactivate the `Edit` toolbar.

Before we add the Edit toolbar, let's set up the application to handle the edit functionality.

NOTE The code for this application is available in the chapter6/part6 folder of the source code included with the book.

CREATING AN EDIT-MODE REQUEST SYMBOL

When users edit a feature on a map, you want to provide an indication that an action is taking place. A good solution is to change a request's symbol while it's being edited. To do that, let's add a new method to the utils/symbolutil module you created in chapter 3. The updated module is shown in the following listing.

Listing 6.13 js/utils/symbolutil.js—add method to supply new symbol

```
define([
  'esri/Color',
  'esri/symbols/SimpleLineSymbol',
  'esri/symbols/SimpleMarkerSymbol'
], function(
  Color,
  SimpleLineSymbol,
  SimpleMarkerSymbol
) {

  return {                                        Provides a method to return
    selectedSymbol: function() {                  a new marker symbol
      return new SimpleMarkerSymbol(
        SimpleMarkerSymbol.STYLE_CIRCLE, 24,
        new SimpleLineSymbol(SimpleLineSymbol.STYLE_DASH,
                             new Color([0,0,255]), 2),
        new Color([0,255,255,0.5])
      );
    }
  };
});
```

This module is similar to what you wrote in chapter 3, but this time, it returns a point symbol that looks like a circle with a dashed outline.

Next, let's create a new Editor widget to perform the edit operations.

CREATING A CUSTOM EDITOR WIDGET

The code for the Editor widget is shown in the next listing. Key steps are labeled in the code and explained in detail after the listing.

Listing 6.14 js/widgets/editwidget.js—custom Editor widget

```
define([
  'dojo/_base/declare',
  'dojo/_base/lang',
  'dojo/_base/array',                             Loads required
  'dojo/on',                                      modules
  'esri/toolbars/edit'
```

```
            'utils/symbolutil',
        ], function(
          declare, lang, arrayUtil,
          on,
          Edit,
          symbolUtil
        ) {

          return declare(null, {
            constructor: function(options) {
              this.map = options.map;

              this.editLayer = options.editLayer;
            },
            init: function() {

              this.editToolbar = new Edit(this.map);

              this.isEditing = false;
              on(this.editToolbar,
                  'deactivate', lang.hitch(this,'onEditDeactivate')
              );

              on(this.editLayer,
                  'dbl-click',
                  lang.hitch(this, 'onMoveFeature')
              );
            },
            onEditDeactivate: function(e) {
              if (e.info.isModified) {

                e.graphic.setSymbol(this.defaultSymbol);
                this.editLayer.applyEdits(null, [e.graphic], null);
              }
            },
            onMoveFeature: function(e) {

              e.preventDefault();
              if (!this.isEditing) {
                this.isEditing = true;
                this.defaultSymbol = e.graphic.symbol;

                e.graphic.setSymbol(symbolUtil.selectedSymbol());
                this.editToolbar.activate(Edit.MOVE, e.graphic);
              } else {
                this.isEditing = false;

                this.editToolbar.deactivate();
              }
            }
          });
        });
```

Annotations:

- **Loads required modules**
- **Gets layer from map to edit**
- **Initializes Edit toolbar with map**
- **Keeps track if in an edit session**
- **When layer is double-clicked, moves the clicked feature**
- **When edit is done, resets to default symbol**
- **Stops the native event**
- **Changes symbol to indicate it's being edited**
- **Deactivates the Edit toolbar**

In this code you load a couple of modules. Here are the steps:

1 Load the `esri/toolbars/edit` and `utils/symbolutil` modules.

2 Retrieve the layer from the map that you want to edit. This is simple since the layer was passed in as part of the options.

3 Initialize the `Edit` toolbar by passing it the map. This will bind some internal functions to the map.

4 Use a variable to keep track of whether or not you're editing. This will make tracking what's happening in your application much easier.

5 Listen for the layer to be double-clicked to start editing.

6 When the `Edit` toolbar is deactivated, apply the updates to the service if the feature has been modified and set the symbol back to the default symbol.

7 Stop the default event behavior of zooming in the map.

8 If user is not already editing, turn on editing for the `Graphic` that was clicked, save the default symbol, and change the symbol to indicate that an action is taking place.

9 If user is already editing, turn off the `Edit` toolbar.

ADDING THE WIDGET TO THE APPLICATION

To use this `Editor` widget in the application, add it to the `controllers/appcontroller` module as shown in the following snippet from the js/controllers/appcontroller.js file:

```
define([
  ...
  'widgets/editwidget'
], function (
  ...
  EditWidget
) {
  ...
  return declare(null, {
    ...
    onMapLoad: function() {
      ...
      this.editWidget = new EditWidget({
        map: this.map,
        editLayer: this.map.getLayer('Requests')
      });

      this.editWidget.init();
    },
    ...
  });
});
```

You pass the custom `Editor` widget a reference to the map and the correct layer to be edited.

Figure 6.12 The request's symbol changes to indicate that its location is being edited.

If you run the application, it doesn't look any different than before. But if you double-click a request on the map, the symbol changes to a blue dot with a dashed outline (see figure 6.12). You can then right-click the request, hold down the right-click mouse button, and drag the request to a new location. Double-click the request again; the symbol returns to normal and the changes are saved to the service. Refresh the map to verify that the new location was saved.

Editing the location of a request is only half of the editing process. The other half is editing the data itself, which we'll look at next.

6.5.2 *Editing a request's attributes*

Like the requirement to a move a request when needed, there may also be situations where the user wants to edit the data associated with that request. In chapter 5, you built custom edit tools to collect the data. To edit the data in this application, you'll use another out-of-the-box widget provided by the ArcGIS API for JavaScript: the `AttributeInspector`. The `AttributeInspector` allows a user to click a feature and then edit the data accordingly, but this widget does require a bit of setup.

> **NOTE** The code for this application is available in the chapter6/part7 folder of the source code included with the book.

CREATING AN ATTRIBUTEINSPECTOR HELPER

You need to let the `AttributeInspector` know which fields to display and of those, which ones can be edited. To make the application more maintainable, let's create a new file in the utils folder called editconfig.js. The purpose of this module is to provide the configurations to the `AttributeInspector`. The code is shown in the following listing.

Listing 6.15   js/utils/editconfig.js—configuration for `AttributeInspector` widget

```
define([
], function() {
  return {
    fieldInfos: [{
      fieldName:'IssueType',          Defines fields to display
      isEditable: true,               in AttributeInspector
```

```
      label: 'Issue Type',
      domain: {                            Defines domains to be used
        type: 'codedValue',                in drop-down menus
        name: 'issueTypeDomain',
        codedValues: [{
          name: 'Graffiti',
          code: 'graffiti'
        }, {
          name: 'Street Light',
          code: 'streetlight'
        }, {
          name: 'Pothole',
          code: 'pothole'
        }, {
          name: 'Other',
          code: 'other'
        }]
      }
    }, {
      fieldName: 'Description',
      isEditable: true,
      label: 'Description'
    }]
  };
});
```

This utility returns an object that contains the fieldInfos that define what fields to display in the AttributeInspector as well as which ones are editable. The new domain property of the IssueType field helps populate a drop-down list in the AttributeInspector from which users can choose a value. Don't get too excited about this feature yet, as it requires more sweat to get it working correctly.

ADDING THE ATTRIBUTEINSPECTOR WIDGET

Adding this widget requires updating the widgets/editwidget module (see listing 6.14). Like the custom Editor widget, this is an in-depth example, so first look at the updated module code in the following listing, and then we'll discuss the details of what's happening in the code.

Listing 6.16   js/widgets/editwidget.js—add AttributeInspector

```
define([

  ...
  'dojo/dom-construct',
  'dojo/on',
  'esri/layers/FeatureLayer',
  'esri/tasks/query',
  'esri/toolbars/edit',                        Defines required
  'esri/dijit/AttributeInspector',             modules
  'utils/editconfig',
  'utils/symbolutil'
], function(
  declare, lang, arrayUti,
```

```
            domConstruct, on,
            FeatureLayer, Query,
            Edit,
            AttributeInspector, editConfig,
            symbolUtil
        ) {
          'use strict';

          return declare(null, {

            map: null,
            editLayer: null,
            attrLayer: null,
            editToolbar: null,
            isEditing: false,
            attrInspector: null,
            editFeature: null,

            constructor: function(options) {
              this.map = options.map;
              this.editLayer = options.editLayer;
            },

            init: function() {

              this.attrLayer = new FeatureLayer(editLayer.url, {
                id: 'RequestsEdit',
                mode: FeatureLayer.MODE_SELECTION,
                outFields: ['*']
              });

              this.editToolbar = new Edit(this.map);
              on(this.editToolbar, 'deactivate',
                  lang.hitch(this,'onEditDeactivate'));
              on(this.map, 'click', lang.hitch(this, 'onMapClick'));
              on(this.editLayer, 'dbl-click', lang.hitch(this, 'onMoveFeature'));
              on(this.map.infoWindow, 'hide', lang.hitch(this, 'clear'));

              if (!this.attrLayer.loaded) {
                on(this.attrLayer, 'load', lang.hitch(
                  this,
                  'onLayerLoaded'
                ));
              }
            },

            onLayerLoaded: function() {
              this.updateFields(this.attrLayer);

              var layerInfos = [{
                featureLayer: this.attrLayer,
                isEditable: true,
                showDeleteButton: false,
                fieldInfos: editConfig.fieldInfos
              }];
```

Defines required modules

Creates layer to edit

Waits for layer's load event if not loaded

When layer loads, finds fields for use in edit tool

Defines the layerInfos for edit tool

Initializes the Attribute-Inspector

```
    this.attrInspector = new AttributeInspector({
      layerInfos: layerInfos
    }, domConstruct.create('div'));

    on(this.attrInspector,
      'attribute-change',
      lang.hitch(this, 'onAttributesChange')
    );

    this.map.infoWindow.setContent(this.attrInspector.domNode);
    this.map.infoWindow.resize(400, 350);
  },
  ...
  onEditDeactivate: function(e) {
    if (e.info.isModified) {
      e.graphic.setSymbol(this.defaultSymbol);
      this.editLayer.applyEdits(null, [e.graphic], null);
    }
  },
```

When map is clicked, checks if currently editing

```
  onMapClick: function(e) {
    if (!this.isEditing && e.graphic) {
      var query = new Query();
      query.objectIds = [e.graphic.attributes.OBJECTID];
```

Selects the feature to edit

```
      this.attrLayer.selectFeatures(query)
      .then(lang.hitch(this, function(features) {
        if (features.length) {
          this.editFeature = features[0];
          this.map.infoWindow.setTitle(this.attrLayer.name);
          this.map.infoWindow.show(
            e.screenPoint,
            this.map.getInfoWindowAnchor(e.screenPoint)
          );
        } else {
          this.map.infoWindow.hide();
        }
      }));
    }
  },
```

Updates the layer with changes in AttributeInspector

```
  onAttributesChange: function(e) {
    this.editFeature.attributes[e.fieldName] = e.fieldValue;
    this.attrLayer.applyEdits(null, [this.editFeature], null);
  },
```

Clears selection of features

```
  clear: function() {
    this.attrLayer.clearSelection();
  },
```

Iterates over configuration to find edit fields

```
  updateFields: function(layer) {
    var domains = {};
    arrayUtil.forEach(editConfig.fieldInfos, function(info) {
      domains[info.fieldName] = info.domain;
    });
```

```
      arrayUtil.forEach(layer.fields, function(field) {
        if (domains[field.name]) {
          field.domain = domains[field.name];
        }
      });
    }
  });
});
```

Iterates over configuration to find edit fields

The steps are detailed here:

1. To use the `AttributeInspector`, add a few more modules, including the `FeatureLayer` and `editConfig`.

2. Create a new `FeatureLayer` for use with the `AttributeInspector`. This layer isn't displayed in the map; it's strictly for editing the attributes. Make sure you specify `FeatureLayer.MODE_SELECTION` as the mode for the `FeatureLayer`, as that's how you determine what features to edit.

3. The layer isn't immediately loaded, so wait for its `load` event.

4. When the layer loads, use `arrayUtil` to iterate over the `fields` property of the layer and find which fields are defined in the `editConfig` module as having domains; then you can assign those domains to the source layer.

5. Create what's called a `layerInfos` array, which tells the `AttributeInspector` which `FeatureLayer` to edit, if it's editable, and provides the `fieldInfos` defined in the `editConfig` module.
   You could also set it so the Delete button is shown, which isn't used in this application, but would make a good exercise.

6. Initialize the `AttributeInspector` and create a new `div` element to contain it. Set this `div` element as the source for the map's `InfoWindow`, which is a pop-up window provided with the map that you can use for the `AttributeInspector`.

7. When the map is clicked, check to make sure the user isn't already trying to move a feature and that the user indeed clicked a `Graphic`. Then grab the `OBJECTID` of the `Graphic`.

8. Select features from the source layer, and once the results are returned, display the `InfoWindow` that allows the user to edit the data. If no features are returned, make sure the `InfoWindow` stays hidden.

9. Listen for when the data in the `AttributeInspector` changes and automatically send the updates to the server so the user doesn't have to click a button to save the data. Because this is a browser-based application for the desktop, this shouldn't strain browser resources.

10. When the `InfoWindow` is closed, be sure to clear the selections made on the map.

11. Finally, you have a method that iterates over the fields in the layer and the fields from the `editConfig` module to populate the domains.

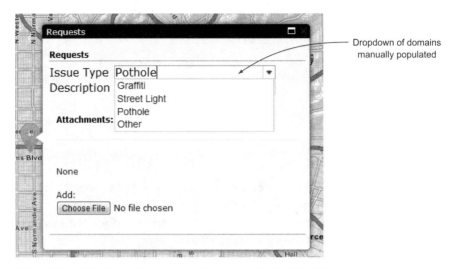

Figure 6.13 `AttributeInspector` **allows users to edit the data.**

That's the basic process of using the `AttributeInspector` to edit the layer's current data. Figure 6.13 shows the `AttibuteInspector` after you click a request on the map.

You may notice the Choose File button at the bottom of the `AttributeInspector`. Go ahead and click it. This button allows you to add attachments to your data, such as images or documents, or anything that you want to associate with this request. That comes for free with the `AttributeInspector`. You don't have to write any extra code for that functionality, which I always thought was neat.

Next, you'll learn how to populate a drop-down list in the `AttributeInspector` with data from a nonspatial web service. This can come in handy when various systems need to be linked together.

6.5.3 *Incorporating a nonspatial service*

You may want to incorporate existing data that has no spatial component with your spatial data—for example, displaying a list of assets, financial information, or employees. The last of those tasks, supplying a list of employees, is what you'll implement to allow users to assign a specific employee to a service request.

CREATING MOCK DATA

You may not have anything to do with the back-end web services that help power your web mapping application. A web service could be written in any number of programming languages, ranging from Java and C# to PHP and JavaScript (using Node), so to save you the time and brainpower of trying to piece together a web service, let's create a mock web service for use in the RequestViewer app.

> **NOTE** The code for this application is available in the chapter6/part8 folder of the source code included with the book.

Create a new file called data/data.json in your project. Notice the .json file extension; this is a JSON file, not a JavaScript file. This file is also available with the source code for the book. The following listing shows the mock JSON data.

Listing 6.17   data/data.json—mock data for application

```
{
  "employees": [{
    "name": "Simon Williams",
    "id": 101
  }, {
    "name": "Sam Axe",
    "id": 102
  }, {
    "name": "Clint Barton",
    "idt": 103
  }, {
    "name": "Kevin Key",
    "id": 104
  }, {
    "name": "Mitchell Hundred",
    "id": 105
  }, {
    "name": "Matt Murdock",
    "id": 106
  }, {
    "name": "Jack Knight",
    "id": 107
  }, {
    "name": "Selina Kyle",
    "id": 108
  }]
}
```

With the data in place, you can move on to the mock web service.

CREATING A MOCK WEB SERVICE

This mock web service is simple. If you're lucky, the various web services you work with return data in an easy-to-use format, and you don't have to spend too much time transforming the data to meet your needs. Because your mock data represents a clean result, the mock web service, shown in the following listing, is clean as well.

Listing 6.18   js/services/employeeservice.js—mock web service

```
define([
  'esri/request'
], function(
  esriRequest
) {
  return {
    getEmployees: function() {
      return esriRequest({          ← Uses esriRequest to load mock data
        url: 'data/data.json',      ← Provides URL to mock data file
```

```
          handleAs: 'json',
          callbackParamName: 'callback'
        });
      }
  };
});
```

Handles file as JSON

Provides a callback parameter name

When working with web services using the ArcGIS API for JavaScript, you should stick with using the `esri/request` module provided by the API. This module handles errors cleanly and also takes advantage of the proxy when needed. As shown in the code, you send a request with the following parameters:

- The URL of the web service; in this case, the JSON file you mocked up (data.json).
- How you want to handle the data; in this case, as JSON.
- A name for the odd property called `callbackParamName`; in this case, it's `callback`.

> **JSON with Padding**
>
> When trying to retrieve data from a server other than the one your application is hosted on, you may need to use the option `callbackParamName`. The value for this option is always `callback`. The purpose of the callback is to take advantage of JSONP, which is JSON with Padding, when needed to make cross-origin requests from the browser. JSONP works by placing a `script` tag in the browser with a URL as the source. The method given to that URL is the callback name.

UPDATING THE EDITOR WIDGET

The final step is to update the `Editor` widget to use your web service and provide the employee information to the layer and the `AttributeInspector`. This last step can get tricky because you have to map the list of employees to a field in the `FeatureLayer`. Look at the updated code in the following listing, and then we'll discuss the details of what's happening.

Listing 6.19 js/widgets/editwidget.js—add web service data

```
define([

  ...
  'dojo/Deferred',
  ...
  'services/employeeservice'
], function(
  ...
  Deferred,
  ...
  employeeService
) {
```

Defines modules for use in file

```
return declare(null, {
  ...
  init: function() {
    ...
    if (!this.attrLayer.loaded) {
      on(this.attrLayer, 'load', lang.hitch(
        this,
        function() {

          this.updateFields(this.attrLayer).then(
            lang.hitch(this, 'onFieldsReady')
          );
        }
      ));
    }

  },

  onFieldsReady: function(fieldInfos) {
    var layerInfos = [{
      featureLayer: this.attrLayer,
      isEditable: true,
      fieldInfos: fieldInfos
    }];

    this.attrInspector = new AttributeInspector({
      layerInfos: layerInfos
    }, domConstruct.create('div'));

    on(this.attrInspector,
      'attribute-change',
      lang.hitch(this, 'onAttributesChange')
    );

    this.map.infoWindow.setContent(this.attrInspector.domNode);
    this.map.infoWindow.resize(400, 350);
  },
  ...
  updateFields: function(layer) {
    var deferred = new Deferred();

    employeeService.getEmployees().then(function(data) {
      var fieldInfo
        , codedValues;

      codedValues = arrayUtil.map(
        data.employees,
        function(employee) {
          return {
            name: employee.name,
            code: employee.id
          };
        }
      );
```

Defines modules
for use in file

Uses fields from
configuration, then
continues setup

Sets up
layerInfos
when ready

Uses employee service
to load employee data

Maps employee data
to values for editor

```
            fieldInfo = {
              fieldName: 'Assignee',
              isEditable: true,
              label: 'Assigned To',
              domain: {                          Sets up employee values
                type: 'codedValue',              to Assignee field
                name: 'employeeDomain',
                codedValues: codedValues
              }
            };

            editConfig.fieldInfos.push(fieldInfo);
            var domains = {};
            arrayUtil.forEach(editConfig.fieldInfos, function(info) {
              domains[info.fieldName] = info.domain;
            });

            arrayUtil.forEach(layer.fields, function(field) {
              if (domains[field.name]) {
                field.domain = domains[field.name];
              }
            });

            deferred.resolve(editConfig.fieldInfos);
          });
          return deferred.promise;          When employee data is ready,
        }                                   continues with application
      });
    });
```

Adds fieldInfo to edit configuration

The steps are detailed here:

1 Load the `Deferred` module, which you used extensively in chapters 4 and 5, as well as in the `empoyeeservice` module.

2 Update the `updateFields` method to return a promise, and, when that promise is complete, launch a new method called `onFieldsReady` to replace the method `onLayerLoaded` from listing 6.17.

3 The `onFieldsReady` method behaves identically to the previous `onLayerLoaded` method, except the `fieldInfos` for the `AttributeInspector` are provided by the `fieldInfos` returned by the `updateFields` method.

4 The `updateFields` method is where most of the code changes have taken place. Call the `employeeService.getEmployees` method to return the mock JSON data.

5 The `arrayUtil.map` method creates a new array of coded values to be used in the application from the JSON results.

6 Create a new `fieldInfo` object that matches the `Assignee` field of the layer you want to associate with the JSON results.

7 Add this new `fieldInfo` object to the array of `fieldInfos` in the `editConfig`.

8 Once the layer has been supplied with all the appropriate domains, resolve `deferred` with the `fieldInfos`, and the application functions as normal.

Figure 6.14 `AttributeInspector` **enhanced with web service data**

If you refresh the application and click a request to edit it, a new drop-down list of employees appears that can be assigned to the `Assignee` field of the request (see figure 6.14).

This is a useful method of linking nonspatial data from a web service with your web mapping application. It's seamless to the user; the employee information isn't part of your spatial data. This is by no means the only way to enhance your application with other web services; sometimes this process can be as simple as opening another web application via a hyperlink and using the `id` of a spatial feature as part of the URL, or as complicated as syncing large amounts of purchasing data with spatial features on the map. Integration needs vary widely, but this exercise should give you a good idea of what's possible.

The edit tools covered in this chapter and the `AttributeInspector` are key to performing edit functions with the ArcGIS API for JavaScript. Once you understand the concepts and uses of these widgets, you can use them in most configurations or customize them to meet your needs. This is a valuable skill set to have when working with the ArcGIS API for JavaScript. In the next chapter, you'll advance the offline editing capabilities of the edit tools for use in your application.

6.6   *Summary*

- This chapter covered a boatload of material. You now have a good idea of how to generate tokens for your secured application, whether you're using ArcGIS Server or ArcGIS Online.
- You saw how to use OAuth 2.0 to handle authentication for your application and even learned a couple of neat methods to save those credentials in the browser.

- You looked at standard widgets, the `Measurement` and `BasemapToggle`, with the ArcGIS API for JavaScript that simplify many tasks.
- You should have a strong grasp of how to use the `Edit` module and `Attribute-Inspector` to edit data in an application, and you even took things a step further by adding custom domain values to the `AttributeInspector` to use a nonspatial web service.

This chapter marks the end of the training-wheels chapters designed to familiarize you with various aspects of the ArcGIS API for JavaScript. I may have let go of the bike on occasion, but I didn't push you down any hills. In the next and final chapter, I'll push you down a hill. Chapter 7 covers advanced methods for loading widgets and map services, all from a single configuration file. Once you write the base project, you can reuse it over and over again. Brace yourself; it's going to get bumpy.

Advanced techniques 7

This chapter covers

- Building an application from a JSON configuration
- Writing a loader class to handle widget loading
- Treating new functionality as a new widget
- Taking advantage of the web map specification
- Implementing advanced offline functionality

By now you have a fairly good grasp of the basics of the ArcGIS API for JavaScript. You've seen how custom widgets are built, and you've loaded default widgets and used them in your applications. You should also have a well-rounded idea of how the Dojo Toolkit is used to build applications using the ArcGIS API for JavaScript. Believe it or not, I've intentionally kept things straightforward and tried to prevent showing overly complicated examples that detract from the core of the tasks at hand.

In this chapter we cover a few advanced techniques that I've found useful over the years. They help focus development on the purpose of the application so you don't have to worry about too much boilerplate code. Many of these techniques involve using basic patterns of the ArcGIS JavaScript API that you may find while building

175

applications. A couple of these techniques take advantage of lesser-discussed tools built into the ArcGIS API for JavaScript, such as how it can build a map from a simple Web-Map ID from ArcGIS Online. This allows you to use specifications of the ArcGIS REST API to your advantage. I also cover more advanced techniques for working with the application when an internet connection is lost.

I'll cover more powerful options available when building a map and adding layers. By the end of this chapter, you'll know how to set up your application so you can add new widgets without writing a single line of additional code. You'll also return to the disconnected editing covered in chapter 5 and look at advanced techniques that can ease the pain of disconnected editing.

These techniques aren't required to be a successful ArcGIS API JavaScript developer, but I believe having them at your disposal will help make you an efficient one.

7.1 Using a single configuration file

One thing I've always found awkward when developing ArcGIS API for JavaScript applications is embedding all my configurations right into my code base. It's not an issue with small apps and a handful of modules, but as an application begins to grow, I have to remember where I defined certain URL paths or widget configurations. I'm not so sloppy that they're hidden away, but when returning to an application a few months after it's completed, there's a cognitive bump I need to get past before I can get back into the groove and update the application. One of the things I think Esri did really well with their FlexViewer application for ArcGIS API for Flex developers is this concept of building functionality in the form of new widgets. Each widget has its own configuration files where you can define parameters, such as Map service URLs and new layers. Maintenance is easy because changes and updates are applied using a configuration file.

This section covers the following:

- Loading a configuration file
- Defining map options in a configuration file
- Defining widgets in the configuration file

NOTE   The code for this section is available in the chapter7/part1 folder of the source code included with the book.

7.1.1 Defining a map

You'll build a small application to load a configuration file that defines many of the settings for the application, including the map and what layers are in the map.

SETTING UP THE APPLICATION

To get started, build the simple index.html file as shown in the following listing. This file references the ArcGIS API for JavaScript, a custom stylesheet you can use with this application, and the JavaScript file that starts the application.

Listing 7.1 index.html—simple HTML file for application

```html
<!doctype html>
<html>
  <head>
    <meta charset="utf-8" />
    <meta name="viewport"
      content="initial-scale=1,
      maximum-scale=1,user-scalable=no"/>
    <link type='text/css'
      href='//js.arcgis.com/3.11/esri/css/esri.css'
      rel='stylesheet' />
    <link type='text/css'
      href='css/main.css'
      rel='stylesheet'>
    <title></title>
  </head>
  <body class="nihilo">
    <div id="map-div"></div>
    <script type="text/javascript"
      src="//js.arcgis.com/3.11compact"></script>
    <script src="js/run.js"></script>
  </body>
</html>
```

Bare-bones HTML file to start the application

This HTML file has only the bare essentials of what's needed to start an ArcGIS API for JavaScript application. The main.css file referenced here is also basic, covering only a few elements, as shown in the following listing.

Listing 7.2 css/main.css—simple style sheet to get started

```css
html,body{
  overflow-x:hidden;
  height:100%;
  width:100%;
  margin:0;
  padding:0;
}

#map-div{
  position:absolute;
  padding:0;
  top:0;
  left:0;
  right:0;
  bottom:0;
}
```

Sets HTML and body to use entire browser page

Sizes map to use entire browser page

You've seen this CSS throughout the book. The run.js file, shown in the following listing, should also look familiar.

Listing 7.3 js/run.js—sets up the Dojo path configuration

```javascript
(function() {
  var pathRX = new RegExp(/\/[^\/]+$/)
```

```
         , locationPath = location.pathname.replace(pathRX, '');        ←─────
     require({                                              Sets up regular expression to override
       async: true,                                         where Dojo looks for modules
       parseOnLoad: true,
       aliases: [['text', 'dojo/text'], ['domReady', 'dojo/domReady']],
       packages: [{                                         ←─────
         name: 'controllers',                                      Defines custom packages
         location: locationPath + 'js/controllers'                 for the application
       }, {
         name: 'widgets',
         location: locationPath + 'js/widgets'
       }, {
         name: 'app',
         location: locationPath + 'js',
         main: 'main'
       }]
     }, ['app']);
   })();
```

Provides aliases for certain Dojo tools

Run.js is a basic module that sets up the Dojo configuration for the application. You've seen this in previous chapters in each new application you've built. This process doesn't change much. It's in the main.js file where you'll see that things are different from the way you've built applications in previous chapters.

LOADING MAP OPTIONS FROM A CONFIGURATION FILE

Instead of defining layers and creating the map in the main.js file, let's create a map based on an external JSON file, as shown in the following listing.

Listing 7.4   js/main.js—loads the config.json file

```
require([
  'esri/request',
  'esri/map',                          Adds esri/request module to
  'domReady!'                          load resources from URL
], function (
  esriRequest,
  Map
) {                                    When a response is returned, creates
  function onConfigSuccess(response) {  map from options provided
    var map = new Map('map-div', response.options);
  }                                    If error occurs, prints
  function onConfigError(error) {       it to debug console
    console.log('ERROR - Loading config file:', error);
  }
  function requestParams() {           Defines parameters
    return {                           to make the request
      url: 'config.json',
      handleAs: 'json'
    };
  }
  esriRequest(requestParams()).then(onConfigSuccess, onConfigError);
});
```

Uses esri/request module to load config.json file

The main.js module now loads a JSON file. Remember, JSON is a subset of JavaScript that defines easy-to-read bits of information. When the JSON file loads, you can create a new map using the options described in the JSON file.

DEFINING MAP OPTIONS IN A CONFIGURATION FILE

Basic map options defined in the config.json file look like this:

```
{
  "options": {
    "basemap": "topo",
    "center": [-118.210,34.285],
    "zoom": 10
    }
}
```

This config.json provides only basic map options, but it's enough to get the party started. If you run the application at this point, you'll see a map similar to what's shown in figure 7.1.

It's fairly straightforward to load config.json and apply the options it defines for the map. This isn't the finished product, but it's a start.

Now suppose you also want to load another widget from the ArcGIS API for Java-Script, such as the Geocoder widget, which allows you to search for addresses. That widget has options you can also define in config.json.

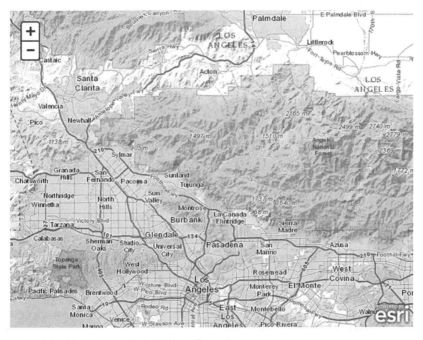

Figure 7.1   Map created from JSON configuration

7.1.2 *Loading the Geocoder widget*

The `Geocoder` widget has a couple of required options, such as the URL for the Geocoder service and a placeholder value to put in the input box. Let's update config.json with the following options for use in the application:

```
{
  "options": {
    ...
  },
  "geocoderOptions" : {
    "arcgisGeocoder": {
      "url": "http://geocode.arcgis.com/arcgis/rest"+
      "/services/World/GeocodeServer",
      "placeholder": "Enter address"
    }
  }
}
```

You can give the `Geocoder` options a unique name to avoid confusing them with the map options. The URL shown is the default used in the widget; this URL is used even if you omit it. I've included it here to clarify that you can change it to a different URL if you choose.

Before you load the `Geocoder` widget, let's add a `div` element to the index.html file that will contain the search box for the widget. You can add it after the `map-div`:

```
<body class="nihilo">
  <div id="map-div"></div>
  <div id="search"></div>
  ...
</body>
```

Next, add styling in main.css to position the `Geocoder` widget:

```
#map-div{
  ...
}

#search {
 position: absolute;
 z-index: 2;
 top: 5px;
 right: 5px;
}
```

This code positions the `Geocoder` widget in the upper-right corner of the browser.

The last thing to do before you load the `Geocoder` widget is to update the main.js file, as shown in the following listing. This file waits for the map to finish loading, and then passes the map and the options from the config.json file to the `Geocoder`.

Listing 7.5 js/main.js—loading the Geocoder widget

```
require([
  'dojo/_base/lang',                    Loads the lang module
  ...                                   and Geocoder widget
```

```
  'esri/dijit/Geocoder',
  'domReady!'
], function (
  lang,
  ...
  Geocoder
) {
  function onConfigSuccess(response) {
    var map = new Map('map-div', response.options);
    map.on('load', function() {
      var geocoderOptions = lang.mixin(
        {
          map: map
        },
        response.geocoderOptions
      );
      var geocoder = new Geocoder(geocoderOptions, 'search');
      geocoder.startup();
    });
  }
  ...
});
```

Waits for map to finish loading

Uses lang.mixin method to create required parameters for the Geocoder widget

Initializes the Geocoder widget and starts it

Now the main.js file loads the Geocoder widget along with another utility module: the dojo/_base/lang module. When the map finishes loading, pass the map as part of the parameters for the Geocoder widget. The lang.mixin method mixes in the fields of

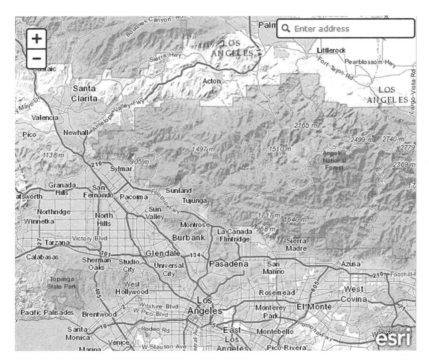

Figure 7.2 Geocoder widget added to the application

one object with another. You can then pass the completed options to the `Geocoder` and run the `startup` method to display it on the page. If you run the application now, you'll see a page similar to figure 7.2, as shown on the previous page.

You can search for an address in the `Geocoder` widget as you would with almost any search engine, and it attempts to zoom the map to the correct location.

I used the `Geocoder` widget to not only show you an example of how widgets are typically loaded with the ArcGIS API for JavaScript, but also to see whether you noticed a pattern with other widgets you've seen throughout the book. If not, don't worry; I'll cover that next.

7.1.3   *Looking for the patterns*

In chapter 6, (see section 6.4), you used the `Measurement` and `BasemapToggle` widget in the browser-based application. You may have noticed that those widgets all followed a pattern similar to the `Geocoder` widget. A widget represents a tool that will be visually accessible in the browser. It's typically designed to interact with the map in a particular manner, such as by changing the map extents, performing measurements, or adding and removing layers or features on the map. Looking at the widgets you've used so far, you can see a pattern begin to emerge:

1   Wait for the map to load.
2   Initialize the widget with options.
3   Pass the widget a reference node.
4   Run the `startup` method.

Given that most widgets in the ArcGIS API for JavaScript follow this basic pattern, it follows that there should be a way to exploit this pattern so you can load nearly any widget with minimal effort. Ideally, you could specify the widget to load and its options, and provide all the information in config.json—without manually loading modules for each new project. This is what you'll set up in the next section.

7.2   *Dynamic widget loading*

Let's think about which critical pieces of information are required to load widgets into an application:

1   Providing a path to the widget with options
2   Loading the widget with the given path and options
3   Designating an HTML element to display the widget

You could also consider the map a fourth component, but let's focus on these three items.

7.2.1   *Widget path and options*

Let's continue using the `Geocoder` widget you defined. To start off small, update config.json to move the options for the `Geocoder` into a `widgets` array. This update allows you to add more widgets as needed.

This time, though, you can provide the path to the widget the same way you would provide it in a Dojo module, as well as what HTML element to bind it to. You can see what this update looks like in the following listing.

Listing 7.6   config.json—updated options for widget

```
{
  ...
  "widgets": [{
    "path": "esri/dijit/Geocoder",
    "node": "search",
    "options": {
      "arcgisGeocoder": {
        "url": "http://geocode.arcgis.com/arcgis/rest"+
        "/services/World/GeocodeServer",
        "placeholder": "Enter address"
      }
    }
  }]
}
```

Widgets array holds configurations for widgets

Path to widget

ID of the HTML element to use for the widget

Widget options

You now have all the items required to build a widget defined in config.json: the path to the widget, the HTML element that displays the widget, and the widget configuration. That was the easy part. Now you need to write code that knows how to handle this configuration.

7.2.2   Building a widget loader

With a pattern defined for building a widget, you need to build a loader module that knows how to parse what's defined in config.json. Remember, you define modules using the `define` method. You need at least one `require` method to start any ArcGIS API for JavaScript application. The key words in that sentence are *at least*. There's no rule that says you can't use a `require` method inside a module.

> **NOTE**   The code for this section is available in the chapter7/part2 folder of the source code included with the book.

Let's write a simple widget loader module called widgetloader.js inside the js/controllers folder of the application. As shown in the following listing, this module iterates over the `widgets` array and creates new widgets based on the configuration information provided in config.json.

Listing 7.7   js/controllers/widgetloader.js—loader module for widgets

```
define([
  'require',
  'dojo/_base/declare',
  'dojo/_base/lang',
  'dojo/_base/array'
], function(
  require,
```

Loads the require module for use in this module

```
      declare, lang, arrayUtil
   ) {
      return declare(null, {
         constructor: function(options) {        ⟵  Copies options to
            this.options = options;                   widget loader
         },
         startup: function() {                   ⟵  On startup, iterates
            arrayUtil.forEach(                        over the widgets array
               this.options.widgets,
               this._widgetLoader,
               this
            );
         },                                                      Mixes in loaders options with widget
         _widgetLoader: function(widget) {     ⟵            options to copy the map reference
            lang.mixin(widget.options, this.options);
            this._requireWidget(widget);
         },                                                   Uses require module to load
         _requireWidget: function(widget) {    ⟵          widgets using path in the config
            require([widget.path], function(Widget) {
               var w = new Widget(widget.options, widget.node);
               w.startup();
            });
         }
      });
   });
```

This little module is working hard:

- It loads the `require` method so modules can be dynamically loaded.
- It iterates over the array of widgets in the config.json file and loads the widgets using the path provided as well as the node.
- When a new widget is created, the `startup` method is initialized (as you've seen before).
- The options passed to this module also contain a reference to the map that has already been loaded.

The following listing shows how to use this module in the updated main.js file.

Listing 7.8   js/main.js—updated to use the widget loader

```
require([
   ...
   'controllers/widgetloader',
   'domReady!'
], function (
   ...
   WidgetLoader
) {
   function onConfigSuccess(response) {
      var map = new Map('map-div', response.options);
      map.on('load', function() {
         var options = lang.mixin(          ⟵  When map loads, pass it to
            {                                    the options for widget loader
```

```
      map: map
    },
    response
  );
  var loader = new WidgetLoader(options);        Initializes widget loader and
  loader.startup();                              runs the startup method
});
}
...
});
```

This doesn't look that different from running any other widget. The key here is to pass the loaded map to the widget loader options so it can be used with other widgets.

7.2.3 *Testing the widget loader*

If you run the application now, it should look no different than figure 7.2, which is the goal. But to show the power of this widget loader module, let's add another widget to the config.json file, as shown in the following code.

```
"widgets": [{
  ...
}, {
  "path": "esri/dijit/LocateButton",
  "node": "locate",
  "options": {
    "highlightLocation": true
  }
}]
```

You also need to add an HTML `div` to the index.html file:

```
<body class="nihilo">
  ...
  <div id="locate"></div>
  ...
</body>
```

Finally, you need to update the main.css file to position the locate button appropriately:

```
#locate {
  position:absolute;
  top:95px;
  left:22px;
  z-index:50;
}
```

With all this in place, if you run the application, you'll see both the `Geocoder` widget and the button for the `LocateButton` widget under the zoom controls. The `Locate-Button` widget pans the map to your location using the browser's HTML5 geolocation capabilities. You didn't have to write additional code to load this widget. The only update was in the configuration file, and `widgetloader` handled the rest. That's a neat feature. The application will look similar to figure 7.3.

Figure 7.3 Two widgets loaded dynamically

At this point, you could continue this exercise with multiple widgets by adding widget entries to the config.json file until you're blue in the face. You can add new functionality to your application with a simple addition to the configuration file and let `widgetloader` handle everything for you.

Now you can focus on building widgets that provide specific functions to your application without worrying about the boilerplate code to load them. You can see how powerful this method is, but you can take it even further. I find it annoying that I have to add a new HTML `div` to the `index.html` page every time I add a new widget. That doesn't seem to fit into the grand scheme of dynamically generated applications. Let's build a solution for that.

7.2.4   *Adding HTML elements*

The third requirement for loading widgets is designating how they're added to the page. Automating this process and eliminating having to update the index.html file every time is achievable in the `widgetloader` module.

> **NOTE** The code for this section is available in the chapter7/part3 folder of the source code included with the book.

Use the `node` option in the config.json file to create a new `div` element and add it to the page. Rather than pass that `node` reference into each widget constructor, you'll create a new element and pass that instead. You can even specify whether the element should be added to another element already on the page; that can be defined by adding a `target` property in config.json with the ID of an element in the index.html file that it'll use as a container. Take a look at the config.json where a target is specified:

```
{
  ...
  "widgets": [{
    ...
  }, {
    "path": "esri/dijit/LocateButton",
    "node": "locate",
    "target": "tool-container",
    "options": {
      "highlightLocation": true
    }
  }]
}
```

The purpose is to specify that the `LocateButton` widget should be placed inside an HTML element with an `id` of `tool-container`. Now you can add this element to the index.html page:

```
<html>
  ...
  <body class="nihilo">
    <div id="map-div"></div>
    <div id="tool-container"></div>
    ...
  </body>
</html>
```

With this in place, you can now modify the `widgetloader` to handle this situation. You need to use Dojo utilities that can handle creating the `div` element when it's needed and append it to the body of the page or another element specified by the `target` property in the configuration for the widget, as shown in the following listing.

Listing 7.9   js/controllers/widgetloader.js—modified to add HTML elements to page

```
define([
  ...                                    Loads Dojo dom utility modules
                                         to help manipulate DOM
  'dojo/dom',
  'dojo/dom-construct'
], function(
  ...
  dom, domConstruct
) {                                      Helper method to return default
  function target(opt) {                 target or document body
    return opt.target || document.body;
  }
```

```
function domNode(opt) {
  return domConstruct.create('div', {
    id: opt.node
  });
}
function targetElem(domTarget) {
  if (domTarget === document.body) {
    return domTarget;
  } else {
    return dom.byId(domTarget);
  }
}

return declare(null, {
  ...
  _requireWidget: function(widget) {
    require([widget.path], function(Widget) {
      var node, w;
      if (widget.node) {
        node = domNode(widget);
        domConstruct.place(node, targetElem(target(widget)));
      }
      w = new Widget(widget.options, widget.node);
      w.startup();
    });
  }
});
});
```

> Helper method to create DOM element sing configuration node as ID

> Helper method that returns default target element or searches for it by ID

> If widget node was specified, uses helper methods to find or create it, then appends to page

The code in listing 7.8 looks at whether a `target` property was provided for the widget. If not, it defaults to use the `document.body` of the browser page. If it was provided, try to find that element on the page. If a new `div` element was created, add that element to the browser page using the `target` as the container. If you rerun the application at this point, it should look identical to figure 7.3.

Because you specified a target for the `LocateButton` in the configuration of that widget, it was added inside that element on the page. You didn't specify a target for the `Geocoder` widget, so it was added to the body of the page. If you inspect the HTML page elements using a browser debugger, you should see the `LocateButton` inside the `tool-container` div, as shown in figure 7.4.

```
<!DOCTYPE html>
▼<html data-ember-extension="1" class="dj_webkit dj_chrome dj_contentbox">
  ▶ <head>…</head>
  ▼<body class="nihilo hasGoogleVoiceExt" data-ember-extension="1">
    ▶ <div id="map-div" class="map" data-basemap="topo" data-zoom="10" data-
      scale="577790 554289" data-loaded>…</div>
    ▼<div id="tool-container">
      ▶ <div class="LocateButton" role="presentation" id="locate" widgetid=
        "locate" style="display: block;">…</div>
      </div>
      <script type="text/javascript" charset="utf-8" src="http://js.arcgis.com/
      3.8compact/js/esri/nls/jsapi_en-us.js"></script>
      <script type="text/javascript" charset="utf-8" src="http://js.arcgis.com/
```

Figure 7.4 `LocateButton` added to `tool-container` div as specified in the configuration for the widget

You now have a fully functional dynamic widget loader. I recommend either appending all widgets to the body of the page or appending all widgets to the `tool-container div` purely for organizational purposes. You no longer need to update the index.html file when you want to add a widget.

Now that widget creation is in place, it would also be convenient to define all map options in config.json, including map services to display and the details for each service. That's what you'll work on in the next section.

7.3 Adding a web map

ArcGIS Online has one simple way to build a map. In chapter 4 you created a free ArcGIS developer account that allowed you to create data you could use in your application or share with others. In chapter 6, you used this account with OAuth 2.0 to provide a layer of security for your application. You can use that same account to log in to the ArcGIS Online website, create a map, and share that map with others.

This section covers the following:

- Defining a web map in ArcGIS Online
- Sharing the web map
- Using the web map in your application

7.3.1 Creating the web map

You can get to the ArcGIS Online sign-in page at www.arcgis.com/home/signin.html. You'll see a page similar to figure 7.5.

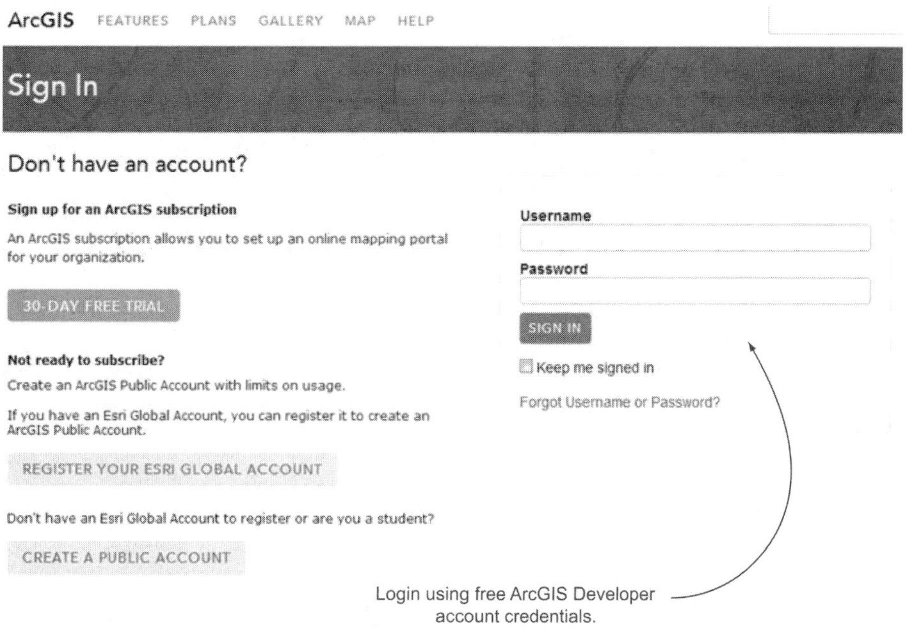

Figure 7.5   ArcGIS Online sign-in page

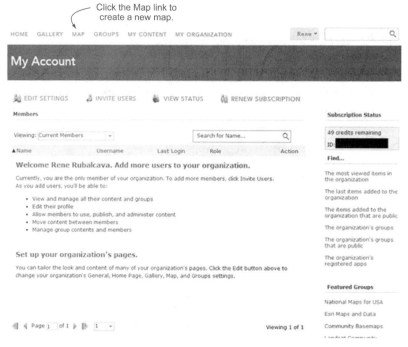

Figure 7.6   ArcGIS Online account page

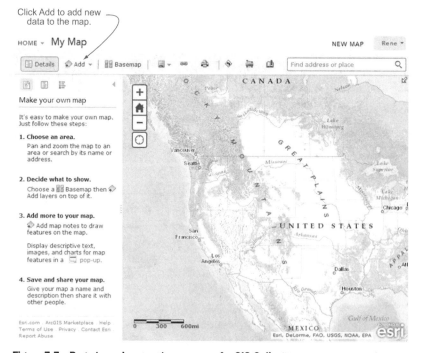

Figure 7.7   Page to make a custom map on ArcGIS Online

Once you log in, you're greeted by the account page, which provides details about how many credits you have remaining, as well as links for managing an ArcGIS Online organization, which is beyond the scope of this book. From this page, click the Map link at the top of the page, as shown in figure 7.6.

When you click the Map link, you're directed to a robust mapping application (see figure 7.7) where you can change the basemap and add new data from your developer account or other services available on ArcGIS Online. Take time to explore this online application. It's meant to provide users a quick and easy way to look at data you want to share.

When you're done reviewing this page and its many options, click Add from the toolbar at the top of the page, and then choose Search for Layers from the menu options. A sidebar window opens from which you can search for layers in different areas. Select ArcGIS Online from the In drop-down menu to see the services available to you, as shown in figure 7.8.

Add the Weather Stations (NOAA) service, and then click the Save icon. Choose Save As to display the Save Map window. Provide a title for your map, a couple of tags, and a summary, as shown in figure 7.9.

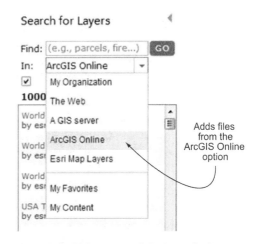

Figure 7.8   Menu to search for layers in the ArcGIS Online map editor

Once you save a map, complete the following steps to share your map:

1 Click the Home button and then click My Content from the menu options.
2 On the My Content page, find the map you saved in the list and click it.
3 On the details page, click the Share button.
4 When the Share window appears, click the Everyone (public) check box to share this publicly, and then click OK.

Save Map ✕

Title:	Weather map
Tags:	arcgiswebdev ✕ *Add tag(s)*
Summary:	Test map for ArcGIS Web Dev book.
Save in folder:	odoenet

SAVE MAP   CANCEL

Figure 7.9   Saving a map in ArcGIS Online

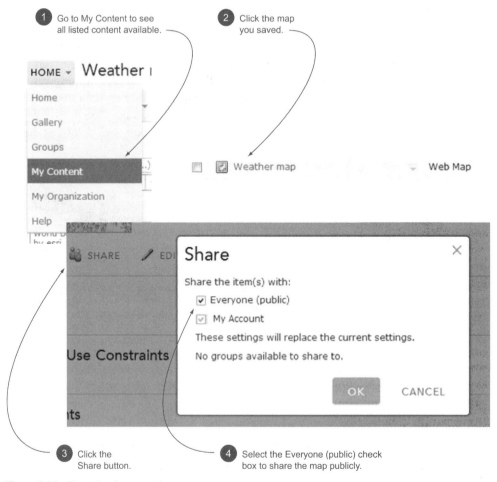

Figure 7.10 **Steps to share a web map**

This process is shown in figure 7.10.

You've created a web map you can share. But you can also use this web map in your web applications. While you're on the same page as the map details, copy the web map ID from the URL in the browser, as shown in figure 7.11.

Save this ID for future reference; you'll use it to create the web map when configuring your application. Feel free to use my map ID if you prefer.

Figure 7.11 **Finding the web map ID in the URL of the map details page**

7.3.2 *Adding the web map to an application*

The ArcGIS API for JavaScript can add web maps created in ArcGIS Online to your custom application. To clarify, think of map creation as another widget.

> **NOTE** The code for this section is available in the chapter7/part4 folder of the source code included with the book.

CREATING THE MAP WIDGET

You can create a new widget called map.js in a folder called map in the widgets directory of your application. This widget's purpose is to create the HTML element that will contain the map, as well as to create the map using the web map ID of the ArcGIS Online map. When the map is ready, it dispatches an event called map-ready so the widgetloader module knows to continue loading widgets, as most of them have a dependency on the map, such as the LocateButton. The map widget is shown in the following listing.

Listing 7.10 js/widgets/map/map.js handles creating map and DOM node

```
define([
  'dojo/_base/declare',              Loads required modules,
  'dojo/_base/lang',                 including ArcGIS utilities
  'dojo/Evented',
  'dojo/dom',
  'dojo/dom-construct',
  'dijit/_WidgetBase',
  'dijit/_TemplatedMixin',
  'esri/arcgis/utils',
], function(
  declare, lang,
  Evented,
  dom, domConstruct,
  _WidgetBase, _TemplatedMixin,
  arcgisUtils
) {
  return declare([_WidgetBase, _TemplatedMixin, Evented], {
    id: 'map-div',
    templateString: '<div></div>',
    constructor: function(options) {        Template for DOM element
      this.options = options;               that contains the map
    },
    postCreate: function() {
      var elem;                             If target DOM element is provided, attach
      if (this.options.target) {            node to that element, or else attach to body
        elem = dom.byId(this.options.target);
      } else {
        elem = document.body;
      }
      domConstruct.place(this.domNode, elem);
    },
    startup: function() {
```

```
    if (this.options.webmapid) {
      arcgisUtils.createMap(
        this.options.webmapid, this.id
      ).then(lang.hitch(this, '_mapCreated'));
    }
  },
  _mapCreated: function(response) {
    this.map = response.map;
    var params = { map: this.map };
    this.emit('map-ready', params);
  }
  });
});
```

↰ **Uses ArcGIS utilities to create map from web map ID**

↰ **When map is created, dispatches an event with map attached**

The ArcGIS API for JavaScript comes with a useful module called `esri/arcgis/utils`. This module takes a web map ID, goes out to ArcGIS Online, and pulls in the defined map, including all layers and extents. This is an incredibly useful way to manage maps and data in the ArcGIS API for JavaScript. If you need to add a new layer to the map in the future, you can update the map in ArcGIS Online, which propagates to all applications that use it.

> **TIP** When a widget extends `_TemplatedMixin`, the ID you provide for the widget will be the ID given to the DOM element that's added to the page. If none is provided, the Dijit library assigns a generic ID.

UPDATING THE WIDGETLOADER

The next step is to update the `widgetloader` module to make sure it creates the map widget before the other widgets, because most of the other widgets are dependent on the map to work properly. This requires more work, because now you have to separate the map widget from the other widgets, load the map widget first, wait for it to load, and then continue loading the other widgets. Because you know that the application has to wait for an action to occur before continuing another action, that's a dead giveaway that this is a good place to use a promise, as was discussed in section 3.2.2. A promise allows you to perform an asynchronous action and wait for it to complete. Now you'll incorporate a promise into the widget creation process. You can see what the updated `widgetloader` looks like in the following listing.

Listing 7.11   js/controllers/widgetloader.js—updated to wait for map to be created

```
define([
  ...
  'dojo/Deferred',
  'dojo/on',
  ...
], function(
  ...
  Deferred,
  on, dom, domConstruct
) {
```

↰ **Loads dojo/Deferred and dojo/on modules to wait and listen for events to happen**

```
function arrange(arr) {
  var mapwidget
    , widgets = [];
  arrayUtil.forEach(arr, function(item) {
    if (item.type === 'map') {
      mapwidget = item;
    } else {
      widgets.push(item);
    }
  });
  return {
    mapwidget: mapwidget,
    widgets: widgets
  };
}
...
return declare(null, {
  ...
  startup: function() {
    var filtered = arrange(this.options.widgets);
    this.widgets = filtered.widgets;
    this._requireWidget(filtered.mapwidget)
      .then(lang.hitch(this, '_mapWidgetLoaded'));
  },
  _mapWidgetLoaded: function(mapWidget) {
    this.own(
      on.once(mapWidget, 'map-ready', lang.hitch(this, '_mapReady'))
    );
  },
  _mapReady: function(params) {
    if (this.widgets.length > 0) {
      arrayUtil.forEach(this.widgets, function(widget) {
        lang.mixin(widget.options, params);
        this._requireWidget(widget);
      }, this);
    }
  },
  _requireWidget: function(widget) {
    var deferred = new Deferred();
    require([widget.path], function(Widget) {
      var node, w;
      if (widget.node) {
        node = domNode(widget);
        domConstruct.place(node, targetElem(target(widget)));
      }
      w = new Widget(widget.options, node);
      deferred.resolve(w);
      w.startup();
    });
    return deferred.promise;
  }
});
});
```

Function returns the map widget separate from other widgets

On startup, filters the map widget from other widgets

Loads the map widget on startup

When map widget is loaded, listens for map-ready event

When map is ready, loads other widgets normally, passing the map with options

Updates the _requireWidget method dojo/Deferred

New functionality is happening in this `widgetloader`. The main change is that the map widget loads first, waiting for the map to be created, and then loads other widgets as needed. This simplifies the widget creation process and avoids any possibility that the map won't be ready for use in other widgets that depend on it.

UPDATING THE CONFIGURATION

The last step is to update the configuration file to add the `map` widget and provide the web map ID it will use. The config.json file will now contain only an array of widgets. You can add the `map` widget parameters as you would for any other widget and provide the web map ID in the options. The configuration looks like this:

```
"widgets": [{
  "type": "map",
  "path": "widgets/map/map",
  "options" : {
    "webmapid": "68d81103c4014bafa886226f15acf6ae"
  }
},
...
]
```

This is bare bones, but it's all that's needed to create the map.

PREVIEWING THE RESULTS

You can now remove the `map-div` element from the index.html file because the `widgetloader` adds the element automatically. If you run the application, you'll see a map similar to figure 7.12.

Figure 7.12   ArcGIS Online web map displayed in ArcGIS API for JavaScript application

This is the same map that was created in the ArcGIS Online environment and made available for use in all your ArcGIS Online applications. The arrows in this map represent wind speed and direction. Any updates made to this map will now be propagated to your application.

That automation simplifies the development process, but what if you come across a situation where you can't use a map from ArcGIS Online and have to build the map manually? You can use the same specifications that a web map uses.

7.3.3 *Using the web map specification*

For the ArcGIS API for JavaScript to load a map from ArcGIS Online, it must follow a standard format so the API can re-create the map as needed. That standard is called the *web map specification.*

> **TIP** The details of this specification are available at http://resources.arc-gis.com/en/help/arcgis-web-map-json/#/Web_map_format_overview/02qt00000007000000/.

The web map specification describes what the JSON format for an ArcGIS Online map should look like, which makes it easy for the ArcGIS API for JavaScript to create a map from this format. The utilities provided with the API provide a JSON object that meets this specification instead of a web map ID. That's something you can use to your advantage to define an entire map in your configuration file without having to write much extra code.

> **NOTE** The code for this section is available in the chapter7/part5 folder of the source code included with the book.

BUILDING A SIMPLE WEB MAP OBJECT

We won't cover the entirety of the web map specification, but we'll stick to the parts that get you the most bang for your buck. Start by adding a `basemap` and `mapOptions` to the configuration and removing the `webmapid` option, as shown in the following listing.

Listing 7.12 `basemap` and `mapOptions`—web map specification

```
{
    "type": "map",
    "path": "widgets/map/map",
    "options" : {
      "id": "map-div",
      "mapOptions": {
        "center": [-118.209,34.285],
        "zoom": 10,
      },
      "webmap": {
        "itemData": {
          "baseMap": {
            "baseMapLayers": [{
              "url": "http://services.arcgisonline.com/arcgis/rest"+
                ➥ "/services/World_Topo_Map/MapServer",
```

```
                "opacity" : 1,
                "visibility": true
            }]
        }
      }
    }
  }
}
```

You now have a mapOptions object as well as a webmap object in the configuration. Use the mapOptions object the same way you'd use a regular map object; in this case, you can define the center and zoom of the map when it loads. The webmap object is where you can define the specification for the web map in the application. The baseMap object contains an array of baseMapLayers. Add a single layer as shown. This is a perfectly suitable JSON object that meets the web map specification.

UPDATING THE MAP WIDGET

Now modify the map widget to use this webmap object when no webmapid is specified, as shown in the following listing.

Listing 7.13   js/widgets/map/map.js—updated to use web map JSON

```
define([
...
], function(
  ...
) {
  return declare([_WidgetBase, _TemplatedMixin, Evented], {
    id: 'map-div',
    templateString: '<div></div>',
    constructor: function(options) {
      this.options = options;
      if (this.options.id) {                      ◁—— Allows map ID to be
        this.id = this.options.id;                      set by configuration
      }
    },
    ...
    startup: function() {
      if (this.options.webmapid) {
        arcgisUtils.createMap(
          this.options.webmapid, this.id
        ).then(lang.hitch(this, '_mapCreated'));
      } else if (this.options.webmap) {          ◁—— If no webmapid provided,
        arcgisUtils.createMap(                         checks for a webmap object
          this.options.webmap,
          this.id,
          {
            mapOptions: this.options.mapOptions   ◁—— Passes mapOptions
          }                                            as another parameter
        ).then(lang.hitch(this, '_mapCreated'));
      }
    },
    ...
});
```

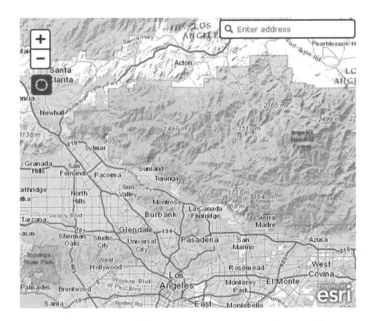

Figure 7.13 Map created from web map JSON

The main change is checking for the `webmap` object if no `webmapid` was provided. The ArcGIS `utilities` module also accepts a third parameter that allows you to add the `mapOptions` object to center and zoom the map. Because nearly everything can be set by the configuration, you can also set the map's ID from the configuration file.

This is only a start, but if you run the application now, you'll see a map similar to figure 7.13.

Admittedly, the map isn't exciting, but the prospect of using a specification from which you can build your entire mapping application in a simple configuration file is exciting. You can now add more layers to the map.

WORKING WITH OPERATIONAL LAYERS

Any map service or layer in the map that isn't a basemap is referred to as an *operational layer*. This layer is composed of unique data, such as census tracts, historical fire data, shipping routes, or locations of your favorite breweries. Operational layers are also defined in the web map specification, which allows you to easily add them to the map.

Adding an operational layer is easy. You can add an `operationalLayers` array to the `itemData` object of the `webmap` in the configuration. You can then define the layer as shown in the following code:

```
"operationalLayers": [{
  "url": "http://services.arcgis.com/V6ZHFr6zdgNZuVG0/"+
         "arcgis/rest/services/CensusLaborDemo/FeatureServer/1",
  "id": "Census_Labor",
  "visibility": true,
  "opacity": 0.8,
  "title": "Census Labor"
}, {
```

```
    "url": "http://services.arcgis.com/V6ZHFr6zdgNZuVG0/"+
            "arcgis/rest/services/la_county_labor_centroid/FeatureServer/0",
    "id": "Labor_Centroids",
    "opacity": 1,
    "title": "Labor Centroids"
}]
```

You could omit everything except the URL, which is the only required property in the configuration. Once the config.json file is updated, you don't need to update the map widget, so when you run the application, you should see something similar to figure 7.14.

As long as you adhere to the web map specification, you can build a highly customizable basic map with only simple additions to the configuration.

DEFINING POP-UPS

A convenient feature of the web map specification is the ability to define what a pop-up looks like. You can define the fields, the labels, and even the format of numeric fields to display when a map feature is clicked. For any particular layer, you can add a popupInfo object that has various options, such as what fields are visible and the title of the pop-up.

You can add this to the layer of centroids for the labor population defined in the configuration, which you can see in the following code:

```
"popupInfo": {
  "title": "{NAMELSAD}",
  "fieldInfos": [{
    "fieldName": "NAME",
    "label": "Tract Number",
```

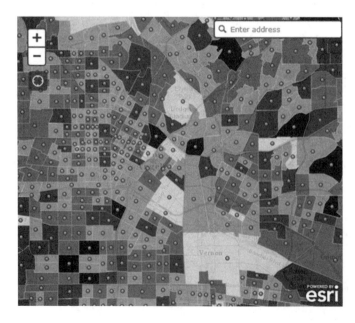

Figure 7.14 Map with operational layers added via configuration

```
      "visible": true
    }, {
      "fieldName": "TOTAL_POP",
      "label": "Total Population",
      "visible": true
    }, {
      "fieldName": "POP_LABOR",
      "label": "Labor Population",
      "visible": true
    }, {
      "fieldName": "LABOR_PCT",
      "label": "Labor Pct",
      "visible": true,
      "format": {
        "places": 2
      }
    }]
}
```

This addition to the configuration file uses the attributes from the layer to define what fields and labels are visible in the pop-up, because a few of the field names are obscure. Once that's done, you can launch the application and click on any census centroid to see the pop-up, as shown in figure 7.15.

I think that's an awesome and easy way to display pop-ups in your map. Because you set up the map widget to use the web map specification as JSON, you haven't added a single line of code to handle these additions to the configuration file. That's slick. The renderer is another great feature you can add to the configuration file.

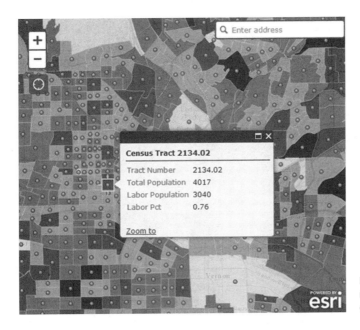

Figure 7.15   Pop-up on map defined in configuration for layer

DEFINING A RENDERER

You learned how to apply a renderer to a layer in section 4.4, so the concept shouldn't be foreign. But the web map specification also allows you to define the renderer in the configuration file. Do this by adding a `layerDefinition` property to the layer, in this case the labor centroids, and in that `layerDefinition`, define a `drawingInfo` property with a renderer that will define how the features in the layer look. This can be as simple or as complicated as you want.

For the labor centroids, define a `classBreakRenderer` that will display larger circles with a higher percentage of the labor population. This may look complicated, but you define a symbol once and change the size for each new category of percentages, as shown in the following listing.

Listing 7.14   `classBreakRenderer`—displaying larger circles

```
"layerDefinition": {
  "drawingInfo":{
    "renderer":{
      "type":"classBreaks",
      "field":"LABOR_PCT",
      "defaultSymbol":null,
      "defaultLabel":"",
      "minValue":0,
      "classBreakInfos":[{
        "classMaxValue":0.25,
        "label":"0 - 25%",
        "description":"",
        "symbol":{
          "type":"esriSMS",
          "style":"esriSMSCircle",
          "color":[115,223,255,255],
          "size":4,
          "angle":0,
          "xoffset":0,
          "yoffset":0,
          "outline":{
            "color":[255,255,255,255],
            "width":1
          }
        }
      }, {
        "classMaxValue":0.5,
        "label":"25% - 50%",
        "description":"",
        "symbol":{
          "type":"esriSMS",
          "style":"esriSMSCircle",
          "color":[115,223,255,255],
```

```
        "size":7.5,
        "angle":0,
        "xoffset":0,
        "yoffset":0,
        "outline":{
          "color":[255,255,255,255
          ],
          "width":1
        }
      }
    }, {
      "classMaxValue":0.75,
      "label":"50% - 75%",
      "description":"",
      "symbol":{
        "type":"esriSMS",
        "style":"esriSMSCircle",
        "color":[115,223,255,255],
        "size":11,
        "angle":0,
        "xoffset":0,
        "yoffset":0,
        "outline":{
          "color":[255,255,255,255],
          "width":1
        }
      }
    }, {
      "classMaxValue":1.00,
      "label":"75% - 100%",
      "description":"",
      "symbol":{
        "type":"esriSMS",
        "style":"esriSMSCircle",
        "color":[115,223,255,255],
        "size":20,
        "angle":0,
        "xoffset":0,
        "yoffset":0,
        "outline":{
          "color":[255,255,255,255],
          "width":1
        }
      }
    }]
  },
  "transparency":0,
}
}
```

Figure 7.16 Renderer of a layer defined in the configuration file

This configuration looks scarier than it is. You've defined the same symbol for each category, but you change the size accordingly. If you run the application again, you should see something similar to figure 7.16.

This capability is why the ArcGIS API for JavaScript is so versatile. If you're unhappy with the default look of a map service, no problem; you can change it. Once again, no extra code is needed because the entire map is defined using the web map specification.

The web map specification has additional options that I'll leave for you to experiment with. The options covered in this section are what I consider the most powerful when building applications: how to better handle working with a web mapping application when an internet connection isn't available.

7.4   *Advanced techniques for offline mode*

In chapter 5, you learned how to build an application that could still function, at least partially, when the user loses an internet connection. This is always a popular feature of working with web mapping applications. Remember, I also said there's no perfect solution, which is true, but that doesn't mean you can't provide more features. In this section you'll learn how to create an application cache and use a third-party library to build your mobile-friendly web mapping application.

7.4.1   *Creating an application cache*

An application cache is an HTML5 feature that caches files so users can browse a website offline.[1] In addition to the benefit of accessing a website offline, an application

---

[1] https://developer.mozilla.org/en-US/docs/Web/HTML/Using_the_application_cache

cache offers a speed boost because files are stored locally without sending requests to a server. This approach works well with most websites, but a web mapping application isn't most websites. Still, you can use it in your applications as needed.

> **Caveat**
>
> If your application cache doesn't refresh in your browser, you may have to manually remove it. Technically, updating the application cache file updates the cache in the browser, but in my experience it can sometimes get stuck.
>
> In Chrome you can manually remove the application cache from the URL chrome:// appcache-internals/. This method works well only if you lose an internet connection; if you refresh the browser without an internet connection, the application won't work.

WHAT CAN GO IN THE CACHE

Static files should go in your application cache, so style sheets and JavaScript files are always good candidates. You can also add images that you may use for icons. The idea is that once someone has used the application, they won't need to download these items again.

Using the sample you worked on in section 7.3, you can build an application cache that lists not only the files you created but also the files that get downloaded from the ArcGIS servers to load the API for JavaScript. In the root directory of the project, create a file called manifest.appcache. You don't have to use that name, but the appcache file extension is standard.

To find out what files to include in the cache, you can run the application in Chrome, and then complete the following steps:

1 Open the Chrome Developer tools.
2 Click the Sources tab.

Locate the small arrow button at the left and click it. A folder structure displays the files in use, organized by the domain they come from (see figure 7.17).

3 Right-click any file, and then choose Copy Link Address to copy and paste that location to the manifest.appcache file.

Although this process of copying and pasting URLs to the appcache file can be tedious the first time you do it, you'll only need to do minor updates in the future.

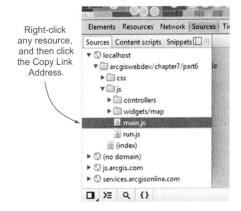

Right-click any resource, and then click the Copy Link Address.

Figure 7.17 List of files used in the web application

NOTE   The code for this section is available in the chapter7/part6 folder of the source code included with the book.

WRITING THE APPLICATION CACHE

When you're done copying the URLs to the appcache file, it should look similar to the following listing.

Listing 7.15   manifest.appcache—URLs added

```
CACHE MANIFEST
# v1
CACHE:
index.html
config.json

## css ##
css/main.css
http://js.arcgis.com/3.11/esri/css/esri.css

## javascript files ##
# esri
http://js.arcgis.com/3.11compact/init.js
http://js.arcgis.com/3.11compact/js/esri/arcgis/utils.js
http://js.arcgis.com/3.11compact/js/esri/nls/jsapi_en-us.js
http://js.arcgis.com/3.11compact/js/esri/tasks/RelationshipQuery.js
http://js.arcgis.com/3.11compact/js/esri/tasks/StatisticDefinition.js
http://js.arcgis.com/3.11compact/js/esri/dijit/Geocoder.js
http://js.arcgis.com/3.11compact/js/esri/dijit/LocateButton.js
http://js.arcgis.com/3.11compact/js/esri/tasks/AddressCandidate.js
http://js.arcgis.com/3.11compact/js/esri/tasks/locator.js


# dijit
http://js.arcgis.com/3.11compact/js/dojo/dijit/_base/focus.js
http://js.arcgis.com/3.11compact/js/dojo/dijit/_base/place.js
http://js.arcgis.com/3.11compact/js/dojo/dijit/_base/popup.js
http://js.arcgis.com/3.11compact/js/dojo/dijit/_base/scroll.js
http://js.arcgis.com/3.11compact/js/dojo/dijit/_base/sniff.js
http://js.arcgis.com/3.11compact/js/dojo/dijit/_base/typematic.js
http://js.arcgis.com/3.11compact/js/dojo/dijit/_base/wai.js
http://js.arcgis.com/3.11compact/js/dojo/dijit/_base/window.js
http://js.arcgis.com/3.11compact/js/dojo/dijit/BackgroundIframe.js
http://js.arcgis.com/3.11compact/js/dojo/dijit/Destroyable.js
http://js.arcgis.com/3.11compact/js/dojo/dijit/Viewport.js
http://js.arcgis.com/3.11compact/js/dojo/dijit/WidgetSet.js
http://js.arcgis.com/3.11compact/js/dojo/dijit/_AttachMixin.js
http://js.arcgis.com/3.11compact/js/dojo/dijit/_TemplatedMixin.js
http://js.arcgis.com/3.11compact/js/dojo/dijit/_WidgetBase.js
http://js.arcgis.com/3.11compact/js/dojo/dijit/_base.js
http://js.arcgis.com/3.11compact/js/dojo/dijit/place.js
http://js.arcgis.com/3.11compact/js/dojo/dijit/popup.js
http://js.arcgis.com/3.11compact/js/dojo/dijit/selection.js
http://js.arcgis.com/3.11compact/js/dojo/dijit/typematic.js
```

Annotations:
- Must have this header so it works correctly. (pointing to `CACHE MANIFEST`)
- Everything under the CACHE: heading will be cached. (pointing to `CACHE:`)
- The # in the file is a way to add comments. (pointing to `## css ##`)

```
# dojo
http://js.arcgis.com/3.11compact/js/dojo/dojo/cache.js

# dojox
http://js.arcgis.com/3.11compact/js/dojo/dojox/gfx/svg.js

# custom
js/run.js
js/main.js

js/controllers/widgetloader.js

js/widgets/map/map.js

NETWORK:
*
```

The asterisk under NETWORK: allows all other traffic to go through.

When writing the application cache file, you can use # to write comments. It's good practice to give your appcache file a version number that you can update when you change the code in your application. The only way the browser will reload the files in the cache is if there's an update in the appcache file. If you don't do this, you'll never see your changes.

USING APPLICATION CACHE

With the manifest.appcache file completed, tell the browser to use it. Do this by adding a new attribute to the HTML node in the index.html file:

```
<html manifest="manifest.appcache">
```

Now when you run your application, prepare to be amazed!

Okay, not that amazing; it probably looks exactly like it did before. But that's okay because you need to load the application at least once with an internet connection for the files to cache themselves. The application cache is a powerful feature, but it's not magic, so reload the page one more time and admire the splendor of fast page load! Sorry if you don't notice incredibly faster page loads in your desktop browser, but on a mobile device, this cache can help speed up the page loads.

If you poke around in Chrome, you can see that the files were loaded from the cache and not from the server. Click the Network tab in Developer tools and look at the Size column (see figure 7.18).

The only items not cached are actual requests that the code makes to the server. You may not see a noticeable difference in your application at the moment, but when you're using a mobile device with sketchy internet, every enhancement is a plus.

If you have an application that loads custom fonts or a set of images that you use to make your application look nice, setting up the application cache can provide a decent performance increase and save on load times. Next, we'll revisit saving data locally.

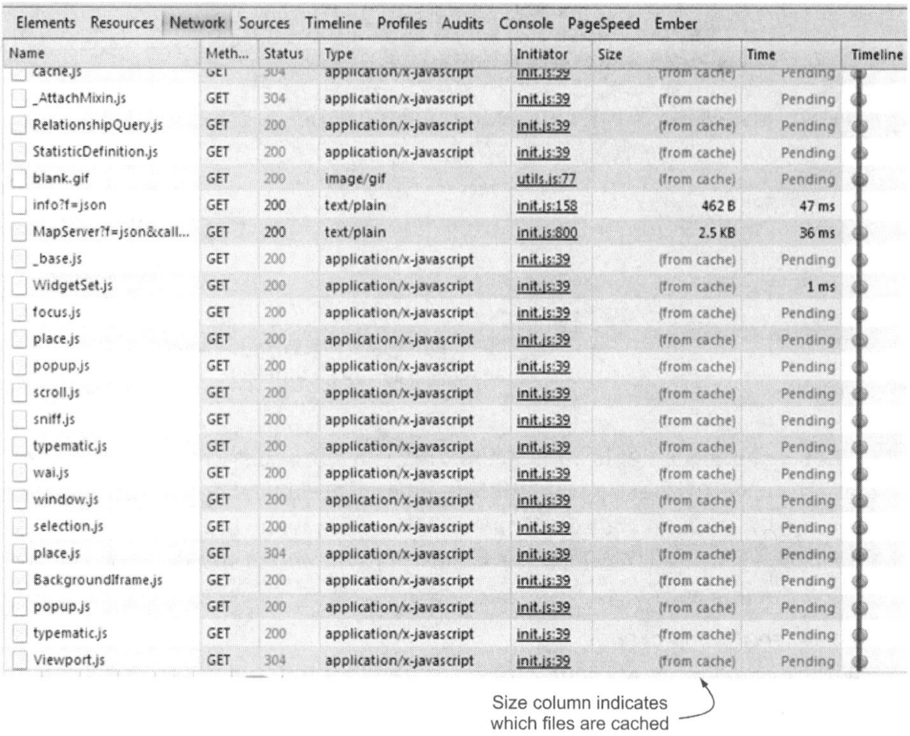

Elements Resources Network Sources Timeline Profiles Audits Console PageSpeed Ember

Name	Meth...	Status	Type	Initiator	Size	Time	Timeline
cache.js	GET	304	application/x-javascript	init.js:39	(from cache)	Pending	
_AttachMixin.js	GET	304	application/x-javascript	init.js:39	(from cache)	Pending	
RelationshipQuery.js	GET	200	application/x-javascript	init.js:39	(from cache)	Pending	
StatisticDefinition.js	GET	200	application/x-javascript	init.js:39	(from cache)	Pending	
blank.gif	GET	200	image/gif	utils.js:77	(from cache)	Pending	
info?f=json	GET	200	text/plain	init.js:158	462 B	47 ms	
MapServer?f=json&call...	GET	200	text/plain	init.js:800	2.5 KB	36 ms	
_base.js	GET	200	application/x-javascript	init.js:39	(from cache)	Pending	
WidgetSet.js	GET	200	application/x-javascript	init.js:39	(from cache)	1 ms	
focus.js	GET	200	application/x-javascript	init.js:39	(from cache)	Pending	
place.js	GET	200	application/x-javascript	init.js:39	(from cache)	Pending	
popup.js	GET	200	application/x-javascript	init.js:39	(from cache)	Pending	
scroll.js	GET	200	application/x-javascript	init.js:39	(from cache)	Pending	
sniff.js	GET	200	application/x-javascript	init.js:39	(from cache)	Pending	
typematic.js	GET	200	application/x-javascript	init.js:39	(from cache)	Pending	
wai.js	GET	200	application/x-javascript	init.js:39	(from cache)	Pending	
window.js	GET	200	application/x-javascript	init.js:39	(from cache)	Pending	
selection.js	GET	200	application/x-javascript	init.js:39	(from cache)	Pending	
place.js	GET	304	application/x-javascript	init.js:39	(from cache)	Pending	
BackgroundIframe.js	GET	200	application/x-javascript	init.js:39	(from cache)	Pending	
popup.js	GET	200	application/x-javascript	init.js:39	(from cache)	Pending	
typematic.js	GET	200	application/x-javascript	init.js:39	(from cache)	Pending	
Viewport.js	GET	304	application/x-javascript	init.js:39	(from cache)	Pending	

Size column indicates
which files are cached

Figure 7.18 Chrome Network tab showing files that are cached

7.4.2 *Storing data locally with the PouchDB library*

In chapter 5, you learned how to use HTML5 storage capabilities to store data locally using IndexedDB. This is a database in the browser for storing complex data structures. Chapter 5 mentioned that IndexedDB isn't supported in all mobile browser environments, even if the desktop browser counterpart supports it. A few mobile browsers support only Web SQL, which is a deprecated HTML5 storage solution. Once something is deprecated, people don't stop using it overnight, so if you want to work with a storage solution on mobile browsers other than Local Storage, you need Web SQL. Using Web SQL in place of Local Storage doesn't have to be difficult. A fantastic JavaScript library called PouchDB can save you hours of hair-pulling.

WHAT IS POUCHDB?

PouchDB is a library that works with data locally and provides the capabilities to synchronize with CouchDB, a document-based database. It's the offline data capabilities that make PouchDB a useful tool for web mapping capabilities. PouchDB provides an interface to work with browser-based data storage solutions.

PouchDB determines whether the browser supports IndexedDB or Web SQL and handles the local database creation, updates, and data retrieval with simple functions. Combine PouchDB with Dojo Store capabilities, and you have a powerful tool. A Dojo

Store is an interface for accessing and manipulating data and is used as a data source for Dijit components.

USING POUCHDB

To get started, PouchDB needs only the name of the database to use. You could use the following code:

```
var myDb = new PouchDB('mydb');
```

That seems simple enough. To add to the database, pass an object to the put method:

```
myDb.put({ _id: new Date().toISOString(), title: 'Hi mom' });
```

PouchDB requires that each entry have a unique _id. Using an ISO standard timestamp will suffice to generate unique _id values. If you don't want to specify one, you can use the post method, and PouchDB will generate a random _id for you:

```
myDb.post({ title: 'Hi mom' });
```

I prefer to use the put method because if you use the put method with an _id already in the database, it updates the data; if the _id isn't in the current database, it adds it.

To retrieve a document, pass the _id to the get method:

```
myDb.get('unique_id', function(error, doc) {});
```

To retrieve all the documents, use the allDocs method:

```
myDb.allDocs({ include_docs: true }, function(error, results) {});
```

When set to true, the include_docs option returns all the documents in the database; when set to false, it returns only the _id field.

PouchDB has other features, but you know enough to start using it in your application.

> **TIP** For more details and documentation about PouchDB, visit http://pouchdb.com/.

CREATING THE POUCHSTORE MODULE

Although PouchDB isn't overly complicated, it would be convenient to wrap its functionality in an easy-to-use module that handles database creation. This neat little module (shown in listing 7.15) exposes a couple of simple methods: add and getAll. It also uses a module for Dojo Store called QueryResults. This module wraps the results of the getAll method with the same functionality of Dojo array utilities, so you have access to methods such as forEach and filter.

Listing 7.16 js/stores/PouchStore—saves data locally

```
define([
  'dojo/_base/declare',
  'dojo/Deferred',
  'dojo/store/util/QueryResults'        ⟵ Loads QueryResults to use
], function (                              in this module.
  declare,
```

```
      Deferred,
      QueryResults
    ) {

    return declare(null, {

      database: null,
      _db: null,

      constructor: function (database) {
        this.database = database;
        this._init();
      },

      add: function (object) {
        var deferred = new Deferred();
        this._db.put({
          _id: new Date().toISOString(),
          item: object
        }, function (err, result) {
          if (!err) {
            alert('Item saved locally');
            deferred.resolve(result);
          } else {
            alert('Error saving item locally: ' + err.message);
            deferred.reject(err);
          }
        });
        return deferred.promise;
      },

      getAll: function () {
        var deferred = new Deferred();
        this._db.allDocs({ include_docs: true }, function (err, response) {
          if (!err) {
            alert('local data retrieved', response);
            deferred.resolve(response.rows);
          } else {
            alert('Error retrieving local data: ' + err.message);
            deferred.reject(err);
          }
        });
        return QueryResults(deferred.promise);
      },
      removeAll: function() {
        this.getAll().then(lang.hitch(this, function(response) {
          response.forEach(lang.hitch(this, function(data) {
            this._db.remove(data.doc);
          }));
        }));
      },
      _init: function () {
        this._db = new window.PouchDB(this.database);
      }
    });
  });
```

Provides database name for the constructor and initializes the module.

Add method takes an object and adds it to database. Returns results as a promise.

getAll returns all documents in database.

Results of getAll are returned as QueryResults.

Function removes all documents from database.

PouchDB is initialized with database name provided.

This module uses the `put` and `getAll` methods of PouchDB but uses promises to return the results to the outside world of the application. Remember, promises work great when you're working asynchronously and you're waiting for something to happen—in this case, read and write from the storage. The PouchDB API isn't particularly complicated, but wrapping this functionality in one place makes it much more reusable.

Okay, great, you have an awesome PouchStore module. How do you use it?

USING THE POUCHSTORE

For this example, you can modify the project you completed in chapter 5 to do disconnected editing. The code for this section is available in the chapter7/part7 folder of the source code included with the book.

In this project, the `editorService` module is responsible for adding the points to the `FeatureLayer`. If an error occurs, it stores the features in `localStorage` and allows the user to sync the data at a later time. You can continue to use this method, but in this case, replace all the code that deals with `localStorage` with the `PouchStore` module. The updated `editorService` module is shown the following listing.

Listing 7.17 js/widgets/edit/editorService.js—using PouchStore to save data

```
define([
  'dojo/_base/declare',
  'dojo/_base/lang',
  'dojo/_base/array',
  'dojo/Deferred',                    Loads the PouchStore
  'esri/graphic',                     for use in this module
  'stores/pouchstore'
], function(
  declare, lang, arrayUtils,
  Deferred,
  Graphic,
  PouchStore
) {

  return declare(null, {
    layer: null,
    hasLocal: false,
                                        Passes the map and
    constructor: function(options) {    initializes new PouchStore
      declare.safeMixin(this, options);
      this.map = options.map;
      this._sync = [];
      this.store = new PouchStore('request');
      this.check();
    },
                                        Method checks if features
    check: function() {                 are stored locally
      this.store.getAll().then(lang.hitch(this, '_onStoreChecked'));
    },

    _onStoreChecked: function(response) {    If graphics are stored locally,
      if (response.length) {                 displays them on the map
```

```
      this.hasLocal = true;
      response.forEach(lang.hitch(this, function(data) {
        var graphic = new Graphic(data.doc.item);
        this.map.graphics.add(graphic);
      }));

    }
  },
```

**Sync function gets all features a
nd syncs them with FeatureLayer**

```
sync: function() {
  this.store.getAll().then(lang.hitch(this, '_onGetAll'));
},
add: function(adds) {
  var deferred = new Deferred()
```

**Add function stores data locally
when fails to save to FeatureLayer**

```
    , req;
  req = this.layer.applyEdits(adds);
  req.then(
    function() {
    deferred.resolve();
  },
  lang.hitch(
      this,
      function() {
        arrayUtils.forEach(adds, function(graphic) {
          this.store.add(graphic.toJson());
          this.hasLocal = true;
        }, this);
        deferred.reject(adds);
      }
    )
  );

  return deferred.promise;
},
_onGetAll: function(response) {
```

**Function handles when data
is synced to FeatureLayer**

```
  if (response.length) {
    this._sync = response.map(function(data) {
      return new Graphic(data.doc.item);
    });

    if (this._sync.length) {
      this.layer.applyEdits(this._sync).then(
        lang.hitch(this, '_dataSynced'),
        lang.hitch(this, '_syncError')
      );
    }
  }
},
_dataSynced: function() {
```

**Data is synced to do cleanup, including
removing data from local database**

```
  this._sync.length = 0;
  this.hasLocal = false;
  this.store.removeAll();
  this.map.graphics.clear();
  this.layer.refresh();
```

```
  },
  _syncError: function() {
    this._sync.length = 0;
  }
});
});
```

If sync error exists, remove graphics from _sync array

The rest of the application can stay the same; you're only changing the editor-Service module. You've left most of the core method names the same, only adding helper methods; this way, other modules that reference editorService won't need to be updated.

The process is the same as before: if features fail to add to the FeatureLayer, they're stored locally, and you display these features on the map in different symbology than other features. When an internet connection becomes available, you can run the sync function to get all the documents from the local database, convert them back to graphics, and add them to the FeatureLayer. When that's complete, remove all the data from the local database and do cleanup, such as refreshing the layer. You can see what this process may look like when adding and syncing data in figure 7.19.

As you can see, you didn't need to tell PouchDB to use IndexedDB or Web SQL because PouchDB determines which is available to use. This application now works on a variety of mobile browsers, and PouchDB handles the heavy lifting behind the scenes for you.

Figure 7.19   Syncing locally stored data to the server

Of course, my caveats from chapter 5 still stand. When it comes to offline web mapping, especially disconnected editing, no perfect solution exists. But this method of using a third-party library to use the available storage is a better solution than doing nothing.

7.5   *Summary*

- This chapter covered a large quantity of material, particularly related to advanced techniques for loading Dojo widgets.

- The goal of this chapter was to introduce you to advanced topics in developing applications with the ArcGIS API for JavaScript and to reinforce the power of reusable code. This isn't to say that my way is the definitive way, as I've seen others create template applications and JavaScript viewers that work differently. But the methods I described here have helped me, through trial and error (lots and lots of error), to go from prototype to production on many occasions.

- The techniques you learned might inch you closer to that coveted perfect disconnected editing web mapping application...almost. The application cache is a good start, and if you're careful to include the files as they're needed, you can save on requests when the application loads.

- Using a library such as PouchDB to handle the heavy lifting of saving data locally ensures that your application will work across multiple platforms. You can even store actual map tiles using PouchDB. The goal here was to provide you with additional advanced methods.

appendix A
Setting up your
environment

You have a few software options when developing web applications. Whether you prefer a visual environment or the command line, the ArcGIS API for JavaScript requires a local server. My three recommendations are outlined in this appendix.

A.1 Visual Studio Express for Web

Web development is easiest with Microsoft Visual Studio Express for Web (www.microsoft.com/visualstudio/eng/downloads#d-express-web). This software comes with a local web server to build your applications. Visual Studio Express is probably the easiest way to get started, as it is both an editing environment and local server in one.

A.2 XAMPP

If you prefer to work in a text editor, one of my favorite lightweight local servers is Apache, which can be installed with XAMPP, which stands for Cross-platform Apache, MySQL, PHP, and Perl (www.apachefriends.org/en/xampp.html). It runs a local instance of Apache HTTP web server on your machine and is easy to work with.

> **TIP** Copy your files to the xampp\htdocs folder to view them in the browser. XAMPP will serve all files from this folder.

A.3 Python

Another option for running a local web server is to use Python (www.python.org). I recommend downloading Python v2.7.

In your favorite command-line tool, navigate to the folder containing your web files and run this command:

```
python -m SimpleHTTPServer
```

This option doesn't provide the fastest server, but it's suitable for running most examples in the book, except when a proxy is required. In that case, I recommend using one of the other two options.

appendix B
Dojo basics

Because the ArcGIS API for JavaScript is built with the Dojo Toolkit, you should be aware of a few details about Dojo. When Esri initially released the ArcGIS API for JavaScript, the company came under scrutiny for using Dojo as the core to the API as opposed to a more popular library such as jQuery. The developers at Esri stated that their reasons for choosing Dojo were that at the time the API was developed, Dojo had better tools for working with web services, and, more important, had better support for working with graphics across a variety of browsers. You can still use jQuery or any other third-party library in your applications, but one way or another, you'll also use Dojo.

As the Dojo Toolkit has been upgraded over the years, so has the ArcGIS API for JavaScript. When the API moved to v3.0, it began using Dojo v1.7 for its core functions, and it continues to keep up with current Dojo updates.

The Dojo Toolkit is a vast resource of modules and utilities for developing robust and scalable applications, which requires an entire book of its own to cover in detail, but you can use this appendix as a starting point for the more detailed coverage in this book. This appendix covers the Dojo loader, the Dijit lifecycle, and common Dojo modules you'll use when building applications with the ArcGIS API for JavaScript.

For more details about Dojo and the Dijit library, visit http://dojotoolkit.org/documentation/.

B.1 *AMD loader*

The introduction of Dojo v1.7 was a big shift for many developers using the ArcGIS API for JavaScript, in part because they were introduced to the asynchronous module definition (AMD) loading system, which is how your individual JavaScript files are loaded into your application. As of this writing, the ArcGIS JavaScript API is at v3.11 and based on v1.9 of the Dojo Toolkit. This isn't an exhaustive appendix on

the Dojo Toolkit, but it's important to be aware of how to use the AMD loading system
when developing your applications.

Prior to v3.0 of the API, you used `dojo.require('my.classname')` to import a
module into your application. The API still supports this, but this method is outdated
and will eventually go away, so it's good practice for developers to take advantage of
the newer AMD loading system. Let's take a quick crash course on AMD.

AMD's define and require methods

Two main components to the Dojo AMD loading system are important to understand:
the use of `define` and `require`. Use the `define` method to define a module you want
to use in your application. Similarly, use the `require` method to use the modules created with `define`. The following listing declares a new class that has a `startup`
method.

Listing B.1   Declaring a new class

```
                          Defines module and
                          provides name          Provides any dependencies
define([                                          for module
'dojo/_base/declare'
  ], function(declare) {
    return declare(null, {                       Provides name for returned
      startup: function() {                        dependencyi n the callback function
        console.log('I am a defined module');
      }
    });
  });

require(['app/sample'], function(Sample) {       Requires the defined modules and
    var s = new Sample();                          gives the returned value a name
    s.startup();                                   Uses the returned
});                                                module as needed
```

Be sure to return
something from
the module

If you're creating a smaller application that doesn't require you to break your modules into multiple JavaScript files, you could do everything inside a single `require`
statement. In applications that may require a couple of widgets and helper modules,
you'll most likely end up having to break up your modules into multiple JavaScript
files, so when you do so, you can require them by path name, as shown in the following listing.

NOTE The following module is defined in the chapter3/app/sample.js file,
and the HTML file is in 3.1.html.

Listing B.2   AMD define and require

```
define([
  'dojo/_base/declare'                           Defines a module without
], function(declare) {                           providing a name
  return declare('Sample', null, {
    startup: function() {
```

```
      alert('I am a defined module');
    }
  });
});

<script type="text/javascript">
...
  require(['app/sample'], function(Sample) {
    var s = new Sample();
    s.startup();
  });
<script type="text/javascript">
```

Requires the module sample.js from the app folder

You can get a better understanding of how the files are related by reviewing figure B.1, which shows how the app/sample.js file is related to the main.js file.

Here you can clearly see that sample.js resides in the app folder, and that main.js requires the module defined in sample.js. This is how dependencies are managed with AMD loading. It allows you, as a developer, to modularize your application into smaller pieces.

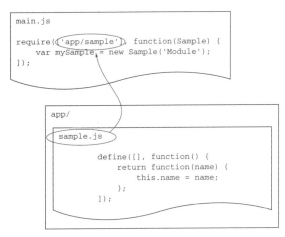

Figure B.1 How files that define modules are related to other files that require them

AMD drawbacks with multiple HTTP requests

One drawback to the AMD pattern, and one that's gotten criticism, is the number of HTTP requests that may need to be made to load many different modules. Although it's true that multiple HTTP requests should typically be avoided in web development, particularly when concerned with mobile devices, the truth is that when dealing with developing mapping applications, this is probably not as big of a concern. Every pan of the map sends a new HTTP request to the server to request new map data to be loaded for areas that haven't been viewed. When all is said and done, mapping applications, by design, send multiple HTTP requests at various stages of use, so loading a few modules separately in your development doesn't typically have much of an impact on performance.

The more you use the AMD pattern, the more familiar it will feel. When it becomes second nature, you won't even think about it anymore.

Another important aspect of working with Dojo is using Dojo Dijits, so it's beneficial to get an overview of the Dijit lifecycle.

B.2   Dijit lifecycle

A widget is typically a module that represents an interface for the user to interact with. If you want to create a widget module for your application, you're likely going to delve into the Dijit library. It could be used to work with HTML forms or a newsfeed widget that could be displayed on the page. The core of the Dijit library is the `WidgetBase` module. When a new class based on_`WidgetBase` is instantiated, it goes through the following lifecycle process:

- `Constructor`—This phase occurs when a class is instantiated with `new`. You usually assign any default properties of the widget in this function.

- `postMixinProperties`–This phase occurs before a widget is rendered on the screen. Variables from inherited classes are mixed in at this point. Properties can be changed here before any DOM (Document Object Model[1]) elements for the widget are created, if needed. Personally, I've never had to do any work in here, but it may be useful to you.

- `buildRendering`–This phase is typically handled by the `Templated` module, but it's when the HTML elements for the widget are created. You could assign properties here that may be bound to something in the DOM element.

- `postCreate`–This is when the DOM elements for the widget are already created, but may not have been added to the page yet, so you could bind up events here or manipulate any DOM elements. I often work in this method related to subscribing to events.

- `Startup`–Runs once the HTML elements are built. If you have to do anything involving style lookups, this is the phase to do it.

- `Destroy`–This method does what it advertises. It destroys your widget and removes it from the Dijit widget registry to free up memory. To remove child widgets, use the `destroyRecursive` method. You don't typically need to override `destroy` yourself, as the Dijit normally cleans things up, but if you instantiate a widget in the module that's not a child widget, it may be necessary to perform the cleanup manually.

You can see what this process looks like in the following listing.

Listing B.3   Sample widget with all lifecycles defined

```
define([
    'dojo/_base/declare',
    'dojo/_base/lang',
    'dojo/dom',
    'dojo/on',
    'dojo/Evented',
    'dojo/dom-construct',
    'dojo/dom-class',
```

---

[1] For more information about DOM elements, see www.w3.org/DOM/.

```
    'dijit/_WidgetBase',
    'dijit/_TemplatedMixin',

    'text!widgets/header/header.tpl.html'
], function(
  declare, lang,
  dom, on, Evented,
  domConstruct, domClass,
  _WidgetBase, _TemplatedMixin, template
) {
  return declare([_WidgetBase, _TemplatedMixin, Evented], {
    templateString: template,
    loaded: false,

    constructor: function(options, srcRefNode) {
      this.set('map', options.map);
    },
    postMixinProperties: function() {
      this.inherited(arguments);
    },
    buildRendering: function() {
      this.inherited(arguments);
      if (!this.domNode) {
        this.domNode = domConstruct.create('div');
      }
    },
    postCreate: function() {
      this.inherited(arguments);
      var nodeCollapse;
      nodeCollapse = dom.byId('nav-collapse-container');
      this.own(
        on(dom.byId('nav-toggle'), 'click', function() {
          domClass.toggle(nodeCollapse, 'nav-open');
        })
      );
    },
    startup: function() {
      var map = this.get('map');
      if (!map) {
        this.destroy();
        throw new Error('A map is required');
      }
      if (!map.loaded) {
        on.once(map, 'load', lang.hitch(this, function() {
          this.set('loaded', true);
          this.emit('loaded', this);
        }));
      } else {
        this.set('loaded', true);
        this.emit('loaded', this);
      }
      this.set('loaded', true);
    },
    destroy: function() {
      this.inherited(arguments);
```

Declares new widget that inherits at least _WidgetBase.

Sets up options

You could change properties of an inherited class here.

You could define the domNode here if it doesn't exist.

You could add any additional event listeners here.

You could check if another widget is loaded here.

You could make sure all child widgets are destroyed here.

```
      this.get('map').destroy();
    }
  });
});
```

This listing isn't a functional example, but it shows you how you might approach working with the Dijit lifecycle.

Throughout the book you've seen various examples of using Dojo widgets, and chapter 7 covers how to use the Dojo lifecycle described here to build applications from a single configuration file. In addition to the Dojo lifecycle, you should also be aware of common Dojo modules.

B.3   *Common Dojo modules*

When working with Dojo and the ArcGIS API for JavaScript, you'll find yourself using a few modules over and over again. This section covers the basics of these common modules.

dojo/_base/lang

The lang module is a common module to use in building applications with Dojo. I use the following methods on a regular basis.

MIXIN

The lang.mixin method does what it sounds like it does: it mixes in properties from one object to another. For example:

```
var options = { name: 'container', width: 25, height: 50 };
lang.mixin(options, { color: 'blue' });
```

The options object now has the property color with a value of blue that was mixed in using the lang.mixin method. This comes in handy when you need to merge datasets from different sources.

HITCH

I use the lang.hitch method in almost all my widgets. It allows you to execute a function in a given context. I often use this in widgets to listen for events to happen in the application and to execute a function on the widget in response to that event. In the following example, when the element with an ID of something is clicked, the handler method is executed, which writes out to the console the event that occurred:

```
require(['dojo/on', 'dojo/_base/lang'], function(on, lang) {
  return function() {
    this.handler = function(e) {
      console.debug('This just happened: ' + e);
    };
    on(document.getElementById('something'),
        'click',
        lang.hitch(this, 'handler')
    );
  };
});
```

You'll probably find that you use this method frequently when working with events in your application.

The `lang` module has a few more methods you may find useful. You can read more about them at http://dojotoolkit.org/reference-guide/1.9/dojo/_base/lang.html.

dojo/_base/array

The module that I probably use the most is the `array` module, which provides support for working with arrays and works well with older browsers. The `array` module makes working with listed data easy and provides a couple of great ways to work with data.

FOREACH

The `array.forEach` method provides a way to iterate over the items in an array:

```
var helper = function() {
  this.doSomething = function(n) {
    console.debug('I am number ' + n);
  };
  array.forEach([1,2,3,4], function(num) {
    this.doSomething(num);
  }, this);
};
```

This method provides a clean interface for iterating over the items in an array. All the `array` methods, including the `forEach` method, even take an optional third argument for the context of how the functions can be called in the method. In this example, you call `this.doSomething`, where `this` was passed as a third argument to the `forEach` method.

MAP

The `array.map` method returns an array that's equal to the results of the callback function:

```
var squared = array.map([2,4,6,8], function(num) {
  return num * num;
});
```

The value of `squared` is `[4,16,36,64]`. This method comes in handy when you need to process all the data in an array.

FILTER

The `array.filter` method is used to filter values from an array that don't meet the criteria as defined in the callback function:

```
var even = array.filter([2,3,4,5,6,7], function(num) {
  return (num % 2) === 0;
});
```

The callback function checks if the modulus (`%`), which is the remainder of the given number divided by 2, is equal to 0. If the remainder is 0, it's an even number. The value of the `even` array is `[2,4,6]`.

There are more methods in the `array` module you may find useful. Details can be found at http://dojotoolkit.org/reference-guide/1.9/dojo/_base/array.html.

dojo/on

The Dojo on module is used to listen for and to emit events in your application. When on is used as a function, you can listen for events to happen:

```
require(['dojo/on'], function(on) {
  return function() {
    on(document.getElementById('something'),
        'click',
        function() {
          console.debug('Something happened');
        }
    );
  };
});
```

The on module listens for an element with an ID of `something` to be clicked, and when it's clicked, it writes out to the console that something has happened. This is a clean interface for listening to events in an application.

EMIT

The on module could even be used to emit events in an application:

```
require(['dojo/on', 'dojo/_base/lang'], function(on, lang) {
  return function() {
    on(document.getElementById('something'),
        'click',
        lang.hitch(this, function() {
          on.emit(this, 'custom-event');
        })
    );
  };
});
```

The on module is used to emit an event from the context of `this`. This is a popular pattern in widgets that you'll become familiar with.

You can find more details about the on module at http://dojotoolkit.org/reference-guide/1.9/dojo/on.html.

appendix C
Configuring a proxy

Using a proxy configuration to access secured services in a browser-based application is optional. You could continue developing the application by requiring a user to log in each time, and the application would still work as expected.

Sometimes you might want to be more lax about security requirements. For example, suppose a handful of users have access to the application—only from within an internal network. You might consider using a proxy page so users don't have to enter their usernames and passwords in the Identity Manager each time the application loads.

Although I encourage you to set up users with their own passwords on your internal ArcGIS Server or via your organization's ArcGIS Online account, this appendix covers the details of using the ASP.NET proxy page provided by Esri (https://developers.arcgis.com/javascript/jshelp/ags_proxy.html). You complete similar steps to set up the application for other proxy pages provided by Esri.

C.1 Setting up the proxy page

Regardless of the proxy page you use (ASP.NET, PHP, or JSP), setting it up involves the same easy process. If using a secured ArcGIS Server service, you can place your username and password in the configuration file for the proxy. In the case of the ASP.NET page, it may look like this:

```
<serverUrl url="http://services1.arcgis.com/"
    matchAll="true"
    username="<USERNAME>"
    password="<PASSWORD>">
</serverUrl>
```

This generates a new token for your application using the provided username and password when you need access to the secure services. Another method if using ArcGIS Online services is to provide the `clientId` and `clientSecret` you would be provided by your application in your ArcGIS Online account. You can configure them like this:

```
<serverUrl url="http://services1.arcgis.com/"
    matchAll="true"
    clientId="<CLIENTID>"
    clientSecret="<CLIENTSECRET>">
</serverUrl>
```

For more details on setting up the proxy configuration, please refer to the documentation at https://developers.arcgis.com/javascript/jshelp/ags_proxy.html.

After you set up the configuration, you can add the proxy page URL to the application.

> **TIP** Add the URL for `static.arcgis.com` as allowed by the proxy as well. This is used to display attribution information on the map; without the URL, you'll see an error in your application.

C.2   *Using the proxy in your application*

To tell your application to use the proxy page for all its requests, add the code as shown in the following listing to js/main.js where the application starts to load.

Listing C.1   Using the proxy page

```
require([
  'esri/config',                    Loads the esri/config
  ...                               module to set the proxy
  'dojo/domReady!'
], function (
  esriConfig,
  AppCtrl,
  mapServices
) {
  esriConfig.defaults.io.proxyUrl = '/proxy.ashx';      Sets the proxy URL
  esriConfig.defaults.io.alwaysUseProxy = true;         Always use proxy
  ...                                                   for requests
});
```

This code adds a reference to the `esri/config` module, which allows you to assign the proxy details. Next, assign the URL. When you're working with secured services and tokens, the most critical step is to set the value of `alwaysUseProxy` to `true`. Otherwise, the proxy is used only if your application makes an HTTP request that exceeds 2,048 characters in length. This is a browser limit, and it's a good idea to use a proxy if you think you may run into this issue. In this case, you want to use it for secured services, so you need to tell the ArcGIS API for JavaScript to always use the proxy.

The proxy page is a great tool to use in a variety of scenarios. As I mentioned, it may even be a requirement if your application makes large requests that could exceed the browser limit. It's also a great option when developing with secured services so you don't have to log in each time. The drawback to this technique is that tokens don't last forever, so you need to set up a schedule to replace the tokens as needed. When using tokens from ArcGIS Online, the maximum duration is 15 days.

index